The Search for Satisfaction

The Search for
Satisfaction

Getting More for Yourself and
Giving More to Others

Ronald H. Rottschafer

BAKER BOOK HOUSE
Grand Rapids, Michigan 49516

142302

To
all who have
allowed me
to join them
on part of
their life-journey

Copyright 1992 by
Baker Book House Company

Printed in the United States of America

Library of Congress Cataloging-in-Publication Data

Rottschafer, Ronald H.
The search for satisfaction : getting more for yourself and giving more to others / Ronald
H. Rottschafer.
     p.   cm.
Includes bibliographical references.
ISBN 0–8010–7762–1
1. Christian life—1960– 2. Satisfaction—Religious aspects—Christianity. 3.
Avarice—Religious aspects—Christianity. 4. Generosity—Religious aspects—Christianity.
I. Title.
BV4509.5.R67   1992
248.4—dc20

                91–31387
                CIP

Contents

Foreword

John F. Kennedy reportedly said that life is a tragic adventure. His life, perhaps more dramatically than our own, was a graphic illustration of his comment. However, calamities are not unknown territory to any of us. Quite the opposite, we do not live long before we are aware of the ambiguity of life: the intriguing adventure that invigorates us and the tragic inevitabilities that damp down our spirits and teach us to withdraw from full-orbed living. There is majesty and malignancy in the human odyssey.

An old Dutch proverb declares, "Ieder huis hat zijn kruis"(Every home has its own private anguish). All of us are suspended between the pleasure of growing into all the marvelous possibilities open to us and the pain of seeing how much life falls short of our expectations and thus grieves us. We long to feel full of the vitality of joyful animation but we often feel empty, depleted by the hard work required to simply survive psychologically, emotionally, and spiritually.

We live in a matrix of pain. Physical pain is relatively minor, however, when compared to the psychological and spiritual pain inherent in being human. Ronald Rottschafer has lived long enough, thought thoroughly enough, and is empathic enough to understand accurately our predicament. In *The Search for Satisfaction* he deals with the human longing to be filled and fulfilled with a secure and satisfying sense of the physical, psychological, and spiritual sensations which can make life seem meaningful, despite its pain.

This graciously humane, sympathetic, and empathic book about us firmly and touchingly illumines the wholesome, as well as the destructive, ways we try to get filled with the sense of being our real selves. As a clinical psychologist, Ronald Rottschafer is intimately acquainted with our psychological sicknesses. He is aware of our deficits and the self-defeating defense dynamics to which they drive us, and speaks as one of us about our struggle to grow.

The Creator has meant for us to grow and he provides opportunities, sometimes tragic events, to help us grow and become what we are capable of becoming.

Self-love is an essential ingredient for growth. In the last two thousand years self-love has gotten a bad name because it was seen as contrary to proper altruism. But Ronald Rottschafer points out the fallacy of that assumption and clearly distinguishes self-care from self-indulgence, selfishness, and narcissism. He wisely asserts that self-nurture is an essential expression of our intrinsic worth. Self-love is the acceptance of God's love for us and affirms the appropriateness of the love of others for us. The fact that self-love often turns into indulgence and exploitation of others does not negate the importance of loving ourselves.

We are hungry, questing beings, longing to be psychologically and spiritually filled because God has made us in his image. We are divinely designed to make judgments, assert ourselves, take charge of our destinies, impose our wills on things and others, and run the universe. We are called by God to assert our genuine and authentic selves. We must see to the nurture, development, filling, and self-actualization of ourselves. God went to immense pain to ensure that we are free to grow, achieve self-fulfillment, and experience the "abundant life." The most important thing about our lives, therefore, is not that we are human, that we have human limitations or perplexities, that we sin, or that we are fractured and imperfect. God seems to have little difficulty accepting and forgiving all of that. What seems to be of considerably more concern to God, as reflected in Scripture, is that we were created to grow along a continuum of development. We can realize in our maturing personhood the flowering of all those potentialities that God invested in us as image-bearers. It is possible for us to come to the total self-actualization of our God-given selves.

Ronald Rottschafer has with great precision and finesse integrated the psychological and spiritual factors that comprise our universal search for satisfaction. He has relieved the tension we feel between our desire for self-satisfaction and God's desire that we achieve according to our capabilities. We need no longer fear that our urge to get all that we can from life is in itself either a selfish or an ungodly act. The perspective has been made clear: As we get more for ourselves we have a heightened opportunity and ability to in turn give more to God and to each other.

There are no losers in this formula!

J. Harold Ellens
Farmington Hills, Michigan

Acknowledgments

A book is not written by the sole efforts of the author but by the interest, support, and critique of all who are involved in its production.

The development of both these written words and the writer has been aided immeasurably by the professional opinion and advice of Lewis B. Smedes, Ray S. Anderson, H. Newton Malony, J. Harold Ellens, David Benner, William Lenters, Michael Bequette, and Guy A. Renzaglia, my former mentor. I am unspeakably enriched and pleased with their invaluable contributions.

I am especially indebted to Mrs. Lois Curley, who as my literary agent, editor, and friend has skillfully helped shape this manuscript into a far more readable form than was initially presented to her.

Finally, I am deeply grateful to my wife, Rhoda, who has shared many of my thoughts, surrendered me to my study, and then has typed this manuscript and its revisions more times than either of us cares to remember.

All of these wonderful people have given of themselves to help me find the satisfaction I have sought in writing this book. Thank you for your gifts: *Sine qua non.*

Introduction

The search for satisfaction is a surging interplay of currents that propels us irresistibly onward from the moment of birth until our last breath is drawn. These demanding human forces carry the traffic of the various needs and wants for which we seek fulfillment. Yet our desires actually ebb and flow like the tides, sweeping us outward to explore the world and get what we can, then carrying us back to our peaceful harbors. Getting all that life has to offer is a reasonable goal, for at stake is not only bare survival but also the quality of our earthly existence. Do we not all journey from infancy through adulthood essentially to find satisfying ways to respond to our various physical, emotional, and spiritual drives?

Unfortunately, the legitimate urge to get all we can out of life has become warped and magnified in contemporary America. No longer do we strive merely to keep body and soul together and be all that we can be, but to prosper on all levels and especially to surpass others' achievements. If we consider it mandatory to maximize our accomplishments according to society-imposed standards, we become preoccupied with "getting more," often mindless of our underlying motivations, the means by which we reach our goals, and the costs our efforts engender for ourselves and others.

The stress induced by this search for ever-enhanced satisfaction takes its toll. As we discover that contentment does not necessarily keep pace with material gain, we feed on our fears that we are never quite secure enough, that our assets can be wiped out in a flash, that others are getting more from life than we are. Today's gratification then seems to be merely a prelude to tomorrow's disappointment.

The issues would be simpler if our concerns were only about acquiring more money and possessions. But "getting more" touches us at a far deeper level. What we define as important enough to seek after shapes the fabric of our individuality. We form our character and establish our reputation according to the beliefs that underlie our getting-and-giving behavior. The "ambitious" seek status through personal gain and may view those who are content with what they already have as "complacent" or even "lazy." The "selfish" care little about others, or so it seems. The "generous" gain satisfaction from giving. The "tycoon" increases his holdings at the expense of others—and so on. Like most stereotypes, such characterizations may at best be incomplete if not unfair. Still, there can be little doubt that our acquisitive behavior flows from our deeply held beliefs about what is important.

The basic assumption of this book is that most of us are looking for ways to feel more satisfied with our lives. We need informed guidance on how to get more of what we truly desire and some perspective on what we *should* be seeking, if we are to avoid self-destructive pitfalls and find meaning and contentment in what we do manage to accomplish. "Satisfaction" has many definitions, of course, but achieving it must start with understanding some principles of human psychology.

One way to approach the subject is to explore the psychology of "getting," a fascinating topic that has immediate application for everyone. The process of getting involves more than the acquisitiveness itself, which is merely the behavior through which we express our needs and wants, since frequently we are unaware of our hidden desires. Therefore, understanding the behavior requires that we know who we are: people who often desperately appeal to consumerism because of our universal sense of inadequacy and our anxiety about survival, happiness, approval, and "success" in a confusing world. We must examine the importance of knowing how much is enough as well as the role of conscience in our search for satisfaction. Whether we assertively take what we want or passively wait to receive it, getting more for ourselves is deeply engrained in the human psyche.

It is enlightening to discover the powerful impact our upbringing has had on our goal setting and the behavior patterns by which we try to fulfill those goals. Whether our parents were generous or withholding, authoritarian or permissive, they have shaped our attitudes and values. In large degree we respond to life's challenges by acting out scripts written for us in our early years. Yet, an essential goal of living effectively is developing one's selfhood beyond the limits our parents have imposed and accepting responsibility for our fortunes. The whole idea of maturation is to achieve independence, to grow beyond a childish reliance on others to provide us with satisfaction.

There is a twentieth-century dimension to my analysis of parental influence: I will propose that pre-1960 parents (and grandparents) had an unintended though no less profound impact on the social-moral-behavioral revolution of the past few decades. I believe it can be argued that these relatively "selfless" elders—frugal, modest, obedient—have unwittingly produced self-centered, value-free offspring who generally reject the codes of conformity as "outdated." The more permissive child-rearing approach adopted by many parents after the 1950s relieved their own unresolved tensions by allowing previously unacceptable behavior to be vented through their children. Many in the "me" generation feel perfectly justified in going after everything their cautious, tradition-bound forebears could only wish for. There are exceptions, of course, as we will see in some of the case histories to be presented; many children blindly *repeat* the behavior of their elders. But those who cater to the self and abandon all guidelines of the past run aground in ways not unlike those of their parents, though for different reasons. One might say that this generation is no more "satisfied" than previous ones.

In this era of self-focus and materialistic excess, we tend to forget that poets, philosophers, theologians, and other commentators on the human condition have always encouraged us to balance what we get with what we give. The ancient Greek warning against the deadly sin of avarice and the biblical reminder that "the love of money is the root of all evil" seem even more appropriate as we approach the twenty-first century. It is my central thesis that whereas it is legitimate to fill ourselves deeply, our satisfaction is incomplete unless we share our input through acts of outreach that show genuine concern for the well-being of others.

Giving is meant to be neither a detrimental emptying of self nor a denial of the importance of claiming something for ourselves. Instead, generosity that enhances the lives of those around us increases our own sense of contentment. Giving is the necessary counterweight to getting, the means by which we avoid the emptiness of self-indulgence. Civilized people have always viewed altruism as mankind's highest virtue, a mark of maturity, a sign of love. Even pagan societies have recognized that individuals must transcend the narrow limits of self-focus and project themselves into others' lives. And, of course, it is irrefutable that the Judeo-Christian ethic has solidified the truth that we broaden our outlook and discover our place and purpose in the universe by discharging our moral and social obligations to others. In the process, we warm our souls over the fires of joy reflected in the faces of our beneficiaries and form meaningful relationships.

However, even if we subscribe wholeheartedly to the Christian ideal that "it is more blessed to give than to receive," for we are to "love one another," we are sometimes leery about its practical application. We may still cling to the fear that charitable acts deplete what is left for ourselves. Some people compensate by giving as little as possible. Others give extravagantly, though only to deny their own hidden hungers by seeking gratitude and/or society's admiration. Seeing corruption in some charitable organizations, and realizing that donations to serve one group of needy persons inevitably brings a flood of mail from other fund-raisers, may also decrease our willingness to subscribe to the wisdom of generosity. If our giving is on a more personal level, we "risk" establishing a deeper relationship than we are comfortable with. Although we are created with the desire and capability to love, intimacy carries obligations we may be unwilling to accept. For these and many other reasons, we are torn between getting for self and giving to others.

Most people devise complicated strategies for balancing their getting-and-giving behavior. Some believe the most sensible course is to press harder, be more clever, get tougher with others and themselves. That way, they can avoid unwelcome commitments and concentrate on pleasure seeking. Even if they are sympathetic to the plight of others, they believe it is justifiable to postpone activating their concern until they feel full enough that sharing is painless. But, for the greedy, that day rarely comes.

Others take the opposite approach, desperately hoping they can establish their own identity in outreach and service. Because this strategy tries to bury the self, yet amounts to waiting expectantly for approval and acceptance, the compulsively generous may still feel empty and victimized. People with a poor self-image are often afraid to internalize the very trophies for which they have worked so hard. Reluctant to claim their victories, they are left dissatisfied, even troubled by guilt for succeeding beyond what they think they deserve.

Regardless of our motives and our style of seeking satisfaction, all of us draw deeply from within our very core—the self—to direct our getting and giving.

Focusing on the self is not necessarily synonymous with being selfish, for judicious attention to our own needs is crucial for sound mental and physical health. But distorted self-care has created two contemporary problems that are opposite faces of the same coin. On the one hand is excessive self-indulgence—the root of modern narcissism and materialistic excess. On the other is the denigration of self—as seen in some ultra-conservative religious circles. Each of these attempts to deal with the self and its needs avoids recognizing the tensions between giving and getting and in essence denies that life becomes imbalanced when there is too much of one and too little of the other.

An important goal of this book is to pursue the details of how our lives can go awry when our behavior overemphasizes either getting or giving. I will critically review the erroneous assumptions of both those who cater principally to self and those who (in light of Mark 8:34) piously deny the need for balanced self-care. Both positions are flawed and incomplete in that they undermine the complementary life goals of finding inner satisfaction and participating in interpersonal relationships. Either self-aggrandizement or self-negation qualifies as an example of what a theologian might define as "sin," since it is a failure to acknowledge God's purposes in our lives.

In considering the complications besetting the integration of psychological and spiritual principles, I will be speaking as a student of both clinical psychology and conservative Christianity. I regard my thirty years as a practicing clinical psychologist and my religious life as a parishioner, teacher, and writer as in-depth resources for my observations on the human condition. Unlike the many mental-health experts who are silent about the spiritual side of life, I will comment appropriately on the problems of those who speak from both the couch and the pew. I will neither try to sell psychotherapy nor witness for Christianity, but will simply write as a healer whose role is to observe, interpret, encourage, and prescribe.

The conclusions and recommendations comprising the final two chapters are designed to provide specific guidelines for enhancing satisfaction. Chapter 12 suggests a three-step program to immediately increase satisfaction on a daily basis. This plan does not require psychological sophistication or individual counseling to increase one's level of contentment, for it provides the reader with a rationale for better utilizing his or her everyday behavior in search of personal and relational satisfaction.

In chapter 13 I conclude by considering some moral-ethical-spiritual principles we can embrace to guide us toward a deeper satisfaction with our lives. I will propose three historic tried-and-true means of pulling together the errant parts of our lives and holding them permanently in place.

Our efforts should begin with a personal adherence to a love ethic that encourages us to reach beyond the limits of self, for we strengthen the self by grasping hands with each other in kindness and mutual care. The second means of solidifying our inner structure is by returning to the principles of self-discipline. Like professional athletes or musicians, we can refine and maximize our skills and talents by following certain success-oriented rules. Finally, enhanced satisfaction requires a commitment to whatever spiritual beliefs and moral values comprise our worldview. Every serious student of human nature concludes with the valid assertion that we are a "religious" people who believe in a divine being and subscribe to spiritual laws and the eternal reality of an unseen world. We will therefore assuredly improve our satisfaction level by affirming those principles in our lives.

Since our central life urge is essentially a search for satisfaction, peace, and contentment, each of us seeks ways to make this pursuit more rewarding. My interest in the topic also springs from a desire to understand my personal quest for growth and fulfillment. Because my own sense of satisfaction inevitably touches others in my life, as I "get" for me and "give" to them, they in turn do the same. This cycle has had many fascinating elements—as I have discovered while researching and writing this book.

1

The Human Condition

The Searching Self

Growth, progress, the idea of "more" is so much a part of our
consciousness that . . . it is our state of mind.

Paul Wachtel[1]

I t is human nature to be always looking for "more." Our needs and
wants seem insatiable, our satisfactions short-lived. As we attend to
our basic necessities and cater to our specific tastes and choices, we
realize over and over again that even momentary satisfaction feels good
and relieves our tensions. We are endlessly driven to search for gratification, to survive, and to attain whatever we have defined as worthwhile
goals. Although we strongly defend our right to exercise our "pursuit of
happiness," we may be unaware of the various factors that determine our
choices and can impede our progress.

First are life's *external* realities—current circumstances that are frustrating, cruel, fearsome, even tragic. Pessimists often view these experiences as a personal affront or see life itself as an ongoing battle against
hostile encumbrances. Others insist that life is basically sweet but provides obstacles to help us develop our survival skills. Whichever position

we take, our life-journey demonstrates convincingly that finding satisfaction demands effort and patience.

Second, even though life's ongoing problems and threats make the going difficult enough, we also must contend with our *internal* realities. What we see within the dark hallways of our mind can be frightening. There we grapple with our inadequacies, our self-doubt, our sense of being flawed—the bitter lessons we believe the past has taught us. We measure the unplumbed depths of our needs and wants, jealously comparing self with neighbor, contrasting the ideal with what seems attainable, and feeding our endless fears and anxieties. Laboring with our awareness of how much we do not know and how weak we are, we grope for someone to trust, for goals of true worth, for the very meaning of life and death. Even our belief in God's providential care may be tempered with doubts about our worth to him. Our hidden demons of self-consciousness, egotism, an inability to love and be loved in return, and our defenselessness against the ticking clock leave us no other course than a lifelong pursuit of relief.

Search Patterns

Each of us is different in our perceptions of reality, our motivations, and our response patterns, all of which develop over time. We are known chiefly by how we handle our search for satisfaction. Some of us focus too sharply on "getting," others are too passive; some people give more than is healthy, while others do not give enough. We will now examine the lives of four individuals who each exemplify one of these four categories. Notice how these people have been imprisoned by habitual patterns of behavior that neither serve their best interests nor bring them satisfaction.

Thomas North: The Successful Loser

Tom, at thirty-eight, is an aggressive achiever, the eldest son in a family with three boys. His parents provided a fairly comfortable living and own a home in a middle-class suburb. They encouraged their children to do their best but were careful not to emphasize riches and worldly success as life's primary goals.

Although Tom's father has worked hard, his cautious business approach has limited the growth of his small company. A modest, quiet man who has carefully planned for his approaching retirement, he is uncomfortable with grandiose ideas, often saying he is from "the old school" that emphasizes thrift, hard work, and saving for the future as three of life's preeminent values. His conservatism is endorsed by a frugal wife whose father had lost everything in the Great Depression. The Norths have no debts but have denied themselves many luxuries they probably could have afforded.

Tom's character reflects a rejection of his parents' tightfisted financial prudence. He grew up resenting his father's dreary lifestyle and his mother's willingness to make do with what the savings-oriented family budget allowed. As a teenager, he came to hate one sentence more than all others: "We just can't afford it." Because Tom wanted "more," he got an after-school job at a supermarket so he could match the spending level of his friends. Tom embraced his father's work ethic, so he earned a supervisor's position by the time he had graduated from high school. Tom was elated about his early success. He had no time for friends now but was making big money for a young man his age. Years later he would recall riding his new ten-speed bike to his job and saying to himself, "Soon I'll be able to afford anything I want."

One need not be a psychologist to analyze Tom North nor predict where his early financial success would lead him. While attending the local junior college, he worked full-time as produce manager at the supermarket. For a year or two he, like his parents, budgeted carefully—but only to save for a small truck. Now he could buy produce at the wholesale markets and sell it at discount rates up and down the streets of his community. But, unlike his father, Tom had an imaginative approach to business. He put advertisements in every mailbox in town and included his time schedule so housewives would know when he would be at their curbside. By age twenty he had borrowed money from the bank to buy a refrigerated truck. His sales soared. Within four years, Tom was a successful entrepreneur on the road to finding the American dream. His risk-taking drive to excel had paid off: He had a wife, a baby on the way, a new home (though heavily mortgaged), and a free-spending lifestyle—though he had little time to enjoy the rewards of his labors.

At age thirty-eight Tom has come for professional help. His marriage has been in serious trouble for some time. His wife has left with their two children to dramatize her unwillingness to live with a man whose workaholism permits him no time for his family. By now Tom owns a huge produce center that makes him very comfortable financially. He is still extremely ambitious, a man determined to make it even bigger. I find it hard to get him to tell me about his marriage. He prefers to talk about employee morale, customer psychology, and the affluence his business success has brought his family. "We spend a lot," he says, "but then I earn a lot, so why not? I hate saying no to myself, and I can afford to buy whatever I want. Is there anything wrong with that?"

Tom has earned the right to spend as he pleases. He, like most of us, believes very strongly that those who make their dreams come true deserve material rewards. But dreams come with a price tag. Not only must we work very hard to achieve them, but also success can entrap us once things are finally going our way. As we get caught up in the motivations that drive us forward, we risk becoming insensitive to the pain our behavior may cause our loved ones and oblivious of the intangible joys we have renounced. We use the fruits of our labors to reward and console ourselves, only to press harder when our trophies leave us unsatisfied. The cycle is addictive. The more we get, the more we want. Getting too much is a risk, because our gains may overshadow our good judgment, our relationships, and inner needs we do not acknowledge.

Tom cannot understand why his wife is not satisfied with all he provides for his family. His mother would have been, he says to himself. "We live like my parents never could have imagined," he boasts. "My brothers don't have even a third of what I've got." Tom cannot admit that his brothers, although not financially successful, have a happy family life, are home for dinner each evening, and know how to have fun. Tom's marriage has been rocky from the start. He has tuned out his wife's complaints that she is lonely and tired of answering the question, "When is Daddy coming home?"

Our total personality is assembled in the kitchen of childhood and baked in the oven of life's experiences. We may not understand our own ingredients well enough to avoid behavior that is not in our best interest. We rationalize our response patterns as unchangeable, as indigenous to our very being. After a bitter argument in which he reminded his wife of the luxuries he had earned ("for the good of the family"), Tom got close to stating this dilemma by asking, "I am the way I am;—what do you want me to be?" This question is in most of our minds at one time or another.

How are you to know who you are and what ultimately you are destined to do with your life? These are soul-searching matters that are easy to avoid as you face the demands of each new day. Even if you take the time to reflect on your ways, you are probably not sure how to alter your thinking or effect changes in your behavior—and it may be hard to admit that it is *you* and not someone else who needs remodeling!

Some issues may be rather obvious. Most of us know about needing proper rest and time for family life and acknowledge the importance of certain values and moral standards. But we may not realize how we are driven by our parents' ways and other remnants of the past or how our successes create attitudes and habits that increasingly control our lives.

Tom does not realize that the first child in a family is often programmed to be an aggressive achiever just by virtue of his or her birth order, the one expected to fulfill unrealized parental dreams. He also does not make a connection between the limited spending money of his childhood and his subsequent drive for more of everything in adulthood.

Tom's classic American success story too often becomes a familiar American tragedy. As we strive for life's pleasures and rewards, we may find it harder and harder to evaluate objectively what we are really searching for. Some of us want worldly success for the shear joy of feeling important and powerful. Others convert all their gains into material goods, whether as proof of their "security" or as sweeteners for the bitter memories of past deprivations. These symbolic Band-Aids and ice-cream cones may heal early pains they do not know how to erase by other means.

But where does it end? How much is enough? Those who press ever onward for more eventually realize that today's relief merely ushers in tomorrow's desire. Getting too much can be as unsatisfying as getting too little.

Ann Southfield: The Missing Person

In an unguarded moment, Ann might wish for some of Tom's style of vigorously pursuing his dreams, whatever the cost. Ann's life is a collage of disappointments. She has never found happiness because she has never searched for it constructively. Although this thirty-nine-year-old woman is bright and attractive, she has gone without satisfaction until the glow has left her face—as well as her life. Ann's story speaks of deprivation, but not because "life is unfair." Ann has learned to deprive herself—to settle for too little.

Ann was the second of four children. Her mother had been reared in a strictly religious home where self-denial in service of others was considered the highest calling for a woman. Her identity had been lost in endless hours of stoic maternalism and devotion to her family's welfare.

Ann formed her personality under the influence of her mother's tired, emotionless face and self-sacrificing ways. Ann has hampered her personal development because she feared that enjoying herself would be unfair, that her own pleasure seeking would only highlight her mother's unfulfilling life. As an adolescent she learned to say no to having fun with peers, volunteering to stay home and help her mother with the younger children. By going without, Ann has bonded herself permanently with her mother, providing herself with a sense of personal identity that gives structure to her life, but no purpose. Getting too little is simply her way of knowing who she is: her mother's daughter.

In my work as a psychotherapist, I often note that many people decide as children what their lives will become and thereafter work at fulfilling their own prophecies. I have had homosexuals tell me they "knew" before adolescence that they were gay. Women have told me of their early decisions to remain childless; men look back and declare they always expected to enter their current professions. Ann decided early in life to ignore herself and her needs, to stifle her dreams. She does not fully understand why she has chosen such an impoverished existence, but her bleak lifestyle is obviously guided by an internal force: the maternal example that consistently holds her to her somber path.

Ann works very hard at a job well beneath her capabilities, but she does not indulge in the chatter and other office frivolities that her co-workers enjoy. She is pleasant but rather somber, friendly to a point but not so as to interfere with her job responsibilities. Although others see her as always willing to lend a helping hand in the office, she puzzles her fellow employees with her unwillingness to accept their praise or appreciation. In fact, Ann seems uncomfortable with personal attention. Because they sang "Happy Birthday" to her once, and she did not know how to respond, they have been careful not to sing to her again. Co-workers see Ann as "rather strange" and tend to respect her apparent desire for privacy. The women in the office do not talk much with her about their boyfriends or husbands because Ann has hinted that she never dates. Ann subconsciously isolates herself further through her disinterest in fashion, cosmetics, even current events. Because she anticipates a minimal response from her peers, she limits her social contacts—and increases her loneliness.

It is ironic that in our efforts to counteract past deprivations, we often invite subsequent loss. Both Tom and Ann have an inner emptiness but try to find life's missing ingredients in radically different ways. Tom's style is to fight aggressively for outward symbols of success; Ann's is to take flight from her needs. One seeks, the other waits passively, but neither finds satisfaction.

One of the major thrusts of this book is to show how the dynamics of getting can be an integral part of making life satisfying—if we are going after the right things in the right way. We learn how to satisfy ourselves to the degree that our parents have encouraged us to pay attention to our needs and wants and to acquire whatever is necessary to maintain our independence. The parental role is to supply love, support, guidance, and discipline as we learn how to reach our goals within the context of common sense, good order, and ethical standards. But we have a decided responsibility to develop our capabilities and make independent decisions.

The lives of Tom and Ann illustrate how critical parental example can be in framing one's overall approach to life. Both case histories reveal how attitudes learned in childhood can interrupt the normal developmental process of becoming one's own person. Tom's acquisitiveness represents a rejection of his parents' financial conservatism, whereas Ann's inertia is her way of handling the inner struggle between being her own person and giving self away as her mother has done. Both will find it hard to change their ways in the direction of healthy self-care unless they shed the emotional burdens they have carried since childhood.

What is most difficult about change is the cross fire of mixed purposes in which we are caught. We must first understand whatever may have impeded us in the past before we can revise our approach. Many of us resist change because we do not want to face our internalized images of our parents. Even if we recognize how our childhood experiences have influenced our present search for happiness, we are not automatically equipped to free ourselves from the past—even if the attitudes that we need to let go of are self-defeating. It often seems preferable to build defenses that temporarily relieve our pains rather than to face and work through the underlying problems. We may actively seek more and more of life's pleasures to distract us from life's difficulties, but because the latter are inevitable, we become divided in our purposes. Like an army that is weakened by having to defend itself on two fronts, we lessen our sense of satisfaction by using many of our accomplishments to ease our sorrow rather than allowing them to bring us joy.

Some people argue that the solution to the problems associated with getting is to focus on giving instead. But, as we shall next examine, the process of giving is also beset with complications that can interrupt our sense of satisfaction.

Betty Eastland: The Not-So-Cheerful Giver

Most of us uphold giving as one of mankind's highest values and acknowledge that sensitive caring for others reflects social and spiritual maturity. But if generosity is virtuous, can we speak of giving too much? We all can think of situations where we and others have not given enough, but the idea of giving too much may sound contradictory to basic moral principles.

Betty Eastland is in her late twenties, single, and known by all as "a very nice person." She enjoys being kind and takes pleasure in the happiness of those around her. Betty compliments them on every success, remembers their birthdays with a card or small gift, and is generous with her time and effort on their behalf. Certainly the world needs more people like Betty Eastland!

Betty's essential dilemma is that her generosity does not stimulate others to give to her in return. Her indiscriminate kindness seems to invite others to take advantage of her. She is reluctant to ask people to repay money she has lent them, and they certainly do not go out of their way to pay her back. She readily fills in for those at work who have to leave early, but they usually find excuses when she needs someone to cover for her. Most people who are treated this way would protest or even be angry about the inequities involved, but Betty has such a poor self-image that she always avoids being "unpleasant" by not taking a stand on her own behalf. She would rather take a loss herself than risk offending someone. The more cynical call her a pushover and do not consider her ways worth emulating because she too often comes out on the short end of things.

When asked why she isn't more assertive, Betty merely replies that she has a lot of faith in people's basic goodness. Because she hates to make trouble, she does not allow herself to be visibly upset about being taken advantage of. Any resentment that brews deep within is quickly squelched. Pleasing others is too important to Betty to risk jeopardizing a friendship over what she calls "little things." She might have gone on this way indefinitely if not for the fact that something happened that was too painful for her to overlook—the breakup of a long-term romance that she expected to lead to marriage.

In our first consultation together, Betty cries uncontrollably. Although she expresses no anger, there is ample evidence that she has been deeply hurt by her boyfriend, Warren, who had recently left her for another woman. Betty describes Warren as a man who "needs a good woman to guide him." According to what she tells me, I diagnose Warren as an inadequate male who manipulates others to compensate for his own lack of direction. He has big ideas that sound good but are more wish than purpose. Warren's reluctance to marry Betty is added proof of his ambivalence about making decisions and commitments. (My guess is that he had finally tired of Betty's "mothering" and was ready to move on to a less one-sided relationship.)

As Betty talks, she demonstrates more concern for Warren's welfare than for her own. She wonders what will become of him, how he will fare without her. She explains that Warren is ten years her senior, a man who was hurt badly by divorce years earlier, but who seemed to finally come alive in their relationship. She tells of how gratifying it was for her to feel needed by him, how he gratefully responded to her loving care.

Betty has failed to realize that Warren's response was selfish, that instead of responding to her caretaking with love or even gratitude, he charged off to pursue his own interests after being rejuvenated by her attentions. Warren was too needy and self-centered to balance getting with giving. Their partnering seemed like a perfect fit to Betty—she gave and he received—but Betty misinterpreted this imbalance as love. When asked what she got out of this relationship, Betty acts as if she has not really thought about the question before. "I guess it's just that he needs me," she replies. "It makes me feel good to be useful, to have people succeed because of what I do for them. Giving makes me feel important."

While it is true that love includes attentively looking after the welfare of the beloved, healthy love demands reciprocity. Betty illustrates the eventual outcome of most relationships in which one person gives and the other only takes. She was so intent on giving that she polarized the relationship and gave Warren no choice but to receive. Partners like Warren are already predisposed to take from a willing giver, to be the objects of generosity. By as early as the first or second date, a covert deal is struck between such partners. A subtle, subconscious agreement is made: "You give and I get." In Betty and Warren's case, each was eager to strike such a deal. Although initially enthusiastic about the arrangement, both have unresolved psychological inadequacies that were not being addressed. Since Betty does not know how to receive and Warren does not know how to give, each looked excitedly to the other for fulfillment. Their partnership failed because healthy love demands that the individuals involved be willing to both give to and get from each other. Unless she comes to accept this reality, Betty Eastland will continue to be unsatisfied in her social encounters and love relationships.

George West: The Angry Tycoon

George is a self-made millionaire in his mid-fifties. He likes to brag about having made his money "the old-fashioned way—I earned it." The Wests live in a fashionable Chicago suburb. They enjoy having a palatial home, expensive cars, and a sailboat on which they and their friends spend pleasant evenings viewing the Chicago skyline from the lake.

George has definite ideas about how to become wealthy and stay that way. "You think success comes easy?" he asks forcefully. "I worked hard for every dime I have, and so should everyone else. I don't believe in this welfare-state mentality. It only teaches people to be lazy." George easily slips into an Archie Bunker philosophy about the have-nots and how they got that way. "They're always complaining about their bad breaks. But you give those people an inch and they want a mile," he says angrily. "Nobody came around to help me when I had nothing, but they sure know how to find me now. The government, the charities, the relatives, the moochers—where were they before? Nothing came to me on a silver platter. I went after what I wanted and I'm going to keep it."

George is not entirely selfish. He provides generously for his wife and children and is the sole support for his immigrant parents who live in a well-managed Florida retirement community. His brothers and sisters all have excuses for not paying a fair share of their parents' upkeep. At the heart of their arguments is the knowledge that George is rich enough to pay it all. He can and he does, but George resents his siblings for their attitude. More than anything else, he wants his family to appreciate his efforts and admire how much he has accomplished.

George deeply believes in pulling one's own weight, in addressing life's problems head-on. "The Lord helps those who help themselves," he states, not as a belief in divine guidance but as an expression of his reliance on himself. His notion of providential care does not extend beyond what he calls "getting lucky." But it is sweat, not luck, that George believes is the reason for his success—the by-product of years of hard work, frustration, and dogged persistence. He is a fighter who believes he can accomplish any task regardless of the odds. He credits no one but himself: "I made it and it's all mine to enjoy."

Despite his affluence, George has a "me against them" philosophy, a pervasive negativism about his fellowman. He blames other people for his social isolation and persistent unrest because he refuses to blame himself. George needs a place to anchor his resentments and an explanation for the insecurities that have spurred him to fight for success and defend what he has. His accumulated negative feelings demand that he never let down his guard against his "enemies." George has painted himself into an existential corner of loneliness. His compulsion to preserve his empire from intruders—both real and imagined—results in an uncharitable philosophy that increases his alienation from others.

Both Betty Eastland and George West have fashioned unhealthy attitudes about giving. Although one gives too much and the other too little, their behavior radically alters the social fabric of their lives. What is noteworthy in these two examples is that neither Betty nor George recognizes why they are dissatisfied with life and why other people continually disappoint them. Betty would say that she doesn't care about her own needs, that she prefers to see people happy—but she is lying to herself. If she can discard her self-assigned role of perpetual care-giver, she will learn to pay more attention to how much she gets in relation to what she gives. Only then will she stop encouraging people to take advantage of her.

On the other hand, if George realized that his reluctance to give is a way of dealing with his hidden resentments, he would be dumbfounded. He, too, has much to learn about himself. Were he to eliminate his anger over his lonely struggle to the top, he would gain the admiration he craves. He could then open his heart more charitably to his fellowman and enjoy deeper relationships that would increase his personal satisfaction in his many possessions.

Balanced Giving and Getting

Betty and George—as well as Tom and Ann—demonstrate incomplete growth in that they have not achieved balance between their giving and their getting. Each lives with a narrow perspective that interferes with the desirable goal of internal and interpersonal harmony. They have not yet discovered how to reach out beyond the boundaries of the self to compensate for past and present problems.

All human beings must learn to deal with their own history, to recognize that they must struggle with the residues of anxiety, fear, anger, inadequacy, and ignorance—the roadblocks constructed out of past experiences. But, somewhat ironically, if our primary purpose is to reach our fullest potential, we can more effectively interact with, contribute to, and make our peace with each other at home and in the community. Focusing only on our immediate needs will stifle the development of our creative, productive, intellectual capacities, the very talents needed to make a difference in the world. Even worse, excessive self-care interrupts our moral, ethical, and spiritual maturation and undermines the values that bind us together in human fellowship.

This is not to say that we should suffocate the self in spiritual zeal for noble causes. Without a solid identity, we have no personal base from which to conduct the crucial business of daily living. So we must feed the self richly and guide it carefully as we come to know our place in the larger picture. The ultimate goal of a mature individual is to be creative and productive and to love generously. It is through work and love that we come to find meaning and satisfaction in life.

Understanding the Search

Each generation has tried to make sense of its hungers and anxieties and take charge of its future. Whereas our grandparents may have struggled to leave their homeland and find their way in a new country, their forebears of ten centuries ago were mainly concerned with plagues and feudal landlords. Throughout all of history, people have faced issues of survival and its attendant fears. They have also desperately searched for answers about the deeper meaning of existence.

One way human beings have sought to understand the universe has been to create mythologies that explain who they are and how they might find satisfaction. In Ancient Greece, imperfect mortals conceived of flawless gods who had all the answers but controlled their destiny capriciously. Although people appealed to the gods to fill their every need and bribed them with sacrificial offerings, it was all too clear that these gods were unpredictable. In time, the ancients realized that the gods themselves were both needy and fallible. Socrates' mentor, Diotima, reminded him that even love was imperfect. She explained that Eros, god of love, was born of Plenty and Poverty and thus had at his very core the seeds of both fullness and emptiness. The Greeks eventually concluded that their search for satisfaction was limited to a reliance on one's own efforts. Freud's student, Theodor Reik, came to the same conclusion 2,400 years later when he suggested that the romantic love that originates in our own inner poverty (our self-dislike) is an attempt to find relief in fantasies of plenty to be provided by a lover—fantasies that always lose out to reality.[2]

Because human beings have typically couched their descriptions of the route to happiness in a religious context, all cultures have a creation story that helps explain the human condition. Judaism, for example, embraces the Genesis account of the beginning of life, the fall from perfection in the Garden of Eden, and the expectancy that a Messiah will provide deliverance from the consequences of human imperfection. Christians, of course, believe that this Creator-Redeemer has already come, has saved those who accept him as Savior and Master, and will come again to establish his eternal kingdom. Religion touches the universal experience of feeling estranged from the cosmos. It comforts us in our struggles with anxiety and provides meaning and purpose to human existence. J. Harold Ellens addresses this aspect of the Genesis account in his book *God's Grace and Human Health:* "The Fall story . . . attempts to explain why humans can conceive of esthetic ideals but hardly create them, long for genuine love but seldom express or experience it, remember and anticipate paradise, yet sense it is eluding us."[3]

Ellens describes the biblical message as a migration from the Old Testament's theme of ignorance, guilt, and punishment by an angry God to the New Testament's theme of loving forgiveness and the grace that brings health and security through Christ. He parallels this religious explanation with humankind's psychological journey from the emptiness of infancy through the adolescent's struggle with authority and reality to the eventual freedom inherent in maturity. We seek the cure for "evil"—all that is empty, ignorant, and chaotic—by finding satisfaction in the "good" of fullness, wisdom, and order.

Theological explanations of human nature rescue us from our helpless twisting in the winds of misfortune and loneliness. Religious belief systems acknowledge our frailties but teach us how to improve ourselves and satisfy our needs in the context of an ordered world formulated by a Being far greater than ourselves.

Modern psychology also attempts to provide answers to many universal questions. Theories about personality structure and how attitudes and behavior can be modified deal with the individual's growth toward the fullest possible satisfaction. Psychology can enrich the fulfillment of life's journey by enlightening the traveler about the most efficient use of his or her mental and emotional characteristics. Like religion and philosophy, psychology examines head and heart as the means whereby we fulfill our needs and wants. "Cognition" (the "head") refers to thinking, planning, understanding, learning—the intellectual aspects of pursuing satisfaction. The "emotional" components (the "heart") include the moods, feelings, and desires that are activated in our search and in many ways have determined our expectations.

The mental-health professional helps troubled individuals understand and alter the patterns of thinking and feeling that have led them to set unrealistic goals or use nonproductive techniques to achieve their desires. For example, consider what a depressed person must pursue with a psychotherapist. There are depressed *feelings*—sadness, apathy and low energy, a sense of powerlessness—and negative *thoughts,* most of which are angry, pessimistic, and self-critical. The initial task of the therapist is to provide a safe, nonjudgmental environment in which to deal with the factors causing the depression. Within that caring atmosphere of acceptance, the therapist then skillfully guides the patient into a detailed review and reassessment of the feelings and thoughts involved in his or her problems. Healing progresses according to how readily the patient can reduce his or her anger level, accept whatever actual losses have occurred, and find a higher level of self-confidence. Evidence of reasonable functioning must occur before the therapist will consider the task finished.

Psychology deals not only with our recognizable and verbalized thoughts and emotions, but with the hidden aspects of our motivations. The case of Tom North illustrates how ambition—the search for total financial security—is often exaggerated by subconscious factors that prod us along an unending treadmill. Tom's drive to succeed is legitimate, but the fact that his insatiable desire for more is rooted in years of repressed childhood anger over his parents' financial caution contaminates both his motives and the outcome of his efforts. Although Tom's way of getting more for himself will bring him many tangible rewards, he is victimized by the compulsive quality of his behavior. He will have troublesome personal relationships as long as he preoccupies himself with the gratification of material wants without considering the origin of his urges or the consequences of satisfying them.

The subconscious elements of who we are may seem mysterious, but the experiences, thoughts, and feelings that we have buried deeply within us are all potentially available for conscious consideration. Although we tend to resist becoming aware of whatever it is about ourselves that is unattractive or painful, self-knowledge holds the key to mental, emotional, and spiritual wholeness. Until we face our fears, accept our inadequacies, and acknowledge the emotional burdens we may be carrying, we cannot fully utilize our capabilities in our search for satisfaction. For some, acquiring insights into what makes them tick as individuals is a relatively uncomplicated process. For others, informal counseling or even intense psychotherapy may be needed to unlock their inner secrets. Whatever approach is used—philosophy, psychology, religion, or a combination of all three—the ultimate aim is to understand the human condition and provide practical guidelines for what I have called "the searching self."

2

The Process of Getting

The Hungry Self

Our ingress into the world
Was naked and bare
Our progress through the world
Is trouble and care.

Henry Wadsworth Longfellow

An old country doctor once told me that of the hundreds of babies he had delivered, not one had ever come out smiling. He was reiterating the truth that life is never easy. The circumstances of life are constant reminders that our task will be long and perilous as we try to discover who we are and why we are here.

Because we all are born hungry, and not just for food, we yearn to get everything we can to make our lives more satisfying. As we develop from a single cell to full adulthood, we passively receive and aggressively take, but we rely on the process of getting as the means whereby we sustain our physical existence and satisfy our less tangible hungers.

In this chapter we will focus on the psychological and physiological aspects of giving without considering the philosophical or theological concepts that affect one's searching. We will first notice how this process originates at conception and attends our every stage of development

31

throughout life. The patterns of getting that we establish early in childhood will generally prevail until death. Understanding some of the
details of this developmental sequence will help us make more sense of
our individual quest for satisfaction.

Next we will briefly view the influences of biological factors on our
search, noting how we carefully gear our getting behavior to satisfy our
needs, some of which are not in our conscious awareness.

The third section will examine the centrality of our thoughts and emotions in acquiring personal satisfaction. Since we act the way we do
largely by virtue of how we perceive the world and feel about our experiences, we can improve our lifestyles through a deeper understanding of
these two major behavioral influences. Central to that examination will
be the thesis that much of what we seek is designed both to provide
pleasure and to reduce our anxiety level.

Finally, we will consider the idea that a healthy and adequate process
of getting must include an eye for the future. By living only for the here
and now, we avoid taking some thought for our tomorrows and suffer
accordingly.

A Developmental View of Getting

The incredibly complicated process of human development begins *in
utero*, where everything we need is automatically supplied. Assuming
that there are no genetic abnormalities or prenatal complications, peace
prevails. This oceanic bliss, as Freud called it, is an important concept,
because uterine tranquility meets its counterpoint in the trauma of the
birth process. As Freud's early disciple, Otto Rank, pointed out, birth is
the most significant crisis we will ever face. Birth removes us from total
peace and marks the beginning of all our later anxiety about separation.

Overwhelmed by a flood of stimuli beyond infantile comprehension,
the newborn is physically aware of profound helplessness, a condition
that is not about to go away. All through life the urge to return to the
peaceful womb prevails, framing and underscoring our life-driving
search for satisfaction. Even at a very primitive level of brain functioning,
where language and logic do not exist, the infant senses vulnerability and
reaches out aggressively for sustenance and rescue. Because every
instinct tells the baby to get what is needed for survival, eye, hand, and
mouth search frantically for Mother, the source of food and physical
comfort.

The desperate outreach by an infant is naturally answered by the loving, reliable care of its mother. This most crucial of human relationships

is so intimate that to the infant the two are bonded as one. We enshrine the concept of motherhood partly because of our own mother's tireless efforts to be available to us. She is the first care-giver we encounter in our perilous journey through life. What we get from Mother is not just her milk but her total person. The gift of herself is the means whereby we once survived, and we never forget that.

We learn as infants the core lesson of survival: To get is to live. But not only does our early acquisitive behavior support life and provide satisfaction, it stimulates growth. A baby's cry for gratification is also the forerunner of language development. Random grasping, kicking, and flailing about become coordinated efforts that proceed to locomotion and small-muscle control, just as focusing on the mother with eyes and ears in search of relief initiates the development of sensory skills that will be needed throughout life. In each series of events, the infant repeatedly reaches out and takes, as well as passively receives, thereby refining the process of getting.

The mother's constant reinforcement leads to what amounts to an inflated sense of infantile power. It is as if the baby concludes, "I cry and she comes. I am hungry so she feeds me. I have it made; she is all mine." Psychiatrist James Masterson states that this infantile narcissism is universal and is a necessary part of the growth process for "regulating self-esteem, for self-assertion, for pursuit of one's unique interests, for one's standards, ideals and ambitions."[1] To the degree that an infant grows within the protection of maternal gratification, he or she develops a personal sense of importance and is boosted up the developmental ladder.

As the infant develops, a powerful cycle is established: Getting stimulates growth—and growth establishes more complex needs that demand satisfaction. Newborns want merely food, warmth, and a comforting touch. Children want bicycles, teens want automobiles, adults want careers, affluence, and society's approval. As we constantly add to our needs and wants, we set new goals and are given added incentive to battle the circumstances of life.

We first sense how tough life is when we realize that gratification is usually incomplete and temporary. The infant becomes aware that Mother is not perfect, that she cannot take away every stomachache or fear, that she does not come instantly every time she is called. Maternal limitations are frustrating and disappointing and become the source of anger toward the parent. But this anger also acts as an impetus for growth; when bliss is not total, the infant cries harder and squirms more for attention. This primitive behavior is rewarded often enough to establish a permanent connection between exertion and satisfaction.

Life itself forces us to grow beyond the narrow limits of what our parents have to offer. Maternal care is crucial in the early stages of life, but the world offers far more complex opportunities for satisfaction than even the most selfless mother can provide. Growth toward maturity as a fully functioning individual demands that a child gradually shed the perception of "mother" (and "father") as an all-sufficient gratifier. It is only by separating emotionally from our parents that we attain our own identity and independence of action. Our essential challenge is to develop our capabilities to the degree that we can gain maximum satisfaction through our own efforts. This is the essence of maturity—the perspective from which we explore the world with creativity, reason, imagination, and tenacity.

Independence is an elixir of life, not just as a joyous feeling of freedom, but as insurance against the ever-present urge to return to the benign passivity of parental care. Mature individuals have been freed from the ghosts of the past, including their infantile dependence on Mother and their fears of growing up and taking on life by themselves. If we are emotionally healthy adults, we have gained enough security and assurance from our early experiences of goodness and love to be able to operate from internal sources of power. We become psychologically mobile, running on our own batteries rather than through the extension cord of parental energy. We face life's challenges with confidence in our own ability to cope—indeed, to triumph.

But independence has a second important characteristic: It stimulates us to give more to others. Although some may argue that self-sufficiency encourages us to avoid relationships because we do not need to rely on the caretaking of other people, the opposite is true. Knowing how to fill our own needs and wants reasonably provides an impetus for social interaction; we can relate interdependently with mutual sharing. The less desperate we are for external support or attention, the less apt we are to manipulate others for selfish purposes. It is easier to affirm the brotherhood of man when we have inner stores from which to draw.

Awareness of our own vulnerability prompts us to become independent of our parents' provision and sphere of influence, but that independence must then spark efforts to become productive. Only then can we get more for ourselves and have something of value to give to others.

A twenty-seven-year-old man recently came for psychotherapy with symptoms of apathy and depression. Sad-faced and listless, he describes himself as "weak," unsure of what to do with his life, although a few months ago he earned a master's degree in electrical engineering. He is obviously out on his own in the world, but he is doing nothing productive with his life and seems unable to move forward.

"My life's just not going anywhere," he mournfully tells me. "I've done a lot to get where I wanted to be, but I seem to have stopped once I arrived."

"Vic, it sounds like you feel powerless to take advantage of your many skills," I comment. "Yet this is a time when you could be making great progress."

"My productivity is nil," he admits. "It's really got me down, but I don't know what's wrong with me."

When I ask Vic when he first noticed a decrease in energy and effectiveness, he tells me that shortly after graduation he sensed a letdown, as if his work was now finished rather than just beginning. Here is a man who has trouble moving from one stage of life to the next. Going back to school for a postgraduate degree has been a way of postponing his baptism into the adult world of responsible self-maintenance. His current lack of productivity reflects a subconscious fear of letting go of what he considers to be security. He left home to go to school, but he was not ready to leave school to go to work. This man's developmental pattern has been to go only as far as his limited self-confidence allows. Now he has reached what he perceives as his limit. Our work together will be to expand his personal view of his abilities and training so that he can become productive in the world at large.

Our productivity stands as a tribute to our imaginations and our skills. The child who builds a sandcastle may someday build a skyscraper. Each of our creations becomes a stepping-stone toward our continual self-development. In a healthy growth pattern there is an ever-widening spiral of productivity and interaction with our environment. This activity helps fill the inner void of self-doubt and dependency. In that onward process of wanting, searching, and growing, we discover many truths about ourselves and other people and find a purpose for life itself.

The Biological Aspects of Getting

Casual observation illustrates how the reciprocal process of getting and giving is central in our biological functioning. Our respiratory, circulatory, and digestive systems constantly operate on the basis of taking in and putting out. Before we can exhale, we first must inhale; the stomach takes in food and then releases nutrients into a bloodstream maintained by the filling-and-emptying action of the heart. The rhythm of these vital organs bespeaks the inherent wisdom of the living organism: There can be no getting without subsequently giving in return. The body "knows" this sequential pattern is crucial for its existence and automatically responds to the underlying physiological principle.

Being healthy demands that we carefully attend to our biological needs. Within us are complicated physiological sensors that monitor the body's condition. The goal is homeostasis, a state of balance for input and output. If we fail to respond carefully to what our internal sensors tell us and to adjust our behavior accordingly, we may experience malfunction or even death.

Theodore Millon describes the profound influence of biological factors on human behavior. He describes how each individual's nervous system has the ability to select, transform, and register objective events according to its own distinctive biological characteristics. In fact, "normal psychological functioning depends on the integrity of certain key areas of biological structure, and any impairment of this substrate will result in disturbed thought, emotion, and behavior."[2]

Millon explains that because each person's chemistry, heredity, genetic makeup, and unique brain structure result in a distinctive pattern of response, all of us will seek to satisfy ourselves in our own individual ways. The energy available for reaching out into the world stems from our biological dispositions and is channeled into stable behavior patterns. The environment shapes these behaviors in various ways, but they arise from internal factors specific to each person. Initial reactions to new situations, sensory alertness, adaptability to change, differing moods, and different levels and intensities of response, distractibility, and persistence—all of these exert their influence on our individual responses.[3]

Those who claim that "biology is destiny" have considerable evidence to support their assertions. My own position is that the process of getting is undoubtedly rooted in human physiology but must also be studied from the vantage point of the behavioral sciences.

Getting Emotional Satisfaction

Humans, unlike other animals, spend much of their time pursuing satisfaction on a nonbiological level. How we feel is important to us and works in tandem with our thinking process. Ideally, we supervise our feelings with good judgment, common sense, forethought, and logic—and we color and brighten our plans and decisions with the full spectrum of positive emotional response. Feeling and thinking perform important functions in human existence, each serving as a check-and-balance to ensure maximum efficiency and satisfaction.

How we act is determined by how we feel and think about ourselves, others, and the physical world. If we are fully functional, we continually move toward obtaining what we desire. However, as we reach toward our various goals, we must exercise good judgment and careful decision making to avoid unfortunate consequences. Self-monitoring allows us the opportunity to preserve what we have obtained and to quit while we are ahead.

The so-called workaholic continues to search for more and more money or success even after having achieved a good deal of both. Tom North qualifies for such a diagnosis. Fed by his habitual desire to escape the childhood pain of never having "enough," Tom presses on, oblivious of all he has already obtained and risking hypertension and a broken marriage. Because his time dimension is stuck in the past, Tom acts obsessively to satisfy "the needy child," which is the perception he has of himself. This self-portrait is drawn so indelibly that Tom does not consider the long-range implications of his quest for satisfaction.

As we progress developmentally from infancy to adulthood, we accumulate experiences that frame our specific ways of thinking and feeling about life. Because many of these patterns are deeply ingrained and will not change much over time, they overlay our basic personality structure, identify who we are, and determine how we behave. Some of us are cautious, some more aggressive. Some are thoughtful, others impulsive. We all have individualized approaches to finding satisfaction because we have developed stylized reaction patterns over the years. Whether or not they are productive, our ways of responding become so automatic that we may be unaware of our motives, our choices, and our own best interests.

Consider, for example, the case of Ann Southfield, the lonely, somber woman who has bound herself to her unhappy mother. Although Ann certainly knows that her life is slipping away quite unfulfilled, she has created her own loneliness by isolating herself from both sociability and personal enrichment. She is not a happy woman, yet she continues her unrewarding behavior patterns as if consulting some inner master plan. Two forces keep Ann locked into her nonproductive behavior. First there is her own personality structure, the consistent internalized way of thinking and feeling that she has fashioned principally on the basis of her mother's example. Everyone is somewhat guided by such outdated and inappropriate "road maps." But most of us do not impoverish ourselves in the process, as Ann does.

There are also external factors that perpetuate Ann's self-defeating behavior, since other people react according to how they perceive her. Ann's quiet blandness evokes quiet aloofness from her associates. As this cycle of limited social interaction becomes established, she seems doomed to an isolated, unsatisfying routine. Ann gets little from life because her demands are so meager.

Changing our ways to get more out of life must begin with an understanding of how we automatically draw upon deeper parts of our beings to make our choices. Asking such questions as "Where did this all begin?" and "What am I getting out of acting this way?" initiates self-discovery. Then we can begin to modify our behavior, substituting more appropriate patterns for those that have been unrewarding in the past.

The Pleasure Principle

Early in his theorizing about human behavior, Sigmund Freud described the search for pleasure as one of the two basic principles governing human nature. He stated that even in infancy we attempt to undo the tensions and pains of being alive. Relief of this stress provides much of the pleasure we experience and is the means whereby we maintain inner balance.

Later theorists explain the search for pleasure as more than an urge to relieve psychic tensions or biological drives. Behavioral psychologist B. F. Skinner describes "pleasure" as the personal satisfaction (or reward) that results from our choices.[4] Each time we experience pleasure, our choices are "reinforced." Thus, whenever we enjoy coffee with sugar, that preference is rewarded, and our future coffee-drinking behavior will be based on those past reinforcements. We seek what has previously pleased us, whether or nor our choices are appropriate to present circumstances.

We can make our lives more satisfying by paying better attention to what pleases us and allowing this knowledge to guide our choices. The more pleasures we seek and find—be they small or large—the more satisfying we make our lives. Yet it is amazing how people limit their repertoire of pleasures! Some know little about having fun; they are too focused on their problems. Ironically, if they allowed themselves more good times, their problems would seem far less overwhelming. Others have narrowed their views of life until they no longer see the pleasures that are available. Whether they are slaves to meaningless traditions or victims of bad habits, far too many people lead routinized and impoverished lives. At the other extreme are those whose principal satisfaction comes in trading up for bigger and better sources of pleasure, as if the real joy is simply having "more." In setting their sights ever higher, they close their eyes to what they already have.

Obtaining more pleasure is certainly a legitimate goal, so long as we keep our desires in a proper perspective. Too often we seek pleasure on the basis of what "feels good" rather than according to what is right for us or anyone else. Many public and private sins involve the human pre-occupation with getting far more than is required to satisfy a particular need.

In reality or fantasy, we seem determined to get our pleasures, whether sensible or foolhardy, and are bewildered when the prizes we win are unsatisfying. Ivan Boesky, Leona Helmsley, and Jim Bakker seem to confirm Plato's ancient observation that "pleasure is the bait of sin." Yet we use our desires to justify our improper choices and find it difficult to delay our immediate gratification or accept substitutes for what we think we want.

It may be especially difficult to control our pleasure seeking if we have stored many memories of bad times. As we evaluate how our lives are going, we often make conclusions rooted in past disappointments that are hard to accept. Previous circumstances may seem so unfair that we believe only extraordinary gains can compensate us adequately. Then we are in danger of risking the greater joy of freedom and personal integrity by rejecting the very standards of decency that preserve our security in a civilized society and reflect the operation of universal moral directives.

Anxiety Reduction

There is a hidden dimension to pleasure-seeking that may account for some of our imprudent methods and our lack of pleasure in what we attain, for we also seek emotional satisfaction to reduce our anxieties. We feel anxiety's sting from birth to death, no matter how successful we are. Because of our distinctly human ability to be aware of ourselves in refer-ence to the universe, we measure our accomplishments according to some inner criteria of security. We are therefore constantly on guard lest we lose what we have or fail to achieve what we seek. Although most of the time we feel more anxious than is warranted—imagining losses that have little chance of occurring or would not be as devastating as we think—we keep ourselves vigilant and self-protective.

If our anxiety manifests itself as a general sense of uneasiness over our human frailty, we may worry for no apparent reason, have insomnia, feel unworthy, and carry an expectation of failure. Anxiety can also appear as a specific fear of loss, such as the impending death of an ailing loved one.

If the fear has a basis in reality, we drop our apprehensions quickly when the crisis passes.

When we are tense or worried, we typically seek ways to relieve these painful feelings through the pleasures of food, love, stimulants, or material increase. As we fill ourselves, we drive out tensions—if only for a few moments. That kind of "pleasure" is not really a positive experience, since it provides only temporary relief and adds nothing to our storehouse of satisfaction.

There are some times of life that are more anxiety-provoking than others. Many young adults, for example, report feeling anxious much of the time. Out on their own and away from the security previously provided by their families or colleges, they actually have much to be anxious about. Many are in entry-level jobs with earnings and opportunities far below their goals or talents. Others are seeking a mate or are in relationships that are frustrating because they are less than ideal. There are often feelings of living under a cloud of pressure to maintain the lifestyles they once enjoyed at home in a family setting. Or there are worries about never fulfilling their "impossible" dreams. These stress factors can easily prod them along in a frantic search for more goods or pleasures to calm their fears.

People over age sixty also report a heightened anxiety level. Whether facing issues of retirement, financial security, health, or concern about their adult children, older people often find that their later years are not necessarily a time of golden contentment. In fact, the crabbiness and possessive ways often found in senior citizens reveal that, despite having already faced and won most of life's major battles, the elderly still struggle with anxiety and insecurities. When they complain about life, they are saying that they remain constantly on guard against trouble.

Although anxiety prods us to get more as compensation, it also puts us at a disadvantage in our searching. When uptight and worried, we are not at our best. Anxious people pay undue attention to their apprehensions at the expense of daily responsibilities, opportunities, and pleasures. If we are preoccupied with grinding away at what is wrong, we are unable to pay attention to solving our problems effectively or even to enjoying ourselves.

When anxiety is deep or persists for a long time, that tension is woven into our personalities. Consider a firstborn child who is anxious over the extra attention given a new baby. The child may experience a jealous anger so intense that it is vented in a secret wish that the baby would die. This hidden desire, along with the urge to get more love and attention, may be covered up by efforts to be extra nice to the baby so that the angry truth will not be revealed. If this superficial show of affection becomes the behavioral pattern in later relationships, honest communication of feelings will have been sacrificed to maximize the chance for affirmation.

When we cover our sore spots, pretending so that others will not know how much we hurt, we also rob ourselves of the potential benefits of self-knowledge. Failing to recognize the seat of our anxieties keeps our successes from feeding the inner person. We remain dissatisfied whenever the payoff is not pleasure but merely anxiety reduction. This outcome may be reflected in the comment, after what *should* have been a fun time, "Well, that's over with!" People who hurry to "get Christmas over with," for example, apply the holidays as a temporary balm for their anxieties rather than enjoy them as a time of happy celebration.

Hidden anxiety that arises from long-term problems or a specific trauma in the past leaves unhealed scars that can be the basis for anti-social behavior. Gene, a young man of twenty-five, was referred to me by his attorney after being arrested for shoplifting. Although Gene has a good job and an affluent lifestyle, he always feels deprived and in need of further symbols of success. Raised in a poor family, Gene earned a college degree by means of a scholarship and his determined desire to escape his childhood insecurities. "My feelings about the past haunt me," he explains. "No matter how good I have it, I often feel this gut-level fear that somehow I'll lose what I have and be left helpless." When walking through a large department store, Gene was overcome with an urge to shoplift a silk tie that he could have easily afforded.

"It was wrong, but it felt very exciting," he explains.

"Like you'd be getting something for nothing?" I ask.

"That's it," Gene replies. "I'm always looking for that little extra because it makes me feel better."

As treatment progressed, Gene learned how feelings of resentment and helplessness from his impoverished past have continued to contaminate his present sense of well-being. Once he identified his inner feeling of anxiety, he saw how to minimize it by consciously decreasing the amount of time he spent reflecting on his bad times and paying more attention to the successes he has earned. He began to give himself due credit for effort, and the resulting good feelings left little room for anxiety. By orienting himself to the present, rather than focusing on the past, Gene has become more optimistic about meeting life's tasks and stresses.

When we are overly anxious, we may develop self-defeating coping mechanisms that do little to reduce the anxiety. If we persist in these ineffective patterns, our behavior is called neurotic. We can easily spot neurosis in others—in people who are desperate for attention and resort to loud exhibitionism to get noticed (and hence are shunned even more) or in chronic worriers who are so afraid of missing out on a pleasurable event that they are too uptight to enjoy it (or even forget to attend). Neurotic behavior is characteristically a futile and aimless attempt to dispel or compensate for unspoken fears that may have no basis in fact.

Probably more personal happiness and productive work hours are lost to anxiety than to any other emotion. To increase our efficiency and level of satisfaction, we must begin by carefully noting the thoughts, words, and feelings that have brought about our self-defeating habits. Monitoring our behavior for several days will give us a baseline from which to compare future levels of progress. If, for example, we notice that we frequently say, "I just can't do this," we must be willing to restate our approach. We can counter our negativism with such positive statements as "I can do this if I work at it." The more aware we are of the reasons for our underlying anxiety, the easier it will be to eliminate neurotic behavior patterns. Relief comes in substituting goal-oriented efforts for our old, counterproductive ways.

We can also decrease our anxieties and thereby increase our satisfactions by carefully noting how well we are doing. When we "count our blessings," we confirm our successes, stamping them deeper into conscious awareness. The power found in positive thinking is twofold. First, we can focus away from real and imaginary losses and minimize the anxieties they engender; second, we strengthen ourselves by more deeply acknowledging life's goodness and claiming our share of this bounty.

Getting as Preparation for the Future

When asked to comment on what had most impressed him about human nature over a lifetime, Rabbi Abraham Heschel replied that it is the amazing ability of people to deceive themselves.

There are indeed many paths to self-deception. One of the most common detours on our journey through life involves our temptation to ignore future needs as we search for present satisfaction. For example, if we regularly eat improperly, we are disregarding implications for our future health. Or, if we live at the edge of our financial limits, with little concern for preserving some of our assets for the retirement years or investment opportunities, we imply that today's pleasures are all that matter.

Mental-health experts recommend that we learn to live in the here and now. Although this is sound advice because the present is all we can experience—the past is gone and the future is yet to come—some people interpret this statement as meaning that we should only live *for* today. That limited perspective provides a motive for obtaining every possible enjoyment today with no regard for what tomorrow may bring.

We live in an era when some claim it makes little sense to prepare for tomorrow, for this world seems headed for destruction. They cite potential for a nuclear and biological warfare, the signs of environmental decay, and the rising incidence of violence and other crimes as good reason to be pessimistic about the future. So why not live it up now? While these arguments let us temporarily avoid some universal questions that seem too difficult to answer, they fail to address our hopeful belief that tomorrow will come, that there is some order to life, and that there is a God who not only has his hand in the destiny of the world but in our personal life as well.

Those who get what they can now but also turn their eyes to the future show the foresight that is characteristic of maturity. Planning for tomorrow's circumstances provides relief from nagging fears of what life will someday be like. As we presently care for our physical, mental, and financial health, we help guarantee a continuation of what we now enjoy.

Part of our preparation for the future involves finding the means to avoid a concept of ourselves as personally insignificant. Ernest Becker points out in *The Denial of Death* that we try to persevere by our persistent consumption and hope to find some sense of significance that will go on after we die.[5] We seek to fulfill our need for self-transcendence through our children, in cultural symbols, or in our beliefs that we are here for the higher purpose of leaving the world a little better than when we entered. All such forms of leaving our mark, says Becker, are attempts to escape our sense that death is final and inevitable.

Whether we believe our existence flows from the Creator's hand and accept the tenets of the Judeo-Christian tradition—or we reject theological explanations in favor of "science"—it is undeniable that ours is an ordered world in which certain principles of human behavior operate. One of those truisms is that life itself is an ongoing process of getting and giving. We must concurrently take and receive in order to survive, to satisfy our desires, and to grow toward maturity.

The expected outcome of this process is a developmental level at which the individual is adequately satisfied by his or her getting behavior and also motivated to give to others in turn. But many of us do not grow sufficiently to transcend self and consider the rights of others, much less their needs. We easily succumb to the allure of materialism, selling our birthright of healthy adulthood for trivial goods and transitory pleasures. As we shall next consider, lust for more and more of everything creates an obsessive consumer mentality that puts self ahead of all else, despite the sometimes heavy cost.

3

Contemporary Getting

The Indulgent Self

"What good is it for a man to gain the whole world, yet forfeit his soul?"

Mark 8:36

Matt and Marla Price have waited almost too long before coming for help. Referred by their attorney for marriage counseling after Marla filed for divorce, this couple must now examine personal and financial issues that they have avoided for a long time.

Matt is thirty-five, Marla thirty-two; they have no children. They met in college where Matt was a finance major and Marla was in elementary education. They fed their love with dreams of the future, which included a high-paying job for Matt, a showcase house, and several children who could have all the opportunities their parents had been given in their own affluent childhood homes.

Matt did very well at the job he got right after college. Intelligent and ambitious, he earned such rapid promotions that after only a year his superiors asked him to take two years off to get an MBA degree. They agreed to pay his tuition and promised him a lucrative position after graduation. Marla, who had been hoping to resign from her teaching job and start a family that year, admitted that they would be better off in the long run if Matt accepted his firm's offer. She consented to work while he was in school and for one year thereafter so that they would have a sizable nest egg.

Unfortunately, the couple's taste for the good life, cultivated as kids in upper-middle-class families, continued to dominate their lives. Matt and Marla easily talked themselves into borrowing money for expensive furniture and a new car, justifying their purchases by dreaming of the big money soon to be theirs. But when Matt received his promised high-salaried position, his urge for spending only increased. He reasoned that by waiting one more year before having a child, he and Marla could pay their debts and also enjoy life and each other more deeply. "We'll be sacrificing for our kids for the next twenty-five years," Matt reminded Marla. "Let's you and I have fun first." The glamorous clothes and expensive vacations felt so right to them. "We have champagne tastes," they joked to their parents.

One year of pleasuring stretched to two. As their income rose, they felt it important to have all the material pleasures that other couples in their social circle were purchasing. Although Marla, now thirty, was troubled over waiting still longer before becoming pregnant, she decided to postpone her maternal plans so they could buy a large home in an exclusive part of town. "In one year we'll be ready for a family," Matt promised. It was a promise he could not keep.

Matt got an opportunity to buy a company with a friend of his, but it meant using their home as collateral for the huge loan that would be needed for the purchase. Marla was absolutely against Matt's idea. She worried about the risk of losing their home if the company failed, and she certainly did not want to wait any longer before having a child. They argued for months. Matt pleaded that this was their big chance to have everything they had ever wanted. Marla gave in, but she became depressed. "Something inside lost hope," she told her friends. "I'm getting so I don't care what he does. All he wants is status and luxury. He'd sell his soul for the right price."

Matt and Marla have embraced a set of values that is common in contemporary America but quite different from the traditional ideas about the good life—working hard for what you want, but buying only what is necessary and saving the rest. Today, because we have expanded our definition of "necessary," we make demands upon ourselves and that can cause financial, personal, and moral problems of a magnitude not previously known. We want to be satisfied fully today and do not easily tolerate second-best or postponing our gratification. Furthermore, we are reluctant to make sacrifices to obtain our goals. Anything that risks personal pleasure while we push ahead is to be sidestepped if at all possible. Matt and Marla, like many of their contemporaries, believe they *must* eat their cake now, so they are unwilling to pay the price of long-range planning that their consumer mentality demands.

The Self As Consumer

Since about 1960, we Americans have dramatically changed our attitudes about the importance of material goods in our lives. As the economy has generally provided us with a better standard of living and the ability to use credit to finance our desires, we have subscribed to a rampant materialism. Many of us believe that (1) more of everything is better, and (2) we should satisfy our desires now, regardless of the wisdom of doing so. This consumer mentality has radically altered our ways of seeking satisfaction from that of our forebears.

We have come to assume that the American way of life means buying new, trading up, doing better than last year. Pleasure and personal indulgence often take precedence over good judgment, common sense, and the ability to pay for our purchases. We demand more of everything regardless of the intrinsic worth of our choices. Our buy-now-pay-later economics does not necessarily mean that we are not value-conscious or are disinterested in saving. But because value and thrift are not the primary determiners for our purchasing habits, appetite and imagination prevail.

Matt's father is a wealthy corporate attorney who came from a humble beginning. In his success, he indulged himself in ways his children came to consider as normative. The father's words, "Never go second-class," have become a core philosophy for his children. This attitude left Matt with the belief that self-worth is increased by material gain, that financial success is more important than any other aspect of life.

Paul Wachtel examines the psychological issues in the American quest for material gain in his book, *The Poverty of Affluence*.[1] He develops the theme that Americans (especially those who are middle-class) deeply believe that more is better, but as a result have suffered a "malaise." In an effort to solve their psychological problems of emptiness, loneliness, and restlessness and discover life's deeper meanings, Americans have substituted economic gains as an answer. Because they have found this answer to be inadequate, they are left feeling disappointed and even depressed. Wachtel explains that at the root of this dissatisfaction is a "miscalculation"—a pursuit of false goals that cannot bring contentment. He argues that people no longer define their aspirations in terms of some specific set of conditions, such as getting married and having a family, buying a house, setting definite economic goals, and living within a budget. Instead, their sense of satisfaction is fed by acquiring bigger and better material goods, just so they can feel they are getting more than they had before and as much as or more than their neighbors. "Our calculations tend to be relative," Wachtel states. "Wanting more remains a constant regardless of what we have."[2]

The more-is-better philosophy seems to have a "trickle-down" quality to it (to borrow a term from Ronald Reagan's economics). That is, we hope that more money, more pleasure, more symbols of affluence, will eventually filter down and satisfy all our inner desires. The naive expectation persists that, given enough of everything, we will finally be content.

Since a consumer mentality interprets any delay in gratification as a source of anxiety and frustration, sometimes we cannot rest until we quiet our nagging desires by satisfying them. Whereas earlier generations suppressed their inner urges if they seemed "unreasonable," now the assumption is that every whim must be gratified if we are to have peace. We often act more to reduce our tensions than to satisfy legitimate requirements, as though being deprived of even trivial pleasures will be the worst thing that could happen to us. If, like adolescents, we imagine that "everyone has one but me," being without something we desire brings a sense of personal failure and embarrassment.

Although the government fosters consumerism as a way to keep the economy strong, we do not base our conspicuous consumption on such patriotic motives. We demand a high standard of living for emotional reasons. Purchasing goods and services is crucial to our sense of personal worth because we believe that the more we *have*, the more we *are*. We tend to judge others and are judged in return by the visible proof of an affluent lifestyle. Our own opinions about how our progress compares with the Joneses' propel us ever harder to keep pace. We spend not just for the intrinsic value of what we buy, but for the internal reassurance that we are really doing well and for the "bragging rights" these items afford us. Affirming our worth through the anticipated applause sometimes seems our most important motivation.

And when we are noticed—even envied—do we find contentment and slow down? No, for a taste of the good life rarely suffices; our successes usually increase our appetites not our satisfactions. Furthermore, most Americans seek not just to consume goods or earn the praise of their fellows, but to take on the world. With the "Westward ho!" adventurism of our forebears, we set out to explore new experiences. Seeking a new twist to our vacations, we lug along bulky videocameras to tape every wiggle and sigh. We discover ethnic restaurants hidden on some back street and rave over strange foods we would never touch at home. Or we travel to faraway countries before exploring our homeland because we want to be children of the universe.

Odgen Nash once quipped that "America is tipped and everything loose rolls down to California." Actually we now roll in every direction. The average family moves once every five years. We willingly uproot ourselves and leave friends or relatives to seek new opportunities for success. Like modern pilgrims in search of a promised land, we seem ready in an instant to trade community, security, and familiarity for "everything that is behind door number two," to quote Monty Hall.

Are we getting anywhere? Is our search for more worth the cost? Of course, the argument for an expansive individualism has some merit, and our efforts to discover more about ourselves and our world takes strength and courage. But this position ignores the evidence that our mobility in quest of more satisfaction is taking its toll on the marriages and families of America. Too often, because we have roots no deeper than the shallow soil of excitement or anticipation, we have no staying power in the inevitable storms of life.

As we earn more, we spend more. If we don't earn "enough," we borrow. Because the pressures of debts and persistent desires give us no peace, we look for other answers. Perhaps we indulge our sexual urges or seek relief in an altered mind state. Some people drink, take cocaine, or bombard themselves with the colors and vibrations of intense sensual stimuli. But when they go up, they must face coming down, so that is no answer. Maybe being "the best" at something is what counts—so we diet and exercise frantically, sometimes to stay healthy, but mainly to have a vague sense of accomplishment. Or we go back to school, read more widely, save to travel, join investment clubs, do yoga, improve the quality of our friendships. All of these efforts may be beneficial, but if there is still a feeling of missing something, the search for more goes on.

The quest for personal enhancement has led to a consumer mentality that provides many opportunities for growth and excitement. However, in our desire for self-improvement, we often descend a spiral staircase into the deeper parts of the self and become lost. If we replace the normal urge for advancement with total self-preoccupation, we can get so caught up in the process of searching that we do not enjoy what we obtain. This kind of frustration leaves us constantly "on the make," investing little effort in anything but our self-oriented goals, yet trapped by our search for answers that escape us.

Becoming Self-Centered

In one sense it is fair to say that we are all centered on ourselves, for the self defines our reality and is the internal base from which we operate. Any act that promotes the self's welfare contributes to our overall health and satisfaction. Because the self requires careful attention, centering on one's needs can be understood not as "selfishness" but as a normal acknowledgment of personal worth. A healthy self-centeredness impels the individual to search for fulfillment and reinforces the self's importance.

Centering our attention on self-care does not necessarily mean that we avoid paying attention to others. If we enhance our own personhood, we have more strength for the task of becoming others-oriented. Furthermore, focusing on the self does not rule out the centrality of God in a religious person's life. Quite the contrary—for if we believe in a loving and purposeful God who has created us in his own image, our individual worth is thereby affirmed, and we are strengthened by our faith in a master plan in which we have an important role to play and will receive intangible rewards. Whatever our view of human existence, it takes much inner strength to discover our own being, yet transcend our self-preoccupation and reach out to others.

Consider the case of a college student who has come for counseling with problems of guilt. He explains that he wants to enter the priesthood but feels guilty because his father has always expected him to join the family business. "I feel my career choice is somewhat selfish," reports the son, "but I want no part of the business world and feel a strong calling from God to take on the spiritual work of a parish priest. If only Dad would approve, I'd feel much better about my decision."

As we discuss his feelings, I point out that no matter how much he loves and respects his father, he has every right to pursue a profession that reflects his own desires. I explain that in being true to himself he is not dishonoring his father. Furthermore, if he ignores his calling in deference to his father's wishes, he will feel a lifelong resentment toward his father and be guilty of neglecting his own dream. The student realizes with considerable relief that the pain he feels is for his father's disappointment and not for his own wrongdoing. He decides to explain to his father that his love and respect for him will not be compromised just because they do not agree on a vocation. "Even if Dad doesn't agree," he concludes, "I know in my heart that my motives are not selfish. I just hope that someday he will understand that I must be me."

Unfortunately, "self-centeredness" is often used only as a negative term to connote a preoccupation with one's own needs and an under-valuing of the needs of others. Although, as we have seen, there are many healthy aspects to focusing on one's selfhood, I will be using the term *self-centeredness* to refer to normal behavior gone awry. In this sense, self-centered people dwell excessively on themselves at the expense of others. Because preoccupation with oneself minimizes the possibility of establishing a rewarding interaction with other people, it limits our overall efficiency. Self-absorbed people bore us because all they talk about is themselves; they also annoy us by dismissing *our* feelings and experiences as unimportant. Others offend by displaying signs of their accomplishments: a montage of diplomas, a Phi Beta Kappa key on a gold chain, framed citations of achievement, or an impressive array of photographs taken with various celebrities. This kind of pretension creates an uneasiness in others but also reveals a lack of good taste, maturity, and a realistic self-image.

The underlying insecurity of self-centered people does not allow any more concern for others than is absolutely necessary. In their neediness, fed by real or imagined deprivation, they frantically pursue satisfaction and are intolerant of outside interference. At its extreme, self-centered-ness involves looking out for oneself at the expense of others, satisfying every personal desire regardless of the appropriateness of the means or even the legality of the end result.

Another way unhealthy self-focus operates is through excessive indul-gence of otherwise normal desires to a point of satiation. If we eat too much, abuse alcohol, drink coffee all day, spend impulsively, or are sexu-ally promiscuous, we risk losing control of the self we are trying to satisfy. Self-indulgence can be described as an expression of the child within us, that urge-dominated and very needy person we all once were. That young child does not care what is right or wrong but simply wants imme-diate gratification. In early infancy this behavior is excusable because cortical reasoning ability is not yet developed. But as childhood pro-gresses into adulthood, we can no longer claim "innocence." Maturity implies an awareness of standards of acceptable behavior, but if we still think as a child, our inner impulses will prevail over the better judgment we should have as an adult.

Self-indulgence can be seen not simply as a childish response to an irresistible urge, but as calculated behavior that the adult personality allows. The reasonable inner adult may comply momentarily with the inner child's demands, thereby permitting an act that may be unwise or antisocial. Why this happens is often revealed in psychotherapy by discovering that the inner adult self has been denying certain experiences or desires that are seen as evil or less than ideal. The adult mind often walls off its "bad" impulses, but later these suppressed feelings can emerge in an unguarded moment. In effect, reason finally gives way to desire. The forbidden act occurs because the inner child, not the adult, is in charge.

When we indulge ourselves by allowing pent-up feelings to emerge, we can gain valuable self-knowledge that helps us avoid further outbursts or shows us how to satisfy those inner urges appropriately. But if we habitually indulge our secret wishes to excess, our self-centeredness keeps us preoccupied with securing constant attention and special treatment, and our relationships are at serious risk.

Contemporary Narcissism

Self-importance may make us so imbalanced that we expect everyone else to defer to us as if we were entitled to some exalted position. This kind of exaggerated self-focus is known as "narcissism."

In Greek mythology the story is told of the nymph Echo who died because Narcissus would not return her love. As punishment the god Nemesis caused Narcissus to spend his life pining away in love for himself after viewing his own beauty reflected in a pool.

Narcissism has become one of those pop-psych buzz words that we bandy about just as flippantly as we use other psychological terminology. Sports announcers refer to a "schizophrenic" game if a team begins to act radically different as play goes on. People call each other "paranoid" when what they mean is suspicious or distrustful. Narcissism is one of these catchy words that is often used incorrectly, even by mental-health professionals, some of whom fail to differentiate between true narcissism (a personality disorder) and narcissistic-*like* behaviors (such as inappropriate spending or excessive boasting over one's accomplishments).

Narcissism as a personality disorder is defined in the *Diagnostic and Statistical Manual of Mental Disorders: Third Edition* (the "DSM III") as follows:

> The essential feature is a Personality Disorder . . . in which there is a grandiose sense of self-importance or of uniqueness; preoccupation with

fantasies of unlimited success; exhibitionistic need for constant attention and admiration; (undue) responses to threats of self-esteem; and . . . disturbances in interpersonal relationships, such as feelings of entitlement, interpersonal exploitativeness . . . and a lack of empathy. The exaggerated sense of self-importance may be manifested as extreme self-centeredness and self-absorption.[3]

True narcissists envy others for who they are and what they have, use surface charm to get what they want, and become cold or even ruthless when disappointed. Psychoanalyst Otto Kernberg observes that they "feel they have the right to control and possess others and to exploit them without guilt feelings. . . ."[4]

Many persons who are not pathological narcissists exhibit mild forms of narcissism in their attitudes and behavior. Some writers describe contemporary Americans as socially and personally narcissistic. Psychoanalyst Aaron Stern states in his book, *Me: The Narcissistic American*, that we are "sailing unsteadily into erosion" much the same as the ancient Romans, caught in a "struggle to prevent our narcissistic selves from overwhelming our caring selves." He believes that "collective narcissism increases individual narcissism and vice versa," and implies that most of us are indulging in a cult of self-love.[5] Stern chronicles ways in which self-preoccupation influences marriage, family life, and male-female relationships. However, in my opinion he does not adequately distinguish between narcissism (as a character pathology) and self-indulgent preoccupation (which is not necessarily a personality disorder). It is not clear how he arrives at the conclusion that someone is narcissistic if his or her life "is governed by forces of narcissism more than fifty percent of the time."[6] Despite these objections, Stern's book is otherwise very readable and informative.

Christopher Lasch's book, *The Culture of Narcissism*, examines the topic more precisely and distinguishes well between narcissism as a personality disorder and narcissism as a popular synonym for "selfishness." But he, too, sees Western cultures as overrun with narcissists and denounces American social and moral values as being in a state of "bankruptcy" to the point that we "cannot face the future." He sees us as "becoming more warlike and barbaric," and generally uses angry language to condemn our excesses.[7] On the other hand, Daniel Yankelovich calls Lasch "a mighty hater, angry and gloom-ridden in his images of American life and the narcissism he associates with the search for self-fulfillment."[8] He describes Lasch's list of traits as "colorful, but arbitrary" and doubts that there is much "evidence that Americans have developed these traits of personality as a response to developments unleashed by late capitalism. . . ."[9]

There remains much controversy about the incidence of narcissism (however it is defined) and its societal implications. Psychologist Paul Wachtel comments that when a term like narcissism can be used "to refer to self-love; self-hatred; self-esteem [or] . . . a genuine regard for oneself; [and] pathological self-regard . . . such a protean term hardly seems like a sound basis for careful and precise analysis of social trends."[10] But the major point drawn from the various writings on narcissism is that there is a continuum extending from normal self-care on the one hand to excessive self-focus on the other, and the latter can easily lead to pathology.

We live in a cultural environment where narcissistic behavior is clearly evident in the wheeling-and-dealing of government officials, the manipulations of Wall Street traders, and the disregard of consumer welfare by certain giant corporations. Less public examples are seen in the "I deserve the best" attitude of ordinary citizens—a self-focused view used to great advantage by the advertising media. Most of us can also cite anecdotal evidence of this gimme-gimme self-centeredness. For example, I know of a wealthy widow who recently paid the traveling expenses of a less affluent friend on a trip to the Caribbean that they took together. The recipient of this generosity was heard to say, while stretching out in a pool-side chair at their luxury resort, "This is how I was meant to live. This is the *real* me!"

Where does such thinking originate? Why should the desire for the good life bring a feeling of entitlement? Most of us have imagined what it would be like to afford whatever we want, and it is hardly abnormal to dream of living in Camelot. We cannot be faulted for wanting the best unless our preoccupation with pleasure takes us beyond the limits of common sense and peace of mind. How have so many people become caught up in a philosophy of excess?

Rhoda Rottschafer, my wife, develops the idea in her research that modern narcissism may be more than a sign of social or individual pathology. She explores the thesis that narcissistic behavior is an effort to adapt to the stressful changes taking place in modern society. When people feel anxious because of excessive pressure, they often compensate by indulging themselves with whatever will make them feel better, sensible or not. This self-focus is designed to replace the missing sense of security and comfort and theoretically should decrease when the life-stresses are reduced.[11]

This point is well taken when seen in the context of the daily bombardment of stress factors we encounter. There are health issues (environmental pollution, toxins in our foods, cholesterol dangers, the AIDS problem, and the like); social problems (crime and other violence, poverty, racial unrest); and personal concerns (marital discord, financial pressures, job security, and other individual worries and fears). Modern living seems precarious indeed!

Robert Anderson of the Department of Family Medicine, University of Washington, defines stress as "any stimulus which demands adaptation on the part of the organism."[12] He goes on to explain that tension is "the biggest single factor in the onset of disability, distress, and death. . . ."[13] From that perspective, narcissistic self-focus can be understood as a way of adapting to the distress we feel because life seems too perplexing, and we cannot feel secure or achieve our goals reasonably. We may prefer not to live selfishly, but it is difficult to avoid selfish motives when other coping mechanisms seem ineffective.

Feeling entitled to the very best in life and seeking it greedily can be understood as a cry of distress. We want to be "happy" but find contentment eluding us. As we notice our neighbors' conspicuous spending and believe the advertising hype that everyone else has more than we do, it is natural to feel deprived and resentful. Then healthy self-care can be exaggerated to the point of scheming, exploitation, and manipulation to achieve material ends that we believe will satisfy our longings.

Jack is just such a man. Resentful of having to drop out of college because of his father's death, Jack began to nurse the fear that he would never achieve as much as his former classmates. Jack got a job with advancement potential, but he was preoccupied with comparing his successes with those of others. As long as his peers also had financial struggles and entry-level jobs, Jack was reasonably comfortable. However, by the time he turned thirty, it became obvious that he was gradually being left behind in the wage race. Although a college diploma does not guarantee professional success, Jack could not stop blaming his slow progress on his limited education.

"It's not fair," Jack told me bitterly. "I deserve more than what I've got. I cringe every time a buddy drives up in his new car or I hear of someone else's job promotion."

Jack has come for psychotherapy after being caught writing bad checks. "I'm not a thief," he argues. "It's just that I'm tired of feeling like a failure." He confesses to running his credit cards to the limit and being in debt to several friends and relatives. "I like to look good and have people notice me. It's not my fault I've had a lot of bad breaks." Jack has crossed the line between taking good care of himself and narcissistic self-indulgence in search of personal validation. Although Jack is an intelligent man, in his frustration over what he sees as life's unfairness, he has allowed his petty desires to overrule his reason (remember that demanding inner child mentioned earlier?). Rather than alter his goal of matching the affluence of his friends, he has tried to reach that level sooner by stealing. Jack's wishes control his life because his personality is twisted by narcissism.

There is a danger that excessive self-focus will continue after the stresses that caused it are reduced. Once an adaptive pattern of self-centeredness is established, the behavior can become habitual. There is increasing evidence that too many of us have already gone too far in our search for security and that a whole new cadre of insatiable young people is following close behind.

If we focus only on ourselves, we are isolated from the very sources of nourishment that promote growth and real satisfaction. As our perspective becomes increasingly narcissistic, our relationships at home and in the workplace are in jeopardy. We are not likely to make love commitments if we are preoccupied with our gratification. Neither will we find it necessary to follow anyone's rules but our own.

4

Dealing with Our Parents

The New Self

> A man performs but one duty—the duty of continuing his spirit,
> the duty of making himself agreeable to himself.
>
> Mark Twain

As we near the end of the twentieth century, we seem to find ourselves "agreeable" in far different ways than our ancestors did. More than ever before, we are demanding our individual rights, pursuing diverse satisfactions, and justifying our acquisitive behavior as an expression of our "free spirits."

An examination of the shifts in values and behaviors since 1960 makes for fascinating reading. Not only have those changes been extremely rapid, but they reflect a dramatic difference in character between today's young people and their parents and grandparents. We have moved culturally from an era of frugality, modesty, and a minimizing of the self to a time of materialistic excess, exhibitionism, and unabashed self-focus. How did the relatively selfless adults of the first six decades of this century produce such egocentric offspring?

This chapter will develop the thesis that the substantial changes in the kind of satisfactions we seek, and how we conduct the search, are in part a result of psychological differences between modern Americans and their parents. Specifically, I will suggest that various cultural, social, and spiritual values of the past fostered an obedient self-denial in many of our forebears. The result has been the personal naivete that is fairly typical of those who subordinate self to others, yet a hidden parental desire to experience their suppressed and forbidden wishes in the lives of their children. In effect, these selfless elders have unintentionally sired self-centered progeny and thereby set in motion a formidable social and psychological revolution.

The End of Innocence

In many ways, the last few decades have marked the end of innocence and a redefinition of the "pursuit of happiness." Social forecaster John Naisbitt discusses in his timely book, *Megatrends: Ten New Directions Transforming Our Lives,* what current influences are restructuring the shape of America as we shift from a largely industrial base to a new "information society" that will activate profound changes in how we act, think, believe, and consume.[1] Naisbitt sees our nation as being in "the time of the parenthesis, the time between eras," a period when people are shifting from national to world issues, from institutional help to self-help, and from what he calls an "either or" society to a "multiple option society." In this transitional time of ambiguity, says Naisbitt, those who can adapt to the shift will be far ahead of those who are wedded to the past.

Since Naisbitt's conclusions are based on the material written by several thousand newspaper editors, one might assume that what he writes reflects what most people already sense (assuming that newspaper editors accurately reflect what the public is concerned about). Many books and movies have described the fifties as a slow-moving time of innocent contentment, an era ended by the "hippie" counterculture and all the rebellious acting-out that eventually touched most strata of society. In the thirty or so years that have followed, there has been a dramatic, if not unsettling, quality to the scientific, sexual, racial, moral, and international changes that have occurred.

Since the early 1960s, we have been witnessing a release from the authoritarianism of a past steeped in the traditions of repressiveness, stoicism, and self-control. It now seems permissible to burst free and indulge ourselves in all the ways that authority figures or conscience have previously forbidden. Although Americans have always found ways to satisfy personal whim or to rebel in small, private ways, never before in our history have we witnessed individual expression in such bold, self-indulgent ways and with such widespread public approval. We insist on exercising our "rights," and we demand answers to previously forbidden questions. The increased affluence that many people enjoy has allowed them the time and money to explore their own personhood more deeply—to feel what they want to feel, see what they want to see, and know whatever is knowable.

This focus on self-awareness is breathtakingly new and very different from the individualistic spirit of past generations. The early settlers came to this New World seeking a better life and more freedom than was possible in their homelands. Although individualism was their ultimate goal, survival required banding together and forming social, political, economic, and family systems that demanded cultural conformity and approval by peers. Pride and individual effort were important, but ethnic solidarity and interdependence limited their expression, as did the strict doctrines of the prevailing religious establishment. Alienation from the group was the fate of those who married out of the faith or tried to advance beyond the cultural directives.

As the country grew from multinational immigration, a central message spread around the world: America provided not just freedom but also boundless opportunity. Stories of unlimited natural resources, free land for those who would work it, and an exploding industrialization challenged millions to pursue their dreams of success. Individual enterprise was amply rewarded; creativity and productivity fanned flames of even greater effort. The sky was the limit.

For generations American ingenuity was rooted in traditional family and community values. Cooperation for the common good, altruism, faith in the democratic ideals of our founding fathers undergirded and shaped personal ambition. The authority of our political, civil, and religious leaders was obeyed and the self was kept under firm control for the good of the majority. An emphasis on selfless duty and public approval prevented brash, egocentric displays; few dared to stand out as "different" lest they be considered selfish.

Nations, like the organizations and individuals that comprise them, grow by gradually developing new ways of solving problems. Until the 1960s "improvement" connoted personal growth for the good of the community. But since that time the American insistence on individual expansiveness has minimized the importance of the welfare of others. We have constructed an idiosyncratic search for satisfaction in ways that have challenged long-standing values and beliefs. Many of us now assume that what worked for past generations no longer seems relevant.

The personal and social changes of the post-1960s era has been most interesting and dramatic. Supposedly, in the quiet, post-World War II era, Americans settled down to a time of domestic tranquility. Our troops were home, the "Baby Boom" generation was being raised, and domestic tranquility was our central concern. Two World Wars and a Great Depression—all within less than thirty years—had exhausted us emotionally and financially; we needed a period of rest.

However, in less than two decades demands emerged and quickly blossomed to outright dissent. Racial minorities, feminist groups, college students, and antiwar protesters arose, not only to claim their rights, but also to shake an established order that had denied them equal opportunities. The young and the disadvantaged were willing to assert themselves emphatically—even violently—to arouse a complacent public that, in their estimation, had been lethargic for too long.

As protesters gained a national audience, they boldly and vigorously asserted themselves. Many people who had been more than willing to suppress personal issues now pursued their hidden agendas. Blatant challenges were issued to hallowed traditions of civil, political, educational, and religious institutions. A sexual revolution confronted our moral rules. A "hippy" generation rebelled against codes of dress, language, and ways of living together; a drug culture sought to free the mind and body from any sense of constraint. This activity was more than civil disobedience, or even consciousness raising. The focus now was on carving out new territories of self-fulfillment beyond that which had worked in the past.

The writers of the sixties and early seventies fanned the flames of doubt and dissent in less violent ways. Martin Mayer took to task Madison Avenue, schools, and television.[2,3,4] Charles Silverman examined the sins of the American educational system and racial issues.[5,6] Garry Wills took a fine-tooth comb to the political establishment in general and singled out Richard Nixon long before his presidential personal crisis.[7] These and other commentators asked questions that disturbed the comfortable—those who wanted to maintain the status quo.

Perhaps one of the most influential descriptions of the movement was that of Charles Reich, author of *The Greening of America*.[8] A professor at Yale Law School, Reich had academic and professional qualifications that added credibility to his evaluation of socio-political trends. In his book (which sold over two million copies), Reich described the evolution of a new way of thinking—one that now put the self into prominence. "Consciousness III" was challenging traditional beliefs and enhancing the self in ways previously ignored. Reich claimed that whereas Consciousness II accepted society, the public interest, and institutions as the primary realities, III declared that the individual self is the only true reality.

Reich proposed that from this new sense of self one could find "genuine values" in a world of falsehoods and distortions. As such, Reich could easily justify the attempts of those operating from Consciousness III to "do their own thing" regardless of social consequences. In fact, Reich naively believed that the pursuit of self-satisfaction would ultimately benefit the society at large, since most people would "put (the) community ahead of their (own) immediate wants."[9] They would "escape from the limits fixed by custom and society (to pursue) something better and higher."[10] Reich's prognosis was based on the assumption that young people had an inherent goodness of purpose and that their rebellion was in the name of progress. He assumed that the whole dying, bloated Establishment needed *any* kind of incision, just so it was guided by what seemed to be good intentions.

Peter Schrag also made a deep cut in middle-class America in his book, *The Decline of the WASP*.[11] He described how the middle class had come to be controlled, mechanized, subservient, puerile, and afraid of personal authenticity. Schrag explained how pre-1960s Americans were slaves to conformity and were becoming detached from themselves. He insisted that "we must learn to discover our own frustrations, our own humanity, our own interests."[12] Schrag, like Reich, saw little with which to be encouraged in the "plastic" middle classes. Comparing Walt Disney, son of an unsuccessful Missouri farmer, with Hugh Heffner, son of a Nebraska preacher, Schrag paralleled their emerging empires as based on an unreal world of make-believe that sold wares to a public eager to fantasize about perfect bodies and a "sanitary Magic Kingdom of Disneyland."[13]

Until the second half of the twentieth century, which marked the end of the age of innocence, most Americans complacently subscribed to the cultural norms that theoretically worked for the common good, even though conformity called for obedient dependency on "the system." It was "against the rules" for an individual to be too hungry for power; one was expected to respect the authority of those who were higher in the pecking order. Ordinary citizens comforted themselves with a childlike faith in the American way of life. Pundit H. L. Mencken captured the

mood of this helpless innocence with his quip that "the normal American
. . . goes to bed every night with an uneasy feeling that there is a burglar
under the bed, and he gets up every morning with a sickening feeling
that his underwear has been stolen."[14]

The fear of individual authenticity prevailed in the older generation.
Consider the 1972 medical advice of columnist Dr. H. Van Dellen in *The
Chicago Tribune:*

> B. J. writes: I get a lump in the throat when I see something that moves
> me, like a parade or a new baby. How can this response be prevented?

> Reply: Some persons are more emotional than others. Recognize it as a
> weakness and let it go at that. These problems are difficult to correct, but
> tend to improve as the individual becomes better adjusted to life situa-
> tions.[15]

Most adults seemed reluctant to acknowledge their real feelings, relying upon emotional detachment and obedience as the best way to avoid
the risk of authentic self-expression. Feelings were considered dangerous,
a threat to the existing order. Children of such parents either conformed
to these traditional ideas or rebelled. Many chose the latter route, especially those postwar baby-boomers who had the financial support, time,
ambition, and energy to do what they believed must be done to improve
their world. They fought for a seemingly noble cause: personal honesty
and release from inhibitions. Schrag noted how "everything that a gray-
ing, nervous civilization kept jammed in [the] closets is coming out—sex
in all forms, feelings, emotions, [and] self-revelations. . . ."[16]

Acting Out Parental Desires

The sixties and early seventies pitted young against old, maverick
against conformist. Probably neither side was aware that this was more
than an attempt to overthrow phony niceties and rigid rules. I believe
that an underlying motive of the young rebels' self-indulgence was to act
out similar but unexpressed wishes harbored deeply within their elders.

As I work with families in psychotherapy, I am always impressed with
the tremendous sensitivity most children have to both the overt and
covert feelings and needs of their parents. Youngsters know intuitively
how, where, and when their parents are hurting. Even when they do not
understand the specific sources of parental conflict, they quite accurately
sense the moods and frustrations these issues create. They also have a

knack for creating "side-shows" so that their parents will stop fighting or ignoring each other and "get together," even if at the children's expense.

I recall a family who came to see me with a problem of constant bickering between their son and daughter, ages twelve and ten. The parents described how the children were forever arguing, engaging in a "yes-you-did/no-I-didn't" debate where the only temporary solution was to separate them in different rooms with the doors shut. The parents had tried threats, bribes, and various punishments to no avail. When asked if the children had always bickered to that degree, the parents stated that this behavior began about two years ago, after the maternal grandmother had died. The children's mother took the death very hard and developed symptoms of depression that required medication. The father, normally passive and quiet, began to complain about his wife's moodiness, even commenting once in front of the children that when his mother-in-law died, he lost his wife, too. The undercurrents of marital unrest made the children very anxious. Without realizing it, they found that fighting between them aroused their mother out of her introspection and also united the parents in a common cause to squelch their children's bickering. The children's problem distracted the parents from their own conflicted situation—for the good of all.

Children often act out their parents' repressed desires and unrest in a desperate attempt to heal the parents, renew family harmony, and acquire the security they need to grow normally. Thus, a parent who cannot make friends may have a child whose schoolwork suffers because he or she is too social; an overly prudish mother will often have at least one promiscuous daughter; professional men who are workaholics frequently have one flunk-out son; and so on. Children often delay their own emotional and intellectual development so as to keep company with a lonely or frightened or troubled parent.

In this light, I want to pursue the point that the uptight, tradition-bound parents of the forties and fifties—parents who feared boasting, standing out, or questioning the established order—reared children who were sensitive to the parents' hidden problems. The children saw that beneath their elders' silent suffering, forced complacency, and unspoken protests was a powerful but repressed urge to cut loose and be themselves without guilt or fear of disapproval. Most kids were experts at spotting those unexpressed feelings: the adventurous, curious, lustful, covetousness urges; the hidden rebellion against the rules of church and state; the financial worries that underlay their frugality; the stored-up resentment toward controlling relatives; the muffled doubts about traditions; and the social bigotries.

The young wondered why their parents denied their own anguish and evaded uncomfortable questions. As tensions rose in the lives of the parents, their offspring were stressed to the point where they had to relieve themselves. Their elders may have been a silent majority, but the children were not afraid to speak out. The emperor was naked, and they said so. They vented their anxieties in protest and self-indulgence, subconsciously showing their parents a way to face problems.

Some may argue that these explanations are far too lenient toward the younger generation, that what the baby-boomers have really done is ungratefully take everything their elders have to offer and then expect the community to indulge them in like manner. A case can be made, some say, that this is a group of spoiled brats who have had it too good and have chosen to climb on the backs of their goodhearted parents to new heights of self-indulgent satiation. They have been described as caring only for personal pleasures—hedonists who spend their substance in brainless, riotous living, continue to sponge off their overindulgent, ever-forgiving parents, and are too selfish to feel remorse for the trail of broken relationships, beer cans, condoms, and hypodermic needles they leave behind. In some instances this angry description may be accurate, but in my practice I have found such cases to be in the minority. Such young people are often the product of severely troubled homes where there has been a lack of effective discipline and meaningful love.

Whatever the causative factors, as young people "act out," they quickly notice how powerful they are in eliciting parental response. Many of us can remember parental disapproval of our long hair or raggy jeans, and their outrage over the issues of sexual freedom and the use of marijuana. Starting in the sixties, parents were forced to turn from their own painful issues and focus their attentions on their children. Although new family tensions arose from these parent-child struggles, they were often more tolerable than before. Acting-out behavior worked quite well, although no one planned it that way.

Over a period of time, the rebellious offspring not only gained considerable attention from their elders, but they also truly enjoyed themselves. Long hair, baggy clothes, and sandals became a fashion statement for both genders, eclipsing the preppie image of the forties and fifties. Young people wore jeans and played guitars, even in church. College students exercised considerable power, forcing universities to alter curricula to accommodate popular demands. Because—whether burning draft cards or bras—the young drew an interested audience, the protest movement now had its own rewards and began to focus on broader issues. Soon there were consciousness-raising groups that addressed a variety of serious concerns: the Vietnam War, civil rights, sexual liberty, women's equality, and abortion (to name but a few). Freedom for the young spawned "power to the people." On many fronts, youthful rebels became the originators and curators of a national movement that, although controversial and divisive, dramatically changed the way all people looked at themselves.

As the older generation noticed these activities, its members responded from deep within their own hidden feelings. Although parental interest often took the form of feigned disgust or outright condemnation, beneath these surface rejections were often themes of suppressed interest—even jealousy.

Consider, for example, a family where a straitlaced, conservative father lectures his son incessantly about the evils of premarital sex. The son is quite the ladies' man and often comes home very late after a date. The son complains in family therapy that his father always waits up for him and presses him for details of the evening. "He forces me to tell him how far I go with a girl," protests the son. "It's weird, as if he likes to hear what I do, even though he tells me I shouldn't do it." Months later the wife calls to tell me she and her husband have had a poor sex life for some time because her husband avoids her when she refuses to engage in all the sexual techniques he likes. "I didn't want to say it in front of the family," she explains, "but I thought you ought to know."

As young people sampled once-forbidden pleasures, they often provided vicarious gratifications for parents who needed deliverance from the authoritarian standards by which they had been reared. "Children are to be seen and not heard," said the grandparents. The proverbial "spare the rod and spoil the child" approach excused the ventilation of parental tensions through what is now considered child abuse. Many parents of the current generation remember how afraid they were of stern discipline as children. They recall how "no" meant "absolutely no!" and how rejection, ridicule, or a hard slap across the face kept them in line. Even in less autocratic families, there was little in-depth concern about whether the children were happy. Moodiness was rarely tolerated. Because it was deemed improper to question older persons' views, much less their commands, many pre–World War II parent-child relationships were grounded in a love that was conditional on showing respect for parental authority.

As parents rejected the rigid rules of their own childhoods, some of them went to the other extreme and allowed their children to explore life much too freely. Of course, not all parents became permissive. There were many pockets of parental authoritarianism, especially among certain ethnic and religious groups, that took longer to change (if at all). But, in general, the more educated and affluent parents became, the more they indulged their children in ways they themselves had rarely experienced. Despite the protests of many parents that they would have been "flattened" for what their children were saying and doing, they allowed them to get away with their rebellious, self-serving acts. Such implicit approval often reflected the satisfaction that the elders experienced through the unbridled behavior of the younger generation. Parents were giving to their children the very freedoms they themselves had never been permitted, but this generosity often became excessive.

In the foregoing paragraphs, I am not "blaming" parents and grandparents for the excesses of their progeny, nor am I condoning the self-centeredness of the young in the past several decades. My purpose is to show how psychological forces come to play between the generations in ways that augment ongoing sociological changes. There are many cultural ingredients in the swing from the conservative mores of the pre-1960s to today's liberality. Such shifts are not without cause or purpose, but not every factor is linked directly to family-related dynamics.

The New Elders

So far we have looked at the interaction between pre-1960 parents and their offspring. It may be interesting to examine the record of the post-1960 generations.

We might assume that the sacrifices of their parents, rebellious indulgence of self, and the chance to act out parental needs would lead to new heights of joy and satisfaction for the upcoming generation. Has it? In some instances, the answer is a definite "yes." Many of today's young adults are brighter, healthier, and happier than their parents ever were. They live more fully, are more self-assured and informed, and feel free to take what is available to develop themselves on all levels. Unburdened by fears of disapproval, they ask whatever questions bother them and are less restricted by guilt than were their conformist elders. If proven wrong, they are more puzzled and challenged than embarrassed. This shift in thinking and behaving has released them from some of the fears and follies, biases and bigotries, and ignorance and insensitivity that plagued their forefathers.

Because the young easily see through hypocrisy and phoniness, they raise questions that challenge the status quo. They demand that professors, politicians, employers, and other authority figures "tell it like it is." An observant group, the rising generation sees things accurately, trusts its observations, and has faith in the individual's ability to improve "the system."

Today's young generally love and respect their parents, but the dynamics of inter-generational relationships have changed. It is hard for the young to understand why the old are so duty-bound. "We want to let our spirits soar, to experience every enjoyment in life. Our folks conformed and sought society's approval; we like to be our own people," they say. Nevertheless, parental influence remains the most significant factor in healthy development.

A principal of a high school in an affluent suburb told me that he can predict which kids have the best chance of becoming the well-adjusted adults of the future. He notes that parents who are sensitive to their children's intangible needs, and show them how to fulfill those desires responsibly, nurture a strong sense of personal identity in their kids. "I see the results over the years," he states, "and there is no doubt in my mind what love tempered with discipline can do."

But there is another group of young adults (below age thirty-five) that has not done as well in its current search for satisfaction. Although typically intelligent and assertive, they show a turmoil and sadness that has short-circuited their progress. Sometimes, for many complicated reasons, selfless childrearing can result in *selfish* offspring who are just as inauthentic, unhappy, and unfulfilled as their parents.

These young persons, whom I have called "New Elders," frequently show the following symptoms: Because of their strong drive to achieve more of everything without expending the patience, discipline, or sacrifice necessary to achieve their goals, they are restless and easily angered. Their hostile, crude language bespeaks a frustration over the ever-present gap between their hungers and their gratification. Raised in middle-class families, these young people have grown up believing they are entitled to a high level of comfort and pleasure, even if their parents did not buy themselves such luxuries. New Elders expect to have a residence at an "in" address and a car that reflects their free-wheeling personalities. They anticipate a job with a future and enough income to satisfy their tastes. When the rewards they believe they deserve are delayed, New Elders may vent their anger by blaming others for their misfortunes, express it in aimless activity, or direct it toward themselves by diving into listless apathy or even clinical depression.

New Elders frequently harbor a deep fear that somehow they are never going to get everything they want. The basis for this negative prediction may be the low stamina level that is often a symptom of poor self-esteem. This deficiency may occur if there has been a history of inadequate love and security. Whether from a family that was unwilling or unable to show love, praise, and encouragement, or from a home broken by divorce, absentee parents, or serious turmoil, an individual may not have developed the emotional strength to face the tough demands of adulthood.

Family love and affirmation can provide the sense of personal worth that encourages perseverance by removing self-doubt. If there are no inner stores of smiles and voices from past and present loved ones, there is fear. The individual then too quickly concludes that a plan is not workable. As New Elders avoid assessing their potential strengths (and weaknesses) and close their minds to avenues of solving difficult problems, they almost eagerly abandon any project at hand. Often, the energy needed to accomplish a task is wasted in preoccupation with seeking proof of self-worth from others. Some New Elders spin off the track into gullies of excessive socializing, jealous put-downs, bragging, or silly exhibitionism. All such attention-getting acts detract from the goal-directed efforts that could yield high satisfaction.

A second cause of the fear of failure is the lack of a meaningful value system to guide daily behavior. Because many New Elders are suspicious of authority figures and their rules, they set their own standards of conduct, often made up to fit particular circumstances. They have chosen to travel less encumbered by the demands of convention or obligation, but they are plagued by doubts that expediency typically brings. Those who are their own rule-makers have no higher power to consult, no confirmation that they are right, no commitment to anyone but themselves. Mavericks often lead an isolated, lonely existence—the bitter price of "traveling light."

When we gallop ahead into new territory without an adequate road map, it is easy to stumble. Being a pioneer, going beyond the accomplishments of parents or peer groups, can be a confusing and unsettling experience. The greater our insecurity, the more vulnerable we become to the lure of offbeat philosophies. This explains why religious and political cults and splinter groups find a receptive audience among young people with bright, creative minds that are grasping for new answers to old questions. In an era of rampant individualism that downplays traditional values and behavior, many people are tempted to do as they please. Then it is easy to lose touch with habits and rules that demand order, discipline, and restraint, thereby winding up with little sense of direction and moral anchoring.

A comparison between the social behavior of the New Elders and their predecessors reveals some interesting contrasts. For example, pre-1960s adults worried that they would be noticed too much. They were careful to be modest and unassuming lest they stand out in the crowd. On the other hand, the New Elders feel uneasy if they are not receiving *enough* attention. They are incredibly ostentatious, desperate to be noticed by the public. See-through blouses, trendy clothes, vivid colors, wild hairdos—all announce loudly, "I'm here!"

New Elders focus on *present* pleasures; they disclaim lessons from the past and are naively unconcerned about the future. Their attitude is really saying, "That was then, this is now—and who knows if tomorrow will ever come?" Although their parents relied on comforting memories from the "then" to hold their lives together until the "now" improved, they also expected that thrift, making do, and going without would make tomorrow even better. Former generations tolerated a period of bad times because they could wait hopefully for an upswing in their fortunes. The New Elders are far too impatient over delays in satisfaction.

Peggy Lee's song, "Is That All There Is?" mirrors the inner vacuousness of many young people today. Because they instinctively recognize that material pleasures bring only momentary satisfaction, New Elders do not really *feel* good about all they are getting. Previous generations believed that feeling good connoted a selfish pride that was socially inappropriate. They readily disowned their achievements by not allowing them to linger in their minds for very long. Humility was an admirable quality, so successes were minimized. Their offspring, by contrast, do acknowledge their own successes, but only long enough to plan hurriedly for the next round of triumphs. Ironically, neither generation seems able to savor its accomplishments, though for different reasons.

The New Elders often live in what e. e. cummings calls "furnished souls."[17] They find nothing that is authentically theirs because nothing has been internalized. Everything brought in is instantly grasped and then released. In that moment of inner encounter there may be a brief sense of fulfillment, but it quickly passes to make way for more satisfaction. To the degree that they ignore the joys of life and furtively seek the new and different, they diminish their inner selfhood. In time the New

Elders starve themselves to the point where there is no inner core from which to draw strength. They may strive to experience "freedom" and give lip service to "authenticity," but their inner selves remain undernourished.

One of the most interesting contrasts between the New Elders and their parents involves their respective attitudes toward sexuality. Although there is ample evidence of a dramatic increase in sexual activity, it is doubtful that sexual freedom has made the New Elders happier either with each other or within themselves. Former generations believed that physical intimacy was inappropriate unless it expressed the broader love and mutual commitment inherent in a marital relationship. The New Elders are too anxious about their sexual urges to delay their gratification. Quick sex helps them handle their apprehensions about not being lovable and relieves them of accepting responsibility for the partner's welfare.

Herbert Hendon's excellent book, *The Age of Sensation,* speaks to this problem as he describes a "war" between the sexes, one based on power motives to get what one can and leave with little sense of caring. He reports on "a general cynicism, disillusionment, and bitterness. . . ."[18] One "scores" or "gets lucky." Because the sexes use each other cleverly and contemptuously, they quickly lose interest after "making it." Sex replaces love, just as the sensations of loud music, vivid colors, and fast cars substitute for real feelings. The sense of self is tenuous and leaves the individual with an inner emptiness that continually needs a quick fix.

Of particular note in Hendon's psychological study of college youth is his finding that sexual impotence is one of the most frequent complaints for college males seeking counseling. Gender competition has robbed male-female relationships of trust, tenderness, and involvement. Males fear they cannot perform well enough to please "liberated" females who demand sexual fulfillment. Women describe an amorous male as someone who "hits" on them, yet men complain that they no longer feel in control of the courtship process. Many males cannot proceed with confidence unless stimulated by the metered ritual of the hunt, the approach, and the "dance" of mating with a passive, modest, and only subtly encouraging female partner. When a man's eager anticipation is replaced with fear of failure, sexual response is jeopardized. Some men hide their fears behind bragging, drugs, and "playing it cool," a euphemism for avoiding pain. To prove their virility to a sexually demanding partner, modern males often resort to "kinky" experimentation or to risk-taking, such as having sex in public places.

A more violent symptom of the struggle for power between the sexes is found in the rising incidence of date rape, especially found on college campuses. Even more alarming are reports of gang rape, which some authorities say is an example of "male bonding"—a sexual ritual of getting closer to other members of a club or fraternity by all having sex with the same woman. The bonding aspect may be true, but we have to look at gang rape as an attempt to feel in control, propelled by a belief that it takes a group of males to combat a newly empowered (and thus feared) female.

Today's young may have had more experience sexually, but they are as uptight about sex as were their forebears. Feature writer Asa Baber writes in *Playboy* magazine: "[T]here have to be some rules or we'll all go crazy. There used to be a sexual waltz. It had its hypocrisies. But now there's a sexual stomp, a form of smash dancing. There are many injured even though nobody's talking about it."[19]

In a study of the sexual behavior of college students from 1965 to 1980, Robinson and Jedlicka conclude that each gender has imposed a standard on the other that calls for a reduction of sexual behavior; but they *both* are actually having *more* sex![20] Both men and women seem to want the sexual pace to slow down; each gender feels things are out of control. But the fact that they *wish* to slow down, perhaps to reduce the constant pressure to perform, does not mean that they *do* go more slowly. Sexual activity is done too compulsively and with too little meaning, as if to hurry up and get it over with.

"Casual sex" was an unfamiliar term in days when the establishment of a sexual relationship generally signified mutual love and a desire to formalize the intimacy in marriage. Even when there was no such commitment, fear of pregnancy and/or disease restricted the sexual activity of most unmarried individuals. Today, however, certain moral and religious directives seem superfluous to a large segment of the population, and high-tech birth-control methods have reduced the possibility of an unwanted pregnancy. (Unfortunately, despite medical advances in treatment and warnings about "unsafe sex," the risk of venereal disease remains, especially in regard to AIDS.) For all these reasons, many moderns believe it is perfectly legitimate to explore their sexuality and gratify their sexual needs freely. That they are also wary about making long-term commitments can be seen in their language. They "see other people," rather than "date," which might imply that a courtship was underway. Today's young people marry later than their parents, have fewer children, and live alone longer than did their parents or grandparents.[21] They are also willing to experiment with such alternate forms of commitment as living together while unmarried, engaging in "open marriage," living in communes, and adopting children without benefit of marriage. As Jessie Bernard states in *The Future of Marriage*, "There is literally nothing about marriage that anyone can imagine that has not in fact taken place."[22]

The apprehension about marriage does not mean that marriage *per se* is distasteful. Most young people still say they want to be married "someday." The problem seems to center on uneasiness about the emotional risks and responsibilities inherent in marital commitments. A young single woman who lives with an older, divorced man recently told me that she is afraid to get married because then she will be less than free. She also said she is afraid to make a "mistake," defined as getting less than she hoped for out of a marriage. This was much less of a problem for her parents. They accepted the risks and pursued mutual goals of community approval, childbearing urges, and financial security.

Today's young often want guarantees that they will get everything they have always wanted. Taking less than a "perfect" mate seems like an unnecessary sell-out to them, a pretense that one could be happy with second-best. The rising divorce statistics reveal the complacency with which many people abandon existing commitments in the hope of finding someone "better." They fail to realize that no partner is perfect and that a successful marriage requires hard work. They also forget that we all change our ideas about what we want as we grow older—almost guaranteeing that no one person could ever satisfy all our needs. The problem is that people in the impatient "now" generation do not want to look at their ambivalence about marriage as something within themselves: their own anxious demand for complete fulfillment.

Many argue that they see their parents unhappily married and thus want no part of marital commitments. They have apparently concluded that the solution is delay or avoidance. Hendon notes how the current emphasis on "disengagement, detachment, fragmentation, and emotional numbness" is so different from his own generation, "which prized commitment and involvement as the source of pleasure and satisfaction in life. . . ."[23]

In their eagerness to "get it on," today's iconoclastic generations feel fettered by a commitment to the traditions, values, and morals of their parents' time. They refuse to invest the time and patience needed to build quality relationships, or even to develop themselves personally. So many say, "I want to see everything, do everything, go everywhere, and get a feel for life!" Unfortunately, since many moderns do not have the emotional maturity to absorb the experiences they encounter, they do not necessarily strengthen their character structure along the way. As they eagerly rush off to the next adventure, they almost guarantee that Narcissus will again meet his Nemesis.

Blending Old and New

The current search for more is so very "oral," as the Freudians would say. Everyone is hurriedly devouring pleasure. It is not surprising that oral sex is the "new intimacy," that fast-food restaurants flourish, that alcohol abuse is epidemic, and that smokers continue to ignore warnings about lung cancer and heart disease. We seem to be "sucking our thumbs," so to speak. Former generations were far more "anal"—withholding, conservative, saving. We do not want to go back to the repressive past with its "sit tight" philosophy, but neither is it healthy to continue our "sucking up" of everything available, unrestrained by guidelines.

The current philosophy of "more is better; winning is everything; and if it feels good, do it" is an inadequate prescription for improving the quality of life. The abandonment of morality, the disregard for traditions, the war between the sexes, and the rejection of discipline have brought about the breakdown of the family and a narcissistic attitude that threatens to destroy every worthwhile human quality.

What can be done to turn our society from its self-destructive ways? Part of the answer lies in a marriage between the past—with its stable structure and its other-centeredness—and the present—with its eager searching and healthy focus on self. Each can complement the other, for the truly mature person is someone who has an inner base of solid values and ideas, but also explores new ideas and experiences that will facilitate his or her personal growth.

The older a person becomes, the more he or she endorses the ideas and values that have stood the test of time. Experience has a way of convincing people that certain practices and ideals are worth preserving: love, honesty, patience, respect, hard work, fairness, generosity, commitment. Such human virtues need to be embraced more passionately by the young in their search for self-fulfillment. On the other hand, life also teaches us that some dreams never come true, that pain, failure, and anxiety can become our traveling companions on life's journey. Older people often become cynical and need to be reminded about dreams, enthusiasm, and continued efforts. The young seem uniquely equipped to provide such encouragement.

Many of the old ways have been swept away in the endless sea of changes that all eras have known, but abandoning the present and returning exclusively to the past would be counterproductive. Authoritarianism and dogmatic decree should no longer be tolerated. We have all learned and experienced too much to be mindless and unquestioning. Although we now know that "the good old days" were not all that good, we also must not continue to tolerate the excess that flagrant self-centeredness demands. The deification of the self at the expense of rules, values, and traditions has proved to be "bogus," to use a favorite expression of the young.

The union of past and present should allow enough individual growth so that something of value can be passed on to the next generations. Young people profit from knowing that an individual's authenticity has its deepest meaning within the context of social responsibility and humanitarian concern. The pursuit of excellence then becomes far more than either personal enhancement or self-indulgence. What the past can teach us is that living only for self is far too narrow a perspective. License is not freedom; aimless wandering does not move us ahead; abandoning morality will not enrich our contentment. We cannot live productively with a credo that puts convenience ahead of character, compromise before conviction. Instead, we must develop a worldview that shows us what is worth living for, and we must behave in ways that affirm everything beautiful and ennobling in us all. Such an approach will best ensure that whatever we achieve will be as free as possible from the possibility of harming others or ourselves.

5

Over-Getting

The Achieving Self

O grant me Heaven, a middle state
Neither too humble nor too great;
More than enough for natural ends
With something left over to treat my friends.

David Mallet

There is a poignant bit of wisdom in the popular saying, "Be careful what you wish for; your wish may come true." Although most of us deal rather extensively in wish making—whether pushing hard to fulfill long-term dreams or playing a state lottery in hopes of instant wealth—we may be unaware of how difficult it will be to manage our gains. When we finally achieve our goals, we may be quite unprepared to handle them. Judging from the acts of unwise investing and excess spending that often characterize the newly affluent, it seems fair to conclude that the ability to manage our achievements and ourselves does not automatically arrive with success.

In times of plenty we live with a dilemma: We have the capacity and encouragement to get even more, yet we must struggle with the personal, moral, and social issues that arise as we obtain more than we need for normal, everyday functioning. To feel comfortable with success, we are first forced to consider whether our gains are legitimately acquired and whether we feel worthy of them. We must also decide what to do with our newfound bounty. Shall we put our goods away? Spend them? Share with others? Invest to make even more? We must deal with the urge to brag, the envious glances of others, the fear of sudden loss. Success creates personal and interpersonal tension and demands personal growth, lest "much" becomes "too much" to handle.

What about our social obligations? It is easy to claim that we have worked very hard for our gains and that we are therefore justified in keeping them all. We may deal superficially with social issues by donating some of our excess to charity without becoming personally involved. If we sense a moral responsibility toward our fellow human beings, we find many avenues of sharing. Yet few of us conclude that we must balance the world's inequities by depriving ourselves, even if we have a nagging awareness that there is more we could and should do.

The problem of limiting our appetites and managing our accumulations is complicated by our annoyance at the thought of restrictions, but we need to ask, "How much is too much?" This question has three aspects. First, we must consider our own well-being: How do our choices affect us personally? Second, there is the issue of conscience: How much should we monitor and control ourselves as we search for more? Finally, we must examine our social responsibilities: How much of our goods should we share with other people?

Making Sensible Choices

To the degree that getting more of everything is a decision-making process, it implies that we have freedom of choice. We hold dear our right to be upwardly mobile, to enhance our pleasures, to pursue our personal desires. For example, why settle for a modest, stripped-down car if we can afford to add the important extras we all value? More than transportation, a car makes a statement about the person driving it. More car means more recognition, a way to show others that we have acquired the ability to choose whatever we want.

"To each his own," we say. Most Americans subscribe to an unwritten social agreement that every person is entitled to his or her personal tastes and has the right to pursue them freely. This philosophy touches our core belief in personal autonomy. We even defend our right to make poor investments or otherwise waste our funds. Who of us has not bought something totally unnecessary or useless, primarily because it was a good deal? This type of acquisition caters to an inner feeling of accomplishment, a satisfaction apart from the actual value of what has been obtained.

Comedian Myron Cohen illustrates this point with a story about two friends who meet and get into the following discussion. One of the men says that he knows someone in the circus who can get his friend an elephant for $100. The friend thinks the whole idea is ridiculous, but the man pushing the sale argues that the elephant is specially trained to sit on a pair of pants and press them or give showers with his trunk. "He could hang your things up high," he argues. His friend responds incredulously, "You crazy? I got a one-room apartment!" After a long pause, the huckster says, "I'll tell you what. I'm going to get you three elephants for $200." "Now you're talking!" replies his friend.[1]

In the haste to exercise our freedom of choice, we may not think about the hidden costs. Go-getters rarely admit that they can get too much. Consider the "Type A" personality—the person who pushes constantly to get ahead, working long hours under tension and refusing to rest until every goal is achieved—all at the expense of good health and interpersonal relations. We know that compulsive achievers eat poorly, usually smoke and drink too much, and do not get enough rest. Since their lifestyle risks heart attacks, ulcers, and hypertension, it seems fair to claim that these individuals are making choices that are detrimental to their own welfare. Although they certainly do not consciously choose bad health or chronic tension, such over-getters are unwilling to moderate drive with good judgment.

We all make choices that can interrupt our composure. I recall a woman in her sixties who came into considerable insurance money after her husband died and could finally purchase some of the luxuries she and her husband had never been able to afford. With the encouragement of well-meaning friends, she immediately bought an expensive townhouse and a luxury automobile. However, even though both were well within her financial means, she soon became tense and sleepless, lying awake worrying whether she really should have spent so much money. Having always lived frugally before, she was totally unprepared to be comfortable with affluence. It would have been better for her to trade up gradually to slowly acclimate herself to the changes in her self-image that wealth had suddenly thrust on her.

What we get has to be digested as systematically as a meal. No one would recommend stuffing ourselves as fast as possible, no matter how tasty the food might be. Manners, digestive comfort, and good health are far more important than the amount of food and speed of consumption. Getting, like eating, should be governed by an inner level of comfort that ensures overall well-being and lasting satisfaction.

Moderation is far more than that, however. A Chinese proverb captures the essence of wise consumption: One should always leave the table a little hungry. If overindulgence causes discomfort, it stifles our interest in proceeding further. The wisdom of the ancient Chinese civilization includes an awareness that desire for more is an integral part of the motivation to keep going. When we get too much, we jeopardize that desire, as if our hungers are enemies to be forever silenced.

Furthermore, when the objects of our attention are too demanding, they risk upsetting our level of comfort. I recall a forty-five-year-old woman who came to me in a state of apathy and withdrawal. This usually bright and personable woman had decided to join a community theater group once she had only one child remaining at home. Hoping to expand her horizons, she threw herself into this new endeavor, going to all the rehearsals and even taking a college class in the dramatic arts. But what began as an exciting adventure became too demanding on her time and personal-emotional resources. She became depressed because she could not remember her lines or emote as freely as some of the other group members. She started to feel guilty because her daughter and husband complained that they saw her far too little and that her "theater job," as they called it, made her tired and jumpy. In time she dropped out of the group and brooded for a long time over having lost touch with herself. Enjoyable activities have to be understood within the perspective of being in service to our total personhood.

As we acquire more, our level of comfort is also influenced by our self-image. To be able to enjoy our increases, we have to see ourselves as worthy. Some people do not let themselves savor what they achieve because they do not feel deserving of success. If we feel awkward or guilty about our gains, we begin to find ways to divest ourselves of our advances. The discomfort may be primarily due to the pressure of managing the new increases. But, more typically, the feelings of unworthiness predominate and prod us to return to a more familiar, pre-success lifestyle.

It takes a very mature person to avoid letting a great deal of money or power interfere with sensible living. When someone suddenly strikes it rich, he or she can fall victim to foolish spending sprees if the riches arrive before the capacity to manage them has developed. In the inevitable discomfort that follows, there is often a hidden desire to eliminate the intrusion of success. The shift from a familiar routine to a new way of living often creates a sense of personal inadequacy. "Too much, too soon" can be upsetting unless we have prepared ourselves for the arrival of prosperity.

When excessive getting produces personal discomfort, the solution may be to consider more carefully why our achievements are causing us pain. Whenever integrity, self-care, and/or our relationships with others are jeopardized, the cost of success is too high. Only if we admit that some gains are not worth the time and energy we have expended are we in a position to change our ways and modify our choice of goals.

Most of us hate to say no to what seems like a surefire opportunity, especially when making money is involved. In our expansive, materialistic society, we become so excited over thoughts of making it big that impulsive risk-taking can easily silence our good judgment. Even if we find our promised pot of gold, the dream will become a nightmare if we are not prepared to handle the responsibilities inherent in getting too much.

The Role of Conscience

There was a time when "conscience" was an important determinant of human behavior, when personal beliefs and social norms governed our actions far more stringently than today. "The word 'sin' has almost disappeared whereas once it was a proud . . . strong . . . ominous word," says Karl Menninger in his book *Whatever Became of Sin?*[2] Raised in a tradition of yielding to authority, earlier generations kept themselves in line by an unquestioning compliance with generally accepted rules. Some may argue that one generation is no more conscientious in following standards of conduct than another, but that is a naive line of reasoning. Some eras do, indeed, permit, even encourage, more acting out of impulses than was previously allowed. It is possible to trace a continuing swing of the pendulum of social conscience from control to permissiveness, from conservatism to liberality—and back again.

Since the early 1960s we have witnessed an obvious swing toward liberality, both at the personal level and in the prevailing attitudes of society. Radical cultural changes now permit casual sexual conduct, abortion, increased personal freedom, and the challenging of hallowed institutions. There is no doubt that removing the rigid constraints of the past has some merit. But, as we have switched from "let the law and your conscience be your guide" to "if it feels good, do it," we have run into trouble. For too many people, freedom has come to be translated as "license," the removal of internal controls on behavior.

The decreased reliance on conscience does not mean that we have become a lawless society. To the contrary, most Americans believe strongly in law and order. In fact, many people accept the conscience not merely as the internalized rules and standards we hold as important (even though sometimes ignored) but also as the vehicle through which universal laws of morality and spirituality are conveyed. Unfortunately, the cry for self-discipline and moderation is often meant to restrain others, not ourselves. Our consciences are curiously one-sided here, but we are most likely to become critical of others in the very areas of offense in which we have personal susceptibilities.

We sometimes believe that we can put our consciences on hold as we pursue our goals. Our middle-class mentality, and hence our morality, endorses getting ahead, even if we have to bend a few rules temporarily. We tell ourselves, "It's dog eat dog. It's a jungle out there—every man for himself!" In a competitive struggle for goods and services, it doesn't seem to matter *how* we get what we want, just that we get our fair share.

The idea of conscience has been beaten senseless in a floodtide of public and private graft and corruption. We read in our newspapers that government contractors charge $9,700 for a $3.00 pair of pliers and cover their greed by listing the pliers as "a mechanical adapter instrument." Televised documentaries expose dishonesty and payoffs in public works projects; widespread tax cheating; Medicare rip-offs by physicians, pharmacists, and patients; crooked lawyers and judges; and insider stock deals. Dishonesty at every level of our society makes it hard to believe in the importance of conscience. But without conscience there is no inner guidance, no self-discipline to direct the impulsive part of the personality. And even an active conscience needs frequent strengthening. There must be encouragement, moral affirmation, and spiritual renewal if the conscience is to remain in control.

Before we can take steps to restore our personal stability, our conscience must tell us that we are wrong. The conscience is an indispensable guide to effective living amidst confusing cultural messages. Although we may not like its nagging or its prohibitions, a guilty conscience comes to our aid by insisting that adhering to the rules will maintain inner harmony. We may quibble internally about why particular rules are necessary, and even hate ourselves for wanting to break them, but—to live with rules peacefully—we have to honor them. Admitting to guilt from wrongdoing is necessary to prevent us from going too far in our acquisitiveness.

For many of us, the conscience is not always infallible. Some of the internal guidelines we have embraced are inaccurate and were self-imposed because of bias or ignorance. We sometimes see this problem in children who have been taught by deeply religious parents that "pride" is sinful. The principle of not looking down on others in conceit is a good one, but not when it produces self-denigration and excessive humility. It is indeed possible to esteem oneself highly without necessarily judging others as inferior. If we grow up feeling guilty whenever we feel proud of our accomplishments, we are our own worst enemies.

Others, because they have been raised in a cultural or family group that has been unduly repressive, have internalized a set of rules so restrictive that they have no freedom to be themselves or to enjoy life. Parents and grandparents of the pre-1960s were far more strictly bound by conscience than most people are today. They refrained from questioning social, cultural, and religious norms too deeply lest they violate the security found in maintaining the status quo. That approach had considerable value in that it established a degree of order during a half-century fraught with the turmoil of two world wars and the Great Depression. Carried to the extreme, however, traditionalism stifles personal growth and the constructive changes that are needed in any healthy society.

Since 1960, conscience has been increasingly overruled by convenience. It is quite accurate to say that ignoring the voice of conscience allows us to justify our current self-indulgence. The excessive reliance on alcohol and drugs in the last several decades not only dulls the pains of life, but silences the voice of conscience. Even if the dictates of conscience are still heard, we tune out messages that might disrupt our plans and limit the personal freedom we prize so highly.

Restoring Wholeness

If the conscience can moderate our getting, what can we do to strengthen its sway over our search for satisfaction? The renewal of conscience begins with an admission that in our pursuit of pleasure we may have neglected to examine our values. It is usually embarrassing to face up to our deficiencies, but personal confessions are easier to bear than revealing our flaws to others. So we *start* by talking silently to ourselves about our standards of conduct, measuring them against what we know to be acceptable to a jury of our peers and deciding what behavioral changes are needed. However, although honest self-analysis is a beginning, it alone cannot re-awaken our conscience. Because we can so easily fool ourselves—lying to cover our wrongdoing and rationalizing bad behavior—we also need very much to talk to someone else.

Considerable relief may come if we admit our faults to someone who epitomizes the forces of conscience—God, a religious person, or a trusted friend or relative whose values and judgment we respect. The purpose of "confession" is twofold. First, as we openly admit our avoidance of conscience and the consequences that have followed, we hear ourselves say these things aloud. When our ears listen to the words of our heart and mind, we are less likely to deny the truths implicit in the message. Open admission makes us confront our own words, which is one of the reasons why psychotherapy is so beneficial in unearthing long-buried secrets.

But there is a second purpose in opening ourselves to others. When we reveal our inner truths to others, we invite their responses. Hearing another person's reactions adds new information we can use if we decide to change our ways. Some of the feedback may include shock and anger, which may be helpful, even though it causes us pain. True friends will respond in nonjudgmental ways that are meant to enlighten or set us straight rather than to reject us. They may be angry because we have been harming ourselves with our unfortunate behavior, but their admonition and advice can fortify our inadequate standards or controls.

What we also get from others are words of love and reassurance. Confession purges us, but it also provides us with a sense of being accepted despite our failings. In the process of getting too much, we may have not only violated our own standards of conduct and used poor judgment, but also left too little time for friendships. When we tell a special friend about our mistakes and receive their comfort and encouragement in return, we fill in the empty places our strivings have generated. We rid ourselves of our burdens, gain insight into how we might improve, reestablish relationships we have ignored, and regain a sense of personal wholeness.

After we have admitted our faults, we must next make a conscious decision to change our ways. We all know that old habits die hard. Fueled by the drive to get more and more, the achieving self often uses short cuts, makes bad choices, and alters the rules. Even those who admit that they should amend their inappropriate behaviors, are usually reluctant to risk decreasing their gains in the process. Yet constructive change often involves the very difficult choice of giving up something that has brought us pleasure.

A young woman consults me as part of her drug-rehabilitation program. She has worked hard to free herself of the physical and emotional problems associated with using cocaine. However, she realizes that continuing to date her boyfriend poses a serious threat to her progress because he still uses the drug. She loves him dearly, but since he refuses to get help for his problem, she must choose between ending the relationship or succumbing to her addiction.

As we work together she reveals deep-seated doubt over her appeal as a woman. She explains that she was shy and self-conscious in high school because she was somewhat overweight. Although she did lose weight in college, she continued to worry that men would not find her attractive, so she was extremely happy when she finally found someone who seemed to care about her. She needed this love so badly that she was willing to compromise her standards by taking cocaine at her boyfriend's request. Despite his promises that they could control their drug habit, they both became addicted and needed professional intervention.

To make the difficult decision to leave her boyfriend, this woman will have to bolster her conscience by finding other sources of self-esteem. She will have to control her weight, remind herself that there are other young men whom she can date, and associate only with young people who avoid drugs. She has a lot of work to do, but her efforts will save her life.

Perhaps the most difficult part of changing is dealing with our inner "urges." An urge is a mindless desire, demanding what it wants regardless of cost because it has no ability to reason or plan ahead. An urge simply wants satisfaction *now.* The conscience and one's urges are enemies, but the more they get into an inner struggle to produce a winner and a loser, the less likely will the solution be adequate. People who are overly rule-oriented become exhausted by constantly increasing their efforts to deny certain temptations and emotions. Like a spring wound too tightly, they either recoil in a flurry of wild indulgence or collapse in helpless anxiety. Suppressing one's feelings can be dangerous. Instead, we must recognize our urges and allow our conscience to address them directly if we are to uncover their source and learn to manage them appropriately.

One way to get more deeply in touch with our urges is to enact a face-to-face confrontation. We can carry on a dialogue between Urge and Conscience by setting up two facing chairs and playing both parts. Each side first states its case as clearly as possible, but it is the ensuing "discussion" that provides information useful in arriving at conciliation and a workable truce.

Consider a man whose quick temper repeatedly gets him in trouble. He has been unsuccessful in controlling his outbursts because he does not acknowledge that it is his mindless urge to assert his autonomy that ignites them. The dialogue between Conscience and Urge might proceed as follows:

> *Conscience:* I'm very disturbed by the way you talk so angrily to people. Please realize what this is costing us and stop it.
>
> *Urge:* I'm sick and tired of being pushed around. I've been hidden for years and now it's time for me to demand my rights. Stop telling me what to do.
>
> *Conscience:* Nothing I say stops you, so I'd better find out *why* you feel so angry. What bothers you most about other people?
>
> *Urge:* I hate being told what to do. It makes me feel stupid, like I'm a little kid again. I had enough orders and demands from my father. Now I can concentrate on what *I* want, not what he thinks I need.
>
> *Conscience:* You sure sound angry at Dad.
>
> *Urge:* That stupid jerk, always making me do stuff I didn't want to do! Never again!

Self-expression that is unrehearsed and spoken directly from the heart will take various directions as it flows. Both aspects of the personality simultaneously hear what comes from within and can profit from the new information that emerges. In this case the impulsive anger arose from the man's repressed hatred of his demanding father and expresses an urge to fight back and assert autonomy. This inner theme remains unresolved, despite pleading by the conscience for reform. Obviously, the anger at the father cannot be directed openly against him, but neither should the hostility be dismissed as unimportant. There must be some kind of truce before both sides can relax the struggle. For example:

> *Conscience:* Please don't misunderstand me. I'm not Dad, but I think I have some reasonable requests. I'm simply trying to help you. The work we have to do is easier when we have a framework of rules.

Urge: So, what's in it for me?

Conscience: Look, there is a reasonable element in what you want, but you go about it in an unreasonable way. We have to separate the two, that's all. You wouldn't mind being less angry, would you, if you didn't have to sacrifice your freedom and satisfaction?

Urge: What do you mean?

Conscience: It is reasonable to want to do some things your own way and get more of what you want. It's just that satisfying your desires by clobbering me and everyone else gets us in more trouble than we need. Can we make a deal? Why not talk to Dad about why you feel angry at him. Even if he denies being overdemanding as a father, your openness with him will help you focus your feelings on their source. Then you won't let your anger infect everything you do.

Urge: Okay. Sounds like I can still be angry at him, but not all the time or at everyone else who makes a request of me.

Conscience: Right, but there's more. Let's rely on each other more amicably. I need you for enjoyment and you need me for direction. Together we can make life better for each other.

Urge [which usually gets the last word]: Sure—I want more freedom and fun. I'll show you a good time and you can keep me on track. Maybe you've got a point. But you'd better be reasonable about it!

The above dialogue is only illustrative and may represent only a small part of what else might be bothering this man. A skilled therapist may be needed to facilitate self-awareness by directing this multi-layered drama. What I am suggesting is that the conscience can be enlisted more effectively by allowing it to carry on a dialogue with the hidden urges that are causing problems. Preoccupation with getting is too costly if it risks violating our rules of conscience.

Interpersonal Responsibility

We have seen that the question of how much is enough should be answered by considering (1) what our gains do to us, and (2) how those gains square with our consciences. One last issue remains: the influence of social responsibility on the process of getting.

In the early 1970s I attended a Gestalt therapy workshop at the University of Chicago. The leader, feeling uptight, suddenly let out an ear-piercing yell that lasted a full ten seconds, though it jolted his audience and disturbed other workshops in the building. No doubt he felt better after relieving his tensions in public, but no one else did. That kind of self-indulgence was a hallmark of the sixties and seventies, an uncontrolled expressiveness that was devoid of social sensitivity.

Other kinds of irresponsible excess have continued and even worsened through the 1980s. We see this evidenced in the entertainment industries over the past twenty-five years. Vulgarity, bloody violence, and borderline pornography are now standard TV fare in living rooms where young minds are being shaped for the future. The show-business media dull our minds and titillate our senses, pandering to what makes the most money. Producers wash their hands of accountability by saying, "We only give the public what it wants."

Social irresponsibility is also obvious in the rape of the environment by corporations and individuals, in the bigot's hardness toward a neighbor, and in the drug dealer's indifference to the moral, social, emotional, and physical health of the country. The world's worst sins seem to be related to a generalized lack of concern for the common good, both present and future.

It is not wrong to pursue our personal welfare, nor should we be expected to exhaust ourselves by carrying everyone else along to share in rewards he or she has not earned. But we must revive our social sensitivity and acknowledge that preserving interpersonal values is a national as well as an individual responsibility. Every democratic nation knows that its most treasured traditions affirm the collective interests of its people. Citizens of every land understand what their countries stand for, what their ancestors have held dear and defended, even with their lives. All these values, morals, and traditions are important and demand responsible preservation. Because we are each other's keepers, and also caretakers of our nation's soul and purposes, we cannot allow the self and its hungers be the sole voice we heed.

We hurt ourselves and future generations if we do not take care of each other and our environment. When tourists deface historical treasures for a souvenir, or corporations bulldoze rain forests for industrial development and thereby threaten the world's oxygen production, they forget that they are undermining their own best interests. Survival also demands understanding and accepting our fellow humans and their differences. If conscience is disowned, guilt and self-destruction cannot be far behind. It is not enough merely to encourage charitable, religious, or governmental organizations to take care of the needy. Our social responsibility must include a personal touch, a genuine prodding from the heart.

The past several decades have witnessed a decrease in social courtesy. Good manners, patience, and consideration for others have disappeared in the frantic pace of modern life. Language in public has degenerated to the point that some of us care very little about who overhears what we say. Are we losing our ability to be embarrassed by bigotry, vulgarisms, and profanity? The general erosion of social graces gives evidence that many of us have either forgotten or rejected the interpersonal guidelines that bring beauty and dignity to a culture. There is a desperate need for courtesy, empathy, tolerance, and etiquette in any civilized society. If we cite saving a little time or money as justification for rudeness and impatience, we will eventually pay the price in our quality of life, both individually and collectively.

The value of getting must be measured not only by *what* we obtain but by *who* we become in the process. We must not make choices simply on the basis of whether our experiences or acquisitions make us feel good, for the pleasure principle is far too narrow a criterion to justify over-getting. Even "security" is insufficient as the ruling philosophy of life if it fails to take into account our deeper purpose: becoming mature individuals who can adapt our personal desires to the practicalities of living at peace with our natural environment and who have developed the interpersonal skills that will enhance all our relationships.

In America brotherly love, fair play, and the good of the majority constitute some of our highest social ideals. If we consider that these lofty principles are rooted in our Judeo-Christian beliefs of the centrality of love as a guide in life, perhaps we will be less ambivalent in deciding how much we will get and how we will get it. The love inherent in spiritual lessons of service, self-control, and even sacrifice will not fail us as we make the tough choice that life always presents to us.

Under-Getting

The Dissatisfied Self

Poverty consists in feeling poor.
Ralph Waldo Emerson

To most of us, the word *poverty* conjures up images of material deprivation—inadequate supplies of food, clothing, shelter, medical attention—in short, a scarcity of what is needed for basic physical comfort and good health. The majority of those who must exist below the statistically defined "poverty level" are victims of complicated circumstances, many of which are beyond their control. However, even those who have material goods adequate for survival may be "poor" in less tangible ways, for we feel deprived, and thus dissatisfied, whenever *any* need or desire is insufficiently gratified.

We will now consider how people can impoverish themselves because of negative attitudes and emotions that impede their search for satisfaction and interfere with their enjoyment of what they do manage to attain.

Destructive Beliefs and Attitudes

Life itself begins with a loss of peace. Even as we are expelled from the Eden of the womb, we sense the sharp contrast between pleasure

89

and pain, serenity and discomfort. We quickly learn to distinguish between what brings satisfaction and what does not, and we do not forget those lessons. All through life our early experiences will remind us that satisfaction is found by increasing our pleasures and finding relief from pain and deprivation.

In *The Minimal Self,* Christopher Lasch points out that the fears, hurts, and disappointments of early childhood bring inevitable anxiety.[1] Children cope with this tension by fantasizing that a return to symbiotic bliss with mother can occur if only the right strategy can be found. When demands for immediate gratification do not work, when fantasies of omnipotence fail to secure total oneness with the mother, when the Oedipal wish for physical union with mother fails, children feel a painful defeat. We learn from our early years that there is much in life that does not satisfy. The satisfying aspects of childhood do register, but the bad parts ("bad mother," as the psychoanalysts say) stick in the throat, so to speak. Whereas the "good mother" is swallowed and digested smoothly, early hurts and losses remain unresolved. Because our early experiences leave memories that persist over the years, they underscore the beliefs and attitudes that will determine the spectrum of personal, material, and experiential objects we will pursue. We sense what has been good, but if our catalogue of painful experiences has too many pages, our basic approach toward life will be negative.

An eighteen-year-old college freshman is referred to me by his parents after dropping out of school. Although he has considerable ability, this young man has trouble getting along with his peers and his teachers. Most of the time he is grouchy and irritable, complaining constantly about anything that does not suit him. People have shunned him, not just because he is so cynical and disgruntled, but because he rejects their efforts to reach out to him.

"Tell me about yourself, Jim," I ask during our initial interview.

"There's nothing to tell," Jim replies. "My life is a big zero."

"Your whole life seems like a waste?"

"That's how it looks to me," Jim answers. "I remember being told that my brother and sister were happy kids. But I was a colicky baby who, according to my parents, bawled my entire first year. My brother and sister picked on me even though I was small and sickly and later on other kids didn't want to play with me. Nothing seemed to go right for me as a child."

"Sounds like you had a really rough time of it," I reply. "Do you think much about those early troubles?"

"All the time," Jim says. "That's the crazy thing about this. You'd think I couldn't wait to get on with life, but all I do is recall how bad everything was before. I can't get it out of my head."

When unhappy adults like Jim consult me, I often must explain that when bad things have happened to us, we may grind away at them over and over, continually reliving the pain. Much of my work in psychotherapy is aimed at helping a client get beyond repetitious thinking about the bad things so that he or she can partake of life's goodness. Negativism is exhausting, draining us of hope and the energy needed to change our lives for the better.

Our impressions about life mold our opinions, beliefs, and attitudes about *ourselves* as searchers. Each of us evaluates our self-worth, the probability of being successful, and our acceptability to others. Negative estimates set limits on how far we are willing to satisfy ourselves. One element in our self-portrait is our sense of where we fit on the social scale. Children from modest backgrounds who have not been praised for their efforts and encouraged to reach higher may see themselves as worthy of only meager rewards, even if they are capable of much more. Our personal estimates about how far we can go may be even more inhibiting than our actual life experiences.

We all carry with us a variety of consciously or subconsciously held beliefs that limit the range of our choices. Whether formed in childhood or shaped from adult experiences, our attitudes about ourselves determine how much we will take from life. As we gradually become what we believe, we fulfill our own predictions. If we automatically see only the bad, we will listen to inhibitory messages from within that tell us to stop trying—which, of course, virtually guarantees our dissatisfaction. Because low self-esteem is an implicit assumption that what we try will probably not succeed, positive effort is avoided. Furthermore, when we do not believe in ourselves, we are quite sure that others will laugh at our failures or walk away unimpressed by our small accomplishments. And so we press onward, restlessly searching for what might possibly fulfill us, but expecting to be disappointed at every turn in the road.

It is easy to devise strategies to rationalize our lack of satisfaction. Some people believe they can keep a sharper, more competitive edge by remaining dissatisfied. They fear that basking in the joys of victory will make them lazy and complacent, thereby forestalling further conquests. It seems easier to visualize even more gains in the future when there is a denial of here-and-now gains—as if the hungrier they are, the more diligently they will apply themselves.

Others continue to foster negative opinions about themselves and of their chances to get more of whatever they need by selectively remembering only their past failures and bad times. The original intention may have been self-protective—past losses remind them not to aim too high. Unfortunately, this kind of selective recall focuses on the fact that they failed, rather than on *why* their efforts were not productive. Even failure has lessons to teach us.

It is common to hide behind negative beliefs and attitudes to avoid facing life's unknowns. Since gains tend to expose us to new ideas and opportunities that can be frightening, we may persist in a low self-appraisal to minimize these risks. The convenient safety of retreat feels good at times, even though the price we pay for clinging to a security blanket is under-getting.

Consider, for example, the possibility that some obese women subconsciously fear the kind of male attention they might attract were they to slim down and look more appealing. Negative feelings about themselves may have lead to self-destructive overeating that has the hidden advantage of avoiding heterosexual involvements they do not think they can handle. At the very least, hiding behind a defensive wall of obesity lets them escape the possibility that they will be rejected. This is not to say that there are no other physical and emotional reasons for maintaining excessive weight. Although sexual avoidance has been used as an example, the point is that negative attitudes toward the self hamper one's personal growth.

Getting is living and living fully gives us the freedom to reach more meaningfully into the lives of others. Under-getting keeps the self puny and compromises our relationships. Getting all that life has to offer is far too important to allow negative attitudes to prevail. We cannot wish away our losses or pretend that our past pains have not been real. But we *can* consciously decide to counterbalance the negative with the pleasures attained by asserting ourselves and reaching out for more of what life has to offer.

Negative Emotions

We have considered how under-getting can be the by-product of our negative beliefs and attitudes. Negative emotions can be equally self-limiting. In particular, fear and anger may prevent us from getting enough to satisfy us and from enjoying what we do obtain.

Fear

Fear of the unknown, or of anything that poses a threat to our security, is no stranger at any age, but it has its genesis in our earliest experiences. The frightening contrast between the dark, quiet womb, where all our needs were satisfied, and the bright, noisy delivery room is only a foretaste of things to come. A newborn infant quickly senses that various noises, movements, strange faces, and other intrusions upset the peace and instinctively signals its fright with crying and primitive withdrawal behavior. If the environment is supportive, the infant is sheltered from fear-producing stimuli and begins to reach out to the world of people and objects. However, if there is insufficient peace and security, the infant is often frightened and quickly learns to protect itself with cautious under-responsiveness to the environment.

Central to the development of a sense of calm and safety is the baby's awareness that Mother's response is predictable. This does not mean that a mother has to be available every moment, only that she has a fairly routine way of interacting with her baby. A solid, almost ritualistic daily schedule of care provides few surprises for the infant and therefore minimizes fear. Maternal inconsistency is especially troubling in early infancy, before verbal communication is possible. A baby is discouraged from reaching out and taking deeply if it does not know what to expect when Mother is erratic—this time loving, the next time cold; on schedule yesterday, but not today.

A pediatrician referred a six-year-old girl to me with symptoms of withdrawal in the classroom. Away at school all day for the first time, the child seems to be too apprehensive and timid to learn what is expected of her academically or socially. The child's early history reveals that the mother, a buyer for a department store, warmly embraced motherhood at first but soon considered it boring to be home full time, so she returned to work. The daily schedule was as follows: Both parents were there until 8:00 A.M., when a baby-sitter arrived; the father returned around 4:00 P.M., and the sitter left; the mother was usually home for dinner but if she had to work late, she was not there for the bedtime story and good-night kiss her daughter expected. Because it was difficult to find and keep satisfactory baby-sitters, the little girl had to adjust to five child-care situations in as many years. The problem was not just one of changing faces but of varying styles of care and an unpredictable schedule. Now that school presents a whole new set of unknowns to cope with, the child has become overwhelmed and withdraws to protect herself from further disappointments.

W. Fairbairn points out that when the natural mother is erratic in her performance, a baby can come to fear that this unpredictability is the baby's own fault, that Mother is driven away by his or her demands.[2] Fearful infants who do not feel protected by the environment often withdraw their attention from the world of people or objects and retreat inwardly for security. If the self-focusing persists, these babies may become adults who trust no one, avoid close contact with people, and see the world as essentially hostile.

Infantile fears can be reinforced in childhood and adolescence by insensitive adults who are too restrictive and use threats to establish their authority. A child who fears being punished for being curious or unconventional learns not only to avoid what is specifically forbidden, but also to ignore the urge to explore the outside world. The conditioned fear of rejection, punishment, and disapproval has a serious consequence. The child begins to downplay self and to rely exclusively on others for instructions about how to act. For authoritarian parents and teachers, such timid compliance seems admirable. But for anyone interested in healthy child development, the focus becomes one of encouraging young people to build confidence in themselves and to take responsibility for making their own decisions.

There are many sources of fear, both real and imaginary: people, situations, natural forces, known and unknown dangers. Whether we fear rejection, physical harm, or failure, we are really describing some anticipated loss. When we are afraid, we try to reduce that unpleasant possibility in any way we can. So we pull back and restrict our natural tendency to reach outward for satisfaction. Yet, even as we shrink our spirits and reduce our exposure to what we perceive as threatening, we concentrate with fixed gaze on the objects of our fear. A dry mouth, uneasy stomach, and tense muscles all demonstrate evidence of self-constriction.

Fearful people may find temporary peace by retreating from freedom and creativity. But as they direct their energies inward, caring less and less for a full interaction with life's normal interests, they abandon the process of getting more for themselves. When in the grip of fear, self-development is put on hold and relationships are merely superficial. The more intense the fear and the longer they suffer, the less satisfaction they get out of living.

A stockbroker consulted me with many anxiety-related symptoms after the October 1987 Wall Street crash. He not only feared that his company would let him go, since many brokerage houses had been failing, but also that––even if he were allowed to stay––his customers might have lost faith in his investing know-how. After a diagnostic evaluation of this man's personality and latent ability to handle a crisis, I reassured him that his job history and personal development gave him every reason for a more positive outlook. However, there was a real possibility that if he shrank from using the aggressive, confident style that had once attracted customers, *he*, not the vagaries of the stock market, would be the cause of his vocational demise. As we worked together, he reviewed his characteristic approach to the market and acknowledged that it had made him successful in the past. My purpose was to turn his attention away from his fearful self and toward the world of finance. Fear had short-circuited his outreach; psychotherapy would restore his confidence in himself and help him channel his energies more productively.

Anger

A second emotion that causes under-getting is anger. When we are angry, we feel unpleasant and upset, but anger bothers our bodies as well as our minds and emotions. We wear threatening facial expressions and hold our bodies more tensely than usual because our internal chemistry changes. Anger, like fear, is accompanied by many physiological reactions. In either case, adrenaline is released into our bloodstream, preparing us to fight or take flight. The heart rate increases, breathing deepens, and sensory perception may become more acute. Just *being* angry wears us out physically, leaving us tired and discouraged, even if we control the impulse to act out our hostility. In that troubled state, we are in no mood to extend ourselves into the world to enhance our satisfaction.

Angry people do not attend to the cues that could help promote the achievement of their goals. As they shift their attitude from positive to negative, their efforts are no longer constructive. An aggressive driver fails to notice the details of the traffic situation and is more prone to have an accident. A resentful student does not pay close attention in class and cannot complete the homework assignment. A boxer who is too angry at his opponent swings wildly and abandons what he knows to be good technique, so his chance of victory becomes compromised.

When we are angry, our judgment and reasoning abilities are clouded. We are less likely to think things over if we are troubled by hostile emotions. In fact, if we are consumed with rage, we may temporarily forget much of what we have carefully learned.

Anger has a second way of jeopardizing our achievement level: When we are angry we offend and even frighten those around us. Anger drives others away either physically or emotionally, so then we must also contend with being rejected. When we allow anger to interfere with our composure and social graces, we risk losing relationships that have provided a network of support in the past. Violence against loved ones and minority groups—even against children—has become a frightening social issue that interferes with the quality of life.[3]

If anger threatens our search for satisfaction, why do we allow it to have such a dominant role in our lives that it easily overpowers reason? First, anger is a primal element of survival that is activated much sooner than higher cortical functioning. Anger is automatic, visceral, basic to the human condition. In one sense it may be accurate to say that we are born angry—if squalling, clenched fists, and a red face are signs of anger. As infants we experience anger whenever we are frustrated by unsatisfied needs. Our angry crying may not always secure for us what we want, but it is an assertive protest that says we are unhappy and want everyone to know it.

Second, because expressing anger is also a demand for attention, we quickly learn as infants that anger can be used to reduce our frustrations. The angry infant usually gets results—a lesson that will be used throughout life to force others to give us what we want.

A third reason why we persist in using anger as we search for satisfaction is that anger reduces our sense of helplessness. As infants and children we must rely on others to gratify our needs because of our limited ability to help ourselves. Our basic dislike of having insufficient power is evidenced in adulthood by the universal fear of being too feeble to be self-sufficient in our senior years. Resorting to anger may not secure our goals, but at the very least it asserts our independence and often can be used to control other people.

Finally, we hold on to anger because it is rooted in envy. Even as infants we experience envy, sometimes called the first deadly sin.[4] As infants we envy Mother's power over us. Although our choice is to be so close to her that the two of us will be one, she has the power to deny us that union and has the final word in providing or withholding nourishment and comfort.

Ironically, infantile feelings of helplessness and envy have a positive side as well. They give us the motivation to assert ourselves, yet teach us that we must also accommodate the demands of others. We have no choice but to moderate our anger and cooperate with Mother, so we learn to control our tempers and channel our energy more constructively. As we mature, we must continually adapt our acquisitive urges to external restrictions. A child's selfhood is subjected to many parental and social directives, creating a tension that is instructive but frustrating. Self, in time, must eventually come under its own control and be able to bear disappointment without excessive anger. Because we will always feel helpless in some situations and can rarely rise above envy, we will never fully sub-due the angry urge to protest and make demands. However, the rational self must begrudgingly agree that restraint is a reasonable compromise.

The most productive way to resolve the tensions between desire and reality is to appeal to reason. Talking over our frustrations mentally or with others will help us understand our motivations and why our efforts are being impeded. With this type of insight we are in a better position to negotiate for what we want, find alternative satisfaction, or—if all else fails—take our loss gracefully. It is ironic that, no matter how fully our basic needs and desires are met, minor defeats are hard to accept. It is as if every wish that does not come true, every project that does not suc-ceed, damages our sense of being in control. We are reluctant to lose a trivial skirmish even though we have achieved many victories.

Reasoning facilitates a compromise between our demand that things must always go our way and the reality that we cannot have everything we seek. When we think things over, we discipline our angry feelings and thereby inhibit the self-defeating responses that typically result when we allow an emotion to govern us. If we can acknowledge that everyone wins some and loses some, that life is not always "fair," and that other people have desires, too, we become strong enough to abide life's frustrations.

This chapter has noted a variety of ways in which the life-sustaining process of obtaining satisfaction can be interrupted by our own inappro-priate behaviors. I have pursued the thesis that we experience the dissat-isfaction of under-getting whenever we allow negative beliefs and atti-tudes to limit our view of what is possible or permit fear and anger to distract us from our goals. Because we are human, all of us encounter these psychological obstructions as we journey through life. We are so vulnerable to emotional pain, so unsure of what is best for us, that we are tempted to take nonproductive shortcuts. Yet, even when we are dead-ended, we stubbornly insist that our methods are correct and our pur-poses legitimate.

Furthermore, even when we are reasonably successful in getting what we seek, we sense that mere acquisition is not enough. We inevitably realize that the trophies of self-aggrandizement are enjoyable only in the context of meaningful relationships with other people. Since relation-ships are, as psychiatrist Heinz Kohut states, "the essence of the individ-ual's psychological life from birth to death," we must go beyond our-selves.[5] Reworded in the language of this text: If we are to become satisfied, we must go beyond getting to giving—which is our next topic.

The Process of Giving

The Generous Self

The only gift is a portion of yourself.
The gift without the giver is bare.

James Russell Lowell

Our obsession with getting is rooted in our biological demands, emotional makeup, mental development, and cultural heritage. Getting more and more for ourselves ensures our survival, provides enjoyment, and is undeniably at the core of our capitalistic system. Acquisition is a remarkably dynamic urge that has motivated exploration, inspired technological advances, and driven entrepreneurs to build giant corporations. (On the down side, it has also led to territorial conquests, recurrent warfare, autocratic governments, and personal greed.)

Our history of giving has been far less newsworthy. Despite dramatic improvements in intellectual and cultural sophistication over the centuries, we have not progressed proportionately in our urge to give. Getting has flourished because it serves the individual directly. Since giving is designed primarily to serve others, it is only indirectly rewarding to the donor. Getting is a human necessity, whereas giving—despite social, moral, and spiritual imperatives—has not been crucial for physical survival.

Ideally, getting and giving relate to each other in a circular fashion: We first get and then give to others in return (but not necessarily to those who are the source of what we acquired). While opposite in direction, getting and giving complement each other to fulfill personal and social obligations. The same type of satisfaction arises if we give before we receive, but getting typically comes first because most people's personal needs overshadow their social needs. The fact that we are more self-centered than others-centered does not necessarily constitute a labeling of the human race as immature or selfish. Sheer expediency demands that we must first take in before we have anything to give.

We are gradually made aware of the relationship between getting and giving if our social development proceeds normally. Even as infants we learn that we cannot have everything our own way, that we must share, wait, and cooperate.

Social reality dictates that as we grow older we must become skilled at noticing the many details of a situation that will help us respond appropriately. We learn to piece together the demands of each situation and relate these to what we know to be a reasonable response. Becoming skilled at suppressing inappropriate reactions, while choosing personally and socially productive behavior, shows social maturation. As we mature, these learned patterns of behavior are fortified and we are encouraged to feel good about giving to others.

Social analyst Daniel Yankelovich points out in *New Rules* that all of us harbor an awareness of the relationship between giving and getting.[1] He refers to unwritten rules that are never explicit but are nonetheless extensive and powerful determinants of how much we will get and give. Yankelovich refers to these important rules as the "giving-getting compact" that governs much of our behavior. We all hold our own private definitions of what we need, what is fair, and how much to give to others. We establish our patterns of getting and giving by deliberately or subconsciously relying on these internal beliefs.

Yankelovich illustrates how the terms of the giving-getting compact have shifted dramatically from the selfless pattern of the past to the self-fulfilling ideology of the present. He condemns this egocentric searching as "defective" because materialistic gain at the expense of the community—that is, failing to share with others—leaves us "isolated and anxious instead of fulfilled."[2] His concern (and mine) is that the process of getting may overshadow that of giving to such an extent that we totally ignore the needs of others. It seems that we continually maneuver to get back as much as, or more than, we give. Erich Fromm calls many of us "marketing characters"—people whose giving reflects an exchange of X for Y.[3] If a genuine concern for the receiver is missing, we are tempted to reduce giving to a businesslike transaction in which personal goals preempt altruism.

Giving is not merely an acknowledgment that being "decent" is a sensible way to maintain peaceful coexistence with our fellow humans. Nor is it necessarily a moral mandate to look after the welfare of others to the exclusion of our own self-interest. This chapter will first examine how we give from our sense of who we are as individuals, what we have learned about being given to, and our private estimates of what we owe to others. Then our attention will focus on how giving benefits not just the recipient; it has built-in rewards for the giver personally and reinforces the spirit of community within a society. Finally we will consider the factor of will in the process of giving.

Giving and Self-Identity

The capacity to give of one's self is truly within every human being, but a person does not have to be rich, mature, or even mentally healthy to have something to share with another. If a baby in a highchair has several grapes and spontaneously thrusts one smilingly toward Mother, the baby is "giving"—as are psychopathic killers in prison who tenderly care for goats and ducks as yard pets, and the severely retarded, the elderly, or the mentally and physically ill who eagerly reach to stroke kittens brought to them for a few hours.

From our earliest years, most of us have had messages about giving drummed into us: "Share your toys!" "Come help me, right now!" "Think of the other guy for once!" These stern commands have made it clear that giving is not optional, that it is an important lesson of life we must learn as soon as possible. Unfortunately, if others mainly evaluate our offerings with a punishing look of "Is that all?" we are more or less shamed into giving during childhood and adolescence and may develop a sense of sharing *only* to avoid social rejection. Internalizing the rules of giving does increase personal acceptance, although—as we will see in the next section—outreach to others brings us direct rewards as well. Whatever our basic motivation, as we develop social etiquette we increase our confidence level.

The process of giving-and-getting, by putting the self in touch with the social environment, establishes a basis for interpersonal relationships. If we find this interaction personally rewarding, we complete the process by acknowledging our obligation to care for others in return. We become comfortable with giving as our sense of social reciprocity is reinforced by our experiences.

Yet, our altruism is usually flawed by personal desire. Few of us find it possible to divorce our acts of giving from our expectations of getting something in return. Our interest in the welfare of others is therefore conditional, tempered by a deliberate or subconscious analysis of potential private gains. We all carry within us a personal accountant who totals up how much is taken in and paid out, decides who owes us and whom we owe in return, and assesses what is fair or unfair. Even the most intimate and permanent of our relationships are subject to such scrutiny. If a spouse or lover is neglectful of our desires, or a busy parent seems preoccupied with other issues, we may withdraw our involvement, despite our need for continued communion with that person. Giving is deeply related to how much we receive.

Consider the case of an eight-year-old girl who was referred to me by her pediatrician because of general apathy, underachievement in school, and poor relations with other children. This child had been a very sickly infant. Her need for months of nursing care literally exhausted her mother, who confided to me that she gradually lost all hope that her baby would ever be well and normal. To protect herself from the pain and disappointment she felt, the mother gradually withdrew emotionally from her daughter. The child's meager response to the mother's efforts prompted little in return. As the years went by, the child recovered physically but continued to be quiet at home and under-responsive in other social situations. Her mother's lack of involvement no doubt contributed to the child's apathy. Each had reinforced the other's withdrawal to the point where very little giving was taking place.

Why is it that we give so conditionally, allowing past experiences to overshadow the importance of giving? To answer this question, we need to examine the nature of the self in greater detail. The self has been generally recognized as the dominant character in our human dialogue with others. Shakespeare advised us that we must first be true to our own selves if we wish not to be false to others. Much earlier, Christ underscored the pivotal role of the self in the act of giving when he urged us to love our neighbors *as we love ourselves* (Mark 12:31). It is clear that the self provides the psychological base from which we operate socially.

Modern theories of human behavior confirm the priority of the self in the process of giving. Psychologists define "self" as the sense of a "me" that is differentiated from the world of human and inanimate objects. This consciousness of personal identity develops early in infancy. When, in the presence of a responsive environment, infants are nourished and supported well enough to begin to differentiate self from Mother, they notice their own body parts and their movements, their own urges, feelings, wishes, and fantasies. They develop, according to Edith Jacobson, "a concept of their sum total, i.e., of the self as a differentiated but organized entity. . . ."[4] The more adequately infants are cared for, the more clearly they are able to perceive themselves as separate from all the objects in their environment. A baby not only looks into the mirror and sees "me," but also mentally adopts this "me" as a source of permanent identity.

As time goes on, babies increasingly sense that there is a relationship between how they behave and how their mothers respond. Eager to please and be pleased, infants form patterns of interacting with the environment, recording all the effects of their behavior, but especially the maternal reactions. In time, images are formed of an idealized self—the "me" that brings the most favorable responses from Mother. In seeking to enhance their pleasure, infants learn to comply with maternal expectations, although this means controlling their own "selfish" instinct to *demand* gratification. The awareness that "good me" gets better results than "bad me" is the beginning of a concept of giving. Through learning that the self's needs must be framed in the context of pleasing the primary care-giver, a baby develops the ability to relate successfully to others in an expanding circle of acquaintances.

In effect, giving is at the heart of all social interchange, but much of our so-called altruism is rooted in a desire to maximize our own satisfaction. From that perspective, we almost always give conditionally, protective of our personal stake in what transpires between the other party and ourselves.

The ideal self is always anchored in the reality of an imperfect self that must find fulfillment or else lose its identity. The "me" I ought to be encourages my actual self to put its best foot forward in interpersonal relations, but the inevitable shortfall can be a source of considerable discouragement. As we sense the distance between who we really are and who we would like to be, most of us feel that we have failed. J. Harold Ellens reminds us that the distance between the real self and the ideal self "is the scope of our pain and emptiness—our neediness for satisfaction, meaning, and the longing for our genuine self." The failure to be as we should be, says Ellens, is what some people call "evil."[5]

Ellens identifies the failure to meet our ideals as a blow to our sense of pride, a loss the self must endure. We therefore acknowledge inadequacy as part of our humanness and suffer daily from not being able to spare ourselves from the pain of being weak. In our loneliness we have two possible sources of relief: we can turn to God and to each other. Because we look to God to do for us what we obviously cannot do for ourselves, we define God in ways that fit the nature of our inadequacy. For the empty, God is a provider; for the lonely, he is a friend and comforter; for those treated unjustly, God is as an avenger. The perfect goodness of this supreme being overpowers the evil of our emptiness—and this dynamic process gives us the strength to persevere.

Another way we ease the anxiety and frustration of not being able to live up to our ideals, is by seeking to relate to other people in some compensatory manner. Especially if we perceive that they view us as unworthy, we decide to act generously to stimulate them to treat us more favorably. We often idealize our image of others, exaggerating how much they have to offer and thereby heightening our expectation of increased gratification. So we try our best to find opportunities to be recognized as caring individuals by people we imagine have goods and answers we lack. Then we can feel justified in asking them for something in return. What we receive from others helps fill some specific needs, but it also eases the pain of knowing we have failed to be all we could be.

The Rewards of Giving

Perhaps one of the most popular questions since 1960 has been: "What's in it for me?" Although it seems to reflect a self-focus that might discount a concern for others, the question has some legitimacy.

All relationships are arrangements between the self and one or more other people, implying that both parties have a stake in what is going on between them. The notion that giving is (and should be) solely for the benefit of the receiver is erroneous. The self always demands its obvious or hidden rewards in all interpersonal transactions, even those involving deep love. Thus, when parents warn their young child not to get into cars with strangers, they are not only thinking of the child's welfare and thus fulfilling their care-giving duties; they are also trying to preserve a deeply satisfying relationship.

"What's in it for me?" can be answered on several levels. First, practically speaking, when you give something away, you leave room for something new to take its place. Consider, for example, what typically happens if you give your used clothing to a charitable organization. As you thin out your drawers and closets, you can more easily justify buying something new to replace what was there. People who hoard their possessions risk becoming saturated with the old and devoid of the pleasure to be found in new purchases.

Compulsive savers—unwilling to part with the old and useless because they imagine that someday those items might come in handy—live with a fear of being caught without enough. As they remind themselves of how bad things used to be and might be again, they are keeping alive some very negative feelings from the past. Miserliness is rarely based only on common sense and prudence. Angry over never having gotten enough, and fearful of feeling deprived in the future, hoarders hold on too tightly to the present status quo. As the old becomes more useless, they become uncomfortably aware that they are missing out on new pleasures others are enjoying. If the price we pay for security is dissatisfaction, we will feel even more insecure.

The dynamics of finding satisfaction dictate that we must give as well as get. We must relinquish the old before taking on the new. Hoarders and compulsive savers violate that principle by refusing to prune the dead wood that is hindering new growth.

The second reason why giving is beneficial for the giver is that it encourages the development of healthy, satisfying interactions with others. In the act of worrying less about ourselves and caring more for others, we become even *more* enhanced. There is a paradox to giving. On the one hand, it appears that giving away our time, attention, or goods leaves us that much less than we had before. According to this simplistic logic, it is sensible to give only when there is a good chance to get back more. The reasoning is that such conditional giving will fortify the self by guarding its personal assets.

However, there is an ironic postscript to this principle of self-preservation: We benefit as givers *because* we then direct our focus away from the self and thereby reduce our ego-centered concerns, especially our fear of rejection. Interacting with others helps us see that they, too, are searching and feel inadequate. When we give, we automatically open ourselves to the broader picture of people and interests beyond ourselves and find reassurance of our acceptability through these involvements. This point is succinctly captured in the biblical paradox that only by losing one's life can one find it (Matt. 10:39).

Over the years I have seen a number of attractive and intelligent people in their mid-thirties who are seeking a mate but still remain single. Invariably, when I inquire into the details of their lives, I find evidence of an excessive self-focus that has kept these young people from marrying. Some are too idealistic, holding out for the perfect mate; others are too passive to circulate in places where a potential partner might be found. Many of them fear intimacy in general and find ways to sabotage relationships. These young people have typically paid more attention to their own needs than to the varied give-and-take details of courtship. Put in the context of our discussion, they have not transcended the narrow limits of self-focus and given enough of themselves to someone else. Their insistence on knowing with certainty who is the "right" one reveals a paralyzing fear that their personal desires will not be sufficiently honored, that a long-term commitment will threaten their autonomy. Whatever the specific underlying psychology, my suggestion to these singles is to reach out and become socially involved: bowling teams, singles groups, church, political campaigns, and the like. As they volunteer to help out or join in such activities, singles redirect the flow of their energies outward and learn that they will receive in proportion to what they give.

Giving benefits the giver in a third way by helping him or her to avoid guilt. When we give to others, we are less bothered by the voice of conscience. We learn early in life to share or else risk feeling guilty of selfishness. We internalize the expected protests of others by thinking to ourselves, "What a weak person I am—always taking and never giving!" The conscience serves as a repository of social standards that we embrace as guides for our behavior.

Social reality dictates that we play by certain rules, treating each other fairly, watching out for the common good. Our urges may drive us to take care of ourselves, but our consciences serve as a check-and-balance to prevent social and personal disharmony. When guilty feelings warn us that we have upset the balance, giving helps us reestablish order.

Many religions teach that we *should* feel guilty if we are uncharitable, for then we are breaking "higher" laws that are more binding than the dictates of social expediency. Non-givers break God's law, not just the practical rules of the conscience. All through the New Testament, for example, Jesus Christ does not merely encourage us to give; he *commands* it. When a lawyer tempted him with the question of what was the greatest of all commandments, Christ's answer was that we are to first love God and then others (Matt. 22:37–40). Elsewhere he indicated the standard for human altruism: "Love each other as I have loved you" (John 15:12). The love ethic that is the core of Christianity calls for a commitment to serving others, but it also implies that generosity will bring joy and contentment to the giver.

Giving and Human Fellowship

While giving strengthens the self by enhancing our acquisitions, building relationships, and reducing guilt, it has an even more important purpose. Giving develops an interpersonal ethic that promotes fellowship within the human family. When we empathize with others—sharing emotions and possessions—we experience an inner peace and freedom from loneliness. This feeling continues to remind us, as we make our way in life apart from the protective and nourishing arms of our mothers, that we can find substitutes for her that will also sustain us. By expressing our filial love in acts of kindness and generosity toward others, we acknowledge our universal needs. If we reach out with gifts to fill the emptiness of our fellow travelers on life's journey, we simultaneously enrich ourselves in our own vital areas. We keep each other alive in empathic communion, for the contact of eye and hand or the gift of time or substance instantly unites people, at least for a moment.

We feel good when we give! Acts of charity remind us that we are decent and generous and that social graces bond us with other human beings for our mutual benefit. Above all, giving provides an inner voice of reassurance that we play an important role in the world community.

Giving calms perhaps the deepest of our fears—that of estrangement and alienation. We all dread the coldness of being alone and uncared for, the emptiness of not feeling affirmed by others. Giving establishes a kinship that erases that sense of separation. As we reduce the gap between self and others by taking their interests and concerns into our hearts, we feel close to them. Caring about someone is an act of intimacy, even if the other person does not know we care.

Who of us never had a sports hero or other public idol? As a child, mine was Andy Pafko, the centerfielder for the Chicago Cubs. I carved his name on my baseball bat and dreamed he would ask me to wash his car or mow his lawn. How I wanted to give selflessly to him. (Well, sort of—I hoped he would give me an autographed baseball, and I still do!) Obviously Andy Pafko did not know I existed, but that did not limit my desire to serve him. Giving was at the core of what bound us together in my mind.

Perhaps that example will illustrate the point that we can feel close to someone who does not know of our interest. When we make charitable donations or volunteer our time in service groups, we have an opportunity to visualize how a recipient's life might be warmed in some way by our generosity. For even the anonymous giver, charity has a potential for intimacy.

On the other hand, if our giving is more personalized, we usually have the chance to observe the receiver's response. Even gifts not altogether appropriate will bring a smile of acceptance, since most people appreciate an act of giving, if not the gift itself. The smile or "thank-you" rewards the donor by affirming his or her generosity. Jesus Christ reiterated this principle of reciprocal benefit: "Give, and it will be given to you. A good measure, pressed down, shaken together and running over, will be poured into your lap" (Luke 6:38a).

What we really look for in the responses of others are signs of the happiness that our gifts have provided. We take pleasure in the moment of seeing another person's joy, partly because we can take that delight and make it our own. We, too, know what it feels like to be given to, and we are reminded of that joy by the positive response of our beneficiary. Under these conditions of mutual satisfaction, we typically do not need any other gift in return. In fact, when others insist on paying us back in kind, we feel awkward and even a little cheated. We may enjoy another's response so much that we do not want to have our pleasure diminished by the insinuation that the gift was given with the idea of getting back something more tangible.

The Will to Give

We have so far considered that every human being has the capacity to give, and the inclination to do so—because there are implicit rewards for the giver. Why, then, are some of us more charitable than others? There are also the related questions of why we give to one person or cause and not to another, and why we give one day and refuse the next. The answer to all of these questions can be found by examining the importance of the will in giving.

Psychologist Rollo May, in his classic study, *Love and Will*, states that "the simple wish [is] the point where every act of will starts."[6] The wish springs in part from a biological urge that pushes us toward some object for satisfaction. But a wish is more than a biological need; the deeper meaning is the desire to assert ourselves and renounce our sense of helplessness. The will to give reflects a deliberate affirmation of self and is a reaction against the temptation to passively let life give to us. May calls passivity "modern man's most pervasive tendency—which has become almost an endemic disease. . . ."[7] As we feel overwhelmed by a sense of helplessness in dealing with personal and social problems, we are tempted to deny the will and to retain our substance by not giving.

Apathy, passivity, and depression are symptomatic of a "frozen" will that no longer senses the purpose of exerting itself. Whether from fear or from a growing sense of personal irrelevancy, when we deny the will we give up wishing for better things. "To cease wishing is to be dead, or at least to inhabit the land of the dead," says May.[8] Where there is apathy, there is a denial of will and a disbelief that we (or forces beyond us) can provide deliverance. No longer do we dream of things to come and imagine ways to obtain them. When we abandon our will to improve ourselves, we give up the very hope that would have led to improvement.

Most psychotherapists have had the experience of working with a depressed patient whose treatment goes on and on with very little measurable progress. I recall a case where a thirty-nine-year-old man stayed faithfully in therapy for over three years but exhibited a marked resistance toward letting go of the rage he felt over childhood disappointments. Born to parents who had married late in life, this man was handled awkwardly and inconsistently as a child—one day indulged, the next deprived. His parents apparently loved him but seemed unable or unwilling to provide the kind of care that reinforces self-worth and fosters independence.

Over the years this man, a successful architect, has acted out the same theme of inconsistency in his self-care. He got into an interesting profession but takes no pride in his accomplishments. He married and had children but is unable to show personal love for his family. He goes on vacations but with an attitude of indifference and even irritability. This man has become an expert at tempting himself with good things and subsequently withdrawing from them. Coming for help but making little progress fits right in with his style of acting in self-defeating ways. It is not surprising that he is depressed.

Why does this man insist on ruining his life? Here we see an example of a person who has refused to use his will to live and enjoy himself. Although he is angry at his parents, he denies the depths of his rage. In fact, by identifying with his parents and acting as they did, he hopes to feel closer to them. This may give him proof that they were not at fault in giving him so little, but it will also remove the justification for the rage buried in his depression. His will to live is frozen in the fear of being honest with himself. His progress in psychotherapy depends on his being able to own up to the truth that he was not raised in a healthy way, that his parents inadequately showed their love. Then he must face his fury and come to forgive them. Only after doing all these difficult tasks can he be free to exert his will to enjoy life and give deeply to others.

The juices of giving flow freely when our urge for self-assertion, the desire to find personal authenticity through selective giving, and our unbounded imaginings are all allowed to stew together in the caldron of self. We may not know why we suddenly decide to give. When that time arrives—when there is harmony between the self and objects of our interest—the will lets go of its inhibitions and giving occurs. For giving to be rewarding, even exciting, there must be a genuine agreement between the inner voices of the self that it is the correct course of action.

If giving is truly against our will, it is dishonest. Too often we give *only* from obligation. As we have seen, we do give partly to preserve personal and social harmony, to enhance our own acquisitions, and to avoid being guilty of stinginess. But those purposes are essentially self-serving. *True* generosity is more others-oriented; it flows from an intentional desire to peek into the soul of the receiver. If we feel oneness with those to whom we give, we can more readily know what they really need or want. For example, the more deeply a husband understands his wife and his feelings for her, the more easily he can exert his will in giving. One Christmas, because a wife is lonely or blue, she may need something cuddly or comforting. Another Christmas she may be interested in expanding her talents or intellectual skills and thus be in need of books or appliances that could foster those specific interests. If a husband pauses to examine his wife's current mood or stage of development, a husband can affirm their human connection by making a purchase that will be most rewarding to her. The question is whether he is *willing* to engage in that kind of search for intimacy.

Genuine giving reflects conscious and unconscious concerns about the relationship between giver and receiver. The fact that we go to great lengths to think of, arrange for, and deliver an appropriate gift shows a high regard for the recipient. Because our gift conveys a message, we take pains to make sure the gift is suitable to the occasion, and to the nature of the relationship. (We do not give something too intimate or expensive to someone we hardly know.) We also want our gifts to express something of who we are as givers—tender, humorous, serious, thoughtful—and how we feel toward the other person.

Giving with sincerity shows an awareness of the needs of others and a desire to improve their condition. The purpose of giving at its finest is to invest the self in an act of loving concern for another person. True generosity is more than a social reflex. It shows that we have matured to the point where we have wrestled with self, others, and things, both conceptually and experientially, and have concluded at the deepest levels of our being that giving is a valuable, necessary, and joyful thing to do. Erich Fromm calls such giving "the highest expression of potency."[9]

Restricted Giving

The Inadequate Self

Selfishness is the enemy of all true affection.

Tacitus

pparently the Roman historian Tacitus, a pagan, shared the view of first-century Christians that taking for self is constantly at war with our impulse to serve others. In considering why his words are still true, philosophers, psychologists, and theologians may argue the point from different perspectives. However, their singular conclusion is most likely that we are primarily takers because we are flawed in some way—that the desire to take more and give less is an inherent characteristic of every human being. Although a mature individual is able to acknowledge that there is personal nourishment and fellowship available in acts of generosity, many factors militate against giving too freely of ourselves. In a very real sense, we are all selfish and therefore very protective of our time, energies, and possessions.

Great thinkers throughout recorded history have sought to comprehend the epic struggle between the will to give and the urge to withhold or to take. They have labored both to define this problem and to prescribe a remedy. The Greek philosophers, for example, described human

wrongdoing primarily in terms of selfishness: envy, lust, greed, and glut-
tony. The remaining three of the "seven deadly sins"—pride, anger, and
sloth—are best described as self-serving rather than selfish, but the gist
of the Greeks' message was to warn against the destructive urge to focus
on self at the cost of being uncharitable.

In ancient Greece, the remedy for human evil was thought to be
found in knowledge. Citizens were urged to travel to Delphi or other
shrines and inquire of the gods what they were to do for relief. The basic
answer was inscribed on the portal of the temple: *"Gnothi se
auton"*—"Know thyself." This meant more than simply understanding
oneself, for self-knowledge implied forgiveness for being merely mortal
and therefore weak and tragically flawed. Even though the Greeks
attributed ultimate wisdom and power to the gods, they could also internalize these positive attributes to foster a deeper sense of personal adequacy. They could then manage their fears and ultimately confront their
sense of weakness by resorting to the power of the mind.

According to Greek philosophy, mankind's destiny was to elevate the
mind *(psyche)* to a God-like control over the body *(soma)* and hence
suppress both the evil passions of the body and the fears stemming from
being human. This "solution" has been far from adequate. J. Harold
Ellens describes what has happened through the succeeding centuries:

> The centuries that follow the golden age, of course, tell an interesting
> story of despair and disillusion. Man as god proved unable to manage his
> "god-ness," or even his goodness. Existentialist loss of meaning set in and
> brought on a wholesale lunge into primitive mystery religions; then
> bizarre supernaturalism followed. That unfortunate course is similar to the
> pattern of history from the humanism of the nineteenth-century Western
> rationalism to existentialist despair with Camus, Sartre, and Kierkegaard
> at the turn of the century and on to the current preoccupation with astrol-
> ogy, karma, and reincarnation in the West.[1]

Interpreting the Human Condition

As we have struggled historically with good and evil, strength and
weakness, we have recognized that this epic battle has no end. We have
had to abandon our aspirations to be God-like, since even the most rudi-
mentary self-awareness convinces us of our insufficiencies. Twenty-five
centuries after the golden age of Greece, mankind is still struggling to
explain the power our self-serving desires hold over us.

I would like to elaborate briefly on how Sigmund Freud has defined selfishness. In contemplating animal urges and social values, good and evil, taking selfishly and giving selflessly, Freud pitted the "good" conscience (superego) against the "evil" urge (id), for the purpose of controlling our selfish thoughts and acts. Although he conceived of a healthful, moderating "ego" to integrate the two, Freud feared that the ego might not be strong enough. Like the early Greeks, he first saw mankind's only hope to be in a self-knowledge that in theory would lead to self-control. But Freud was uncomfortably aware of how deep and unstoppable our aggressive urges are.

R. Sampson reminds us that deep within every individual are the murderous demons, the Oedipal lusts, the universal guilts, the self-anger over our many failures.[2] Sampson quotes Freud as saying, "[T]he more a man checks his aggressive tendencies toward others the more tyrannical, that is aggressive, he becomes in his ego ideal."[3] Freud saw people as capable of turning their aggressive instincts against themselves if unable to direct their urges against others. He tried to explain the problem of aggressive, selfish urges by calling the demand for self-serving power a mark of psychic realism. To be sick, said Freud, is to deny the power, to be dishonest with oneself, and to be a slave to the pleasure principle. In effect, he encouraged people to assert themselves and to choose freely as a sign of wholeness.

But Freud actually had little faith in human beings. He pessimistically described the common man and woman as untutored and unalterably and forever linked to personal, aggressive self-interests. Freud doubted that people would voluntarily forestall or discipline their urges. It would seem to follow that society must curb the monster within us, so he prescribed group force for purposes of control. But, we might well ask, if our aggressive instincts are only to be controlled by social restriction and punishment, what of the possibility that higher social or spiritual values could be utilized to provide some similar sense of control? Is mankind too animalistic to voluntarily accept moral codes?

Sampson concludes that Freud's later writings soften his skepticism about mankind's moral impotency. In fact, he came to describe people as possibly having the ability to direct their libidinal energies toward the altruistic goals of giving. Freud even brought his atheism into close proximity with Christianity when, in *Civilization and Its Discontents*, he considered the importance of love as a means of disciplining one's aggression. He wrote, "From one ethical standpoint . . . this inclination towards an all-embracing love of others and of the world at large is regarded as the highest state of mind of which man is capable."[4] Freud came closest to acknowledging the importance of giving out of love in this statement: "And in the development of mankind as a whole, just as in individuals, love alone acts as the civilizing favor in the sense that it brings change from egoism to altruism."[5]

However, Freud failed to link the theory and practice of love to a divine energy or a religious, moral structure. Until his death he remained skeptical that either he or anyone else had accomplished much to solve the depressing human dilemma of how to transcend selfish goals.

Selfishness has always been described as evil, while the sharing of one's substance has always been seen as good. The green-eyed monster exists now, as it did historically. But is it true that we are still primarily animalistic in our motives, untouched over the centuries by social and spiritual values?

In all fairness, most of us cannot be described as creatures who generally *enjoy* being selfish and withholding of our substance, although we may sometimes look for excuses not to give. Yes, we can be coldly indifferent to others, but this is not usually the case. Most of us are not entirely uncharitable—unwilling to share at all—because we accept the social reality that we must learn to share, that tightfisted withholding may hurt us even more than others. We know it is reasonable to assume that one hand washes the other, even if we do not faithfully practice this principle.

There is no doubt that we look after our own best interests but, as Ayn Rand points out in her classic work, *The Virtues of Selfishness,* this kind of self-focus is not "selfish" in the traditional sense of the word.[6] The fact is, most of us dislike truly ungiving people and do not want to be that way. Common sense dictates that each of us must learn to give voluntarily and to see the wisdom of giving. There must be a healthy balance between the two: some getting, some giving; something for self, something for others. We learn to strike this balance as we mature, but our social development is never complete, so we constantly struggle with a darker, selfish side.

Our Generic Inadequacy

What is it about our human condition that fosters selfishness? I want to develop the thesis that the psychological root of selfishness is found in our sense of inadequacy. I believe that the more adequate we feel, the more we are willing to give to others. We are born with an awareness of our weaknesses and therefore fear the wiles of a capricious world. We tremble in considering how much we do not know, in realizing how vulnerable we are. This sense of inadequacy defines who we are, but it can also guide us toward relief—if we fill the "evil" of our emptiness with the "good" of personal growth, wisdom, moral fiber, interpersonal relating, and spiritual communion.

Alfred Adler, one of Freud's early disciples, split with him over the issue of what causes anxiety. Whereas Freud claimed that anxiety is based in sexual instincts, Adler attributed anxiety to universal feelings of inferiority. Adler explained that these feelings "supply the motive power for compensatory striving. . . ."[7] Therefore, everything we seek after (and accomplish) stems from our discomfort over being and feeling inadequate.

To build upon the Adlerian theory of universal inferiority feelings, I want to add my belief that while all of us are strongly motivated to feel adequate, we also harbor a desire to *retain* our sense of helplessness. We have learned that, despite the natural urge to develop ourselves, it sometimes feels good *not* to grow. As we use our feelings of inferiority for a variety of self-serving reasons, we are also less motivated to share with others, despite our ideals and the inherent rewards of giving.

One way we use inadequacy is as an excuse to avoid facing changes. We basically fear and dislike change because of the risks involved. Playing it safe by staying with the familiar is so strong a protective impulse that we find ways to resist moving beyond the tried and true. Even our inadequacy affords us a certain amount of security—a safe place to rest until we feel comfortable about proceeding.

Listen to a man in psychotherapy who is struggling with inadequacy. We have been talking about this man's boredom after seventeen years in a mediocre job and have come to the point where I have asked why he has put up with the monotony.

"I've thought about trying some other kind of work, but for some reason my ideas don't seem too strong," he says. "I want to get away from my job, but I still stay there."

"You seem to hope your ideas will motivate you and are disappointed when they fade," I comment.

"Exactly, as if the ideas are supposed to force me to move whether I am ready or not. It's weird! Here I am hoping for a way out of boredom, but I don't really do anything about it. I guess it's just too familiar where I am."

"As if your work situation is too comfortable to get into the pain of changing jobs?"

"Yes, like it's my place to hide out."

"And you oblige the urge to stay put by avoiding anything that would jeopardize your familiar hiding place."

"It sounds horrible when I hear you say that, but that's exactly what I'm doing. It's almost as if I'm fighting being successful."

This man's progress in treatment will require him to shift from feeling helpless—a victim of "weak motives" and self-doubt—to acknowledging that he has made no effort to grow. Now that he has admitted he is hiding in excuses, he will have to take steps to resist feeling inadequate and get on with finding a new job. Our next steps in therapy will be to have him review his talents and then make specific plans for a job change.

It is ironic that we sometimes resist solving the very problems that give us pain because our sense of vulnerability makes us reluctant to upset ourselves further. We prefer to tolerate unfortunate circumstances rather than do something constructive. Nevertheless, our inadequacy can actually have motivating power. When we decide to promote ourselves in any form, the pain of feeling inadequate is a starting point. The difficulty is in *admitting* that discomfort.

Let us listen in again on the case previously cited to illustrate this principle. In the next session the man begins:

"You know, I've been reviewing what I've said the last few times, and what I hear is that I don't like my inactivity. I seem to find excuses for not advancing myself, not just in changing jobs, but as a general way of life."

"And you are unhappy about the way you feel?"

"Yes, I'm sick of feeling weak and scared. It stops me from getting where I want to go. The best way to get rid of unhappiness is to get going."

This man finally realizes he has spent years trying to get comfortable with a painful situation. Once he sees that he has been making excuses and avoiding progress, he uses this awareness to prod himself into action. "I'm sick of feeling weak and scared" is the turning point. Now he is motivated to move.

There is no pleasure as rewarding as the ending of pain. Relieving the pain of inadequacy adds to our enjoyment of success. We appreciate the contrast in "before and after" pictures and stories of those who overcame defeat. When we exhaust our excuses, our inadequacies spur us on and help us celebrate our achievements more deeply. Not coincidentally, once a degree of success is attained, we may go into another slump and gravitate back down to earlier levels of impoverishment.

Feeling inadequate has other self-serving features. There is, for example, the lurking thought that when we feel weak or tired, we will be excused from giving to others.

During a marriage-counseling session, a wife complains that her husband always "plays dead" when he arrives home after work: "Ed walks in the door, plops down, and says, 'I'm dead; get me a beer.' I don't mind his relaxing a little, but he ignores us. The kids are eager to see him and I'd like some conversation, but he doesn't say a word. It's like he has nothing left in him for his own family."

"Look, I've had it by five-thirty," Ed says resentfully. "What do you want, blood?"

His wife replies, "On bowling nights you're not the least bit tired, and the other day, when Tina from next door came over, you were real chatty. How come you're there for others but not us?"

Ed angrily responds, "You're crazy. I'm just exhausted."

"What's Louise's point, Ed?" I ask.

"The point is, he doesn't care about us," Louise interrupts.

"The real point is that no matter how hard I work, it's never enough for her," Ed answers.

I comment, "From my side of the desk it looks like Louise and the kids want you to give them more than a hard day's work, Ed. You have a right to feel tired and to relax for a while after work, but not at the expense of these important family ties. You are more than a paycheck to them. Louise, suppose you tell Ed right now how important he is to you and what you appreciate about him. After that, Ed, why don't you tell Louise what she means to you and what you love about her."

The tired, the poor, and other "unfortunates" are not *expected* to have anything to give. If we look inadequate, we get deferential treatment from others that allows us to keep what appears to be the little bit we have. Heroes who claim their success was won by luck or by others' help are often merely asking not to be expected to repeat their victories. Poor-mouthing is a clever strategy.

Similarly, when we look or act inadequate, we can more easily ask for help or special consideration. "Who could turn down someone in need?" we reason subconsciously. The worse our impoverishment, the less our guilt in asking for more. In fact, some people even use this "poor me" feeling to justify cheating a corporation or the government, because these organizations are seen as having so much that it would only be "fair" for them to share with those who have so little. With this kind of thinking, we may come to assume that our employers or elected officials owe us a reasonable standard of living, whether or not we deserve it.

Others assume that by remaining inadequate they will move others to be generous to them. Street beggars, for example, survive primarily by this kind of appeal—but so do children who always claim to be tired when asked to do their chores, and certain charitable organizations that are forever discovering some new "crisis" to manipulate the public into making contributions. Pretending to be weak, and therefore needy, is a clever manipulation to get more and give less. Such pretenses easily become habitual.

We may also unconsciously nourish our sense of inadequacy by ignoring the very accomplishments we have worked so hard to achieve. If we have pressed vigorously toward some goal, we can become so enamored with the process of striving that reaching that goal feels somewhat uncomfortable.

Many people have a very low tolerance for feeling good about their talents and victories. We need to savor our accomplishments, yet we so easily take them for granted and focus more on how we might have done even better. It seems easier to dwell on the problems at hand, stewing and worrying about their solutions—as if we forget how well we have handled other problems. We too infrequently say to ourselves that the next challenge will be even more interesting, an opportunity to once again use our abilities. Rather, we sigh, "Now what? Is there never any relief?" Our short memory for past victories builds a barrier between the ego-building events of our lives and our sense of achievement. If we fail to integrate our positive qualities into our self-structure, we remain dissatisfied—obsessively worried or discouraged about the problems before us instead of enjoying the fruits of our best efforts.

An upwardly-mobile young woman who is developing her own company recently said to me that she *knows* she has a fine husband, loving and well-behaved children, financial security, good health, nice friends, and a bright future, but she *feels* restless and unhappy. She is too busy working to really enjoy anything and recently wondered if she might find some excitement by having an affair. For this woman, and for many other high achievers, the barrier is between knowing and feeling. Although she comprehends the elements of her success story, she does not experience the joy of triumph.

"You seem to have a lot of trophies, Angela," I begin. "Yet they're out there somewhere rather than in here [as I point to my heart]."

"I don't understand why I do that," Angela responds. "I'm familiar with pushing on for more because everything I've ever gotten has come from my own efforts. So why can't I enjoy my gains?"

"You are telling me that you operate from a formula that goes, 'I push and things happen.' Let's try an experiment, so you can hear from your feeling side. Rest your arms on the arms of the chair and raise each hand upward. Let's call your right hand the one that drives hard to accomplish and your left hand the one that experiences the gains. I'd like you to speak for each side. Left hand, tell us what it feels like to know you are a competent mother."

"Well, I guess you could say—I know: I love my children very much," Angela tells me.

"Yes, it's true that you love your children," I agree. "Now I'd like you to feel good about that love rather than make statements about it."

As Angela allows her warm feelings of love to be experienced, all goes fairly well because her maternal emotions are instinctive. But when I suggest that she feel good about her success in life, Angela gets defensive.

"I don't know where we are going with this."

"Which hand is talking right now?" I ask.

"I guess that's me, the impatient pusher—my right hand," she replies.

"Exactly. Now try again to feel good about *everything* you've accomplished. Just let a good feeling radiate within you," I suggest.

After pausing for a while, her left hand rises up and she whispers, "I can't; I feel scared to."

"Say it again, Angela," I urge.

"I'm afraid to let my feelings come."

"Again."

"I'm afraid to feel successful." Suddenly she bursts into tears. "The things I like—they always go away. It always seems that once I really enjoy something, it's just a prelude to losing it."

"So if you don't let yourself feel for something, you won't get hurt when it goes away," I reflect.

"Yes, and pushing hard for more makes me feel doubly sure I won't get hurt."

Angela is moving nicely into an exploration of the reasons she remains emotionally inadequate. Her formula—less feelings means less hurt—will have to be explored in more detail to see how she has come to embrace such a position. But for now she has made a significant connection between how she is using her emotional inadequacy for her supposed benefit, and why she pushes so hard to get more for herself.

Somehow she has not let go of past losses; she uses the memories of those disappointments to generate a vigilant defense against further loss.

Most of us have learned to protect our private interests by remaining underdeveloped in some way. Eric Berne catalogues the many ways we manipulate others for our own purposes in *Games People Play*.[8] He illustrates how our subtle (and yet fairly obvious) pretenses at being weak are designed to get what we want while not giving up our native inadequacies. A game familiar to us all is called, "Ain't It Awful." The idea is for the player to complain to others about how bad things are for him or her and thereby manipulate the others into concerned words, advice, or pity. As long as the "sufferer" plays the part well, the audience's attention can be held. On good days this game can even result in offers to solve the problem for the player. The better the outcome, the greater the chances the game will be played often—and the longer the inadequacy will be maintained.

In summary, we resist feeling adequate for two basic reasons, neither of which necessarily increases our long-term satisfaction.

First, we use feelings of inadequacy to stimulate ourselves to take action *temporarily*. While we work or create or solve problems, we feel more potent during that period of time. Like an angry dog snapping at our heels, inadequacy in a specific situation can get us moving, if only to escape the pain of staying put. However, unless this avoidance behavior also brings us pleasure and a sense of accomplishment, the feelings of inadequacy remain after that particular problem is solved.

Second, although we may sometimes make short advances, we like to feel inadequate so we can stay close to the overall security of inactivity. Nothing ventured, nothing lost! We are afraid of change. Not using our talents keeps us more dependent, more safe. Ignoring our triumphs works the same way. Besides, we feel more justified in manipulating others to give us what we want if we feel we have nothing.

Both of these expressions of inadequacy seem degrading and even self-destructive, especially the latter. What is so important about being dependent and safe that we would risk keeping ourselves underdeveloped? Indeed, why are we alive if not to develop ourselves to the fullest? Even using our feelings of inadequacy to spur us onward seems shallow if relief from pain is our only motivation. Can we not create products and answers out of the joy of using our skills? Is there nothing to be said for personal development as an expansion of self-care rather than from the fear of going without?

Reducing Our Sense of Inadequacy

In many ways, the inner child of our past, the progenitor of our universal and inevitable inadequacy feelings, is still searching for the "good mother" who can fulfill our deepest longings through her benevolence. But what can we do to reduce our sense of inadequacy through our own efforts?

Samuel Johnson once referred to the life-journey as "a progress from want to want." His words, as well as those of other wise commentators on the human condition, find ready confirmation in our own personal experiences. Life indeed has a way of surfacing our sense of inadequacy. Even riches, power, fame, and love do not take away the painful awareness of our weaknesses.

Given our indigenous frailty, there seems to be no chance of overcoming our apprehension that we cannot properly manage ourselves or our environment. We can, however, reduce our universal sense of being deficient—of "not being equal to that which is required" as one dictionary defines inadequacy.

Avoiding Self-Anger

We must first stop the frequent self-punishment—especially the name-calling—that so easily tears down our character and our spirit. This suggestion is aimed primarily at those readers who have an overactive conscience that (like the parental voice it imitates) means well but does a lot of harm. If you seek to control and improve yourself by browbeating your weaknesses out of existence, it won't work. Self-condemnation is not generally helpful! In fact, handling yourself angrily and impatiently undermines your general sense of well-being and makes you feel even more inadequate. The child who is yelled at for spilling his milk is then even more anxious at the table and thus more likely to spill again.

The analogy of how to instruct children most productively is well applied to the example of how we should treat ourselves. Ridiculing, shaming, condemning, insulting, or rejecting ourselves (or our children) is an ineffective way to eliminate inappropriate behavior. With others and with ourselves, change comes about more readily through instruction in avoiding mistakes, in practicing or learning new skills, and in being rewarded for small increments of success. Because such efforts are aimed in a positive direction, the human spirit is not torn down in the process. Self-hatred neither reduces inadequacy nor increases performance.

A young man of twenty-three was referred to me by the physician who had treated him for an infection caused by a paper clip the patient had inserted under his skin. The number of scars on the man's arms indicated that he had been engaging in this form of painful and dangerous self-mutilation for years.

The young man's history revealed that he had been emotionally immature from an early age. Physically awkward and small, he was ignored by a robust, aggressive father who could hardly contain his disappointment in his offspring. As the father harshly and impatiently criticized him, the mother moved closer to protect the boy. The combination of a rejecting father and a solicitous mother compromised the boy's identity to the point of underachievement in school and inadequate social skills with peers. Too afraid of his father to show his anger, the boy suppressed these feelings. But they surfaced later in disguised ways. When the boy was twelve, his father died. At that time he took it on himself to fill his father's place as head of the family, partially to escape the sense of failure he already felt, but also to gain a sense of closeness with an absentee father who had never paid the boy much attention while he was alive. His efforts only led to further failure, for—of course—he was too young to take on such responsibilities.

After several sessions, this troubled young man revealed that he has always seen himself as worthless. As his peers all seem well on the way to success, he has felt more and more angry at himself. Harming himself has had a variety of meanings for him. First, and most obviously, self-mutilation is a way of punishing himself for his inadequacies. (The fact that he has always dreaded going for shots as a child and was now giving himself "shots" with a paper clip is not coincidental.) Second, his masochism provides an outlet for the deep anger toward his father that has never been vented. The son was symbolically stabbing the father, not to kill him but to punish him for his neglect and rejection. Third, there is a subconscious motivation to join his father in death, thus finally finding the togetherness the father never provided.

The treatment goals were first to work through the anger that was being displaced against himself, and then to focus on enhancing this man's sense of adequacy. He has been very hard on himself and has been deprived of the kind of positive, caring attention that could have strengthened his self-image. His repeated failures are understandable, considering the apathy and depression rooted in his rejection as a child. From his earliest years, this youth avoided the good feelings that self-esteem and success could bring, by constantly playing out his father's assessment that he was "no good." He had been fulfilling this prophecy by failing.

Applying Self-Affirmation

Closely related to the recommendation that we reduce our sense of inadequacy by avoiding self-anger is the suggestion that we acknowledge our assets and accomplishments more openly. It is ironic that we can work so hard to be successful without taking the time to reflect on and appreciate all that we have done. We must, in simple terms, be more generous with our self-praise. If we congratulate ourselves for our victories and our finished tasks, we are helping to ensure that we will direct our energy and talent to the next challenge we encounter. Belief in our competence should surface in the wake of success, and that sense of adequacy is necessary to generate further success.

Realistic self-praise does not in and of itself lead to exaggerated pride or conceit. That occurs only when we let our inner voice of happiness get so out of hand that we lord it over others in a haughty manner.

Most psychotherapists are constantly aware of how hard it is for people to credit themselves. Even those who brag a lot do not really believe what they are saying. They are merely asking others to confirm their statements. We need to be aware of the importance of giving ourselves credit for who we are and what we have achieved. Self-praise in the form of a brief pat on the back and a smile of inner happiness does much to dispel feelings of inferiority.

It is interesting to note that all too often those who are high achievers—the successful, ambitious, talented, and respected—are prone to ignore their assets and press on in a search for perfection. Take the case of a man who quits his job and puts his ideas profitably to work in his own business. As he succeeds more and more, he realizes how good it feels to accomplish his dreams, but he is so busy striving for even bigger or better holdings that he becomes extremely intolerant of mistakes, especially his own. He says to his peers, "We all have to win a few and lose a few," but these are hollow words. Deep inside, his philosophy tells him that errors are a total waste and are inexcusable.

As he angrily curses his mistakes, this man is increasing the pressure on himself to dangerous levels. His self-criticism and push for more and more indicate that he does not feel more adequate when he does well, so that all that counts is pressing onward. Because he ignores his own success, he works even harder to increase his productivity. He cannot afford to relax and take time for leisure or mindless fun. Even his family's interests are sacrificed to the cause. When he plays golf or tennis, he is not really "playing" at all. Once again he is forcing himself to a high performance level. Even if he wins the handball championship, he does not feel good about it, at least not more than momentarily. He is too busy calculating how he can improve his game next time.

The starving inner self must be fed generously rather than pushed impatiently. The high achiever often seems unable to internalize success, which leaves the self more, not less, impoverished. We all need to be positive about who we are—realistically appraising our abilities, accepting our limitations gracefully, and celebrating our victories. It is healthier to be a "B+" worker with a degree of inner peace than an "A+" worker who is still dissatisfied.

Validating the Self

When we contribute to our own or to another's sense of adequacy, we are encouraging healthy self-development. It follows that having our feelings of worth reinforced by other people allows us to give more easily. All of us operate best when frequently encouraged, lovingly supported, carefully listened to, respectfully treated, and honestly taught to reach toward personal fulfillment. When we are urged to cast off unrealistic self-hatred and impatience, we respond positively and come to see ourselves as being more adequate. It is at this point that we are best able to share our time and assets.

At times the reduction of inadequacy requires professional intervention. Psychotherapists are trained to relieve problems by encouraging personal growth. Unfortunately, many mental-health professionals have not done enough to reinforce the concept of giving as a valuable aspect of feeling adequate. Although they truly care about their clients' development, they may terminate therapy after a specific problem seems to be relieved. Therapists, like physicians, may focus too much on illness and be relatively unversed in the concept of wellness. Some, for example, consider love and altruism to be issues only for poets or theologians. I believe there needs to be more scientific inquiry into when and why and how people give to each other. S. L. Halleck has the right idea when he states that his work as a family therapist has taught him to be "more committed to values of fairness, cooperation, mutuality, and harmony than to values of self-actualization, individual success, and unlimited freedom."[9] Halleck's work seems to underscore the importance of behaviors related to giving, and more research should be done in this regard.

Becoming one's own person is vitally important for emotional health, but that goal is merely a prelude to interacting with other people. When we authenticate who we are, we are finally in a position to decrease our self-preoccupation and be more others-centered. Although balanced giving-and-getting is at the heart of the love ethic and social harmony, this message has been discounted in our times. Some misunderstand self as an isolated entity that is continually at war with others. Quite the opposite is true. The validated self becomes a vehicle whereby others can be served, because it is a mature self that can put back into human relationships as much as has been taken out, thus completing a cycle of mutual sharing. The self dominated by a sense of inadequacy can neither savor the rewards of getting nor internalize the benefits of giving. Then there is personal impoverishment—no wholeness, no resting, no overall satisfaction.

$\mathcal{9}$

Disproportionate Giving

The Imbalanced Self

Human benevolence is mingled with vanity, interest, or some
other motive.

Samuel Johnson

In the preceding two chapters, we have examined some of the
dynamics and psychological elements involved in behavior described
as "giving." When we give, we are essentially sharing the self with
others, continually balancing intake with output. Generosity is, at least in
theory, beneficial for the giver in terms of validating his or her personal
identity, establishing supportive human relationships, and increasing the
overall satisfaction derived from acts focused on getting more for self. It
follows, however, that the quality and the degree of any individual's charitable outreach are determined by a complex mix of motivations and past
experiences. Furthermore, since any act of giving involves *two* participants, it must also be considered from the receiver's perspective. For a
gift to be mutually rewarding, it must be appropriate to the needs and
wants of both giver and recipient and to the nature of the relationship
itself.

I have already set forth the thesis that our giving is significantly affected by our sense of personal worth—how realistically we view our assets and liabilities and handle our feelings of inadequacy. Branching out from that general theme, we will now explore the concept of disproportionate giving. It is clear to even the most casual observer of human behavior that some people give too much for their own or anyone else's good; others give far too little. Either pattern is flawed and even emotionally unhealthy, since it thwarts our continual search for a satisfying and productive lifestyle.

Giving Too Little

Literature has frequently warned us about the problems engendered by getting too much and giving too little. For example, in Charles Dickens's familiar *A Christmas Carol,* one of the frightening messages that changed Ebenezer Scrooge from heartless miser to generous giver was delivered by the ghost of Jacob Marley, his deceased partner. Marley moans that in the hereafter "we wear the chains we forge in life" and that those who give too little are forever cursed with unhappiness. From cradle to grave, through religious doctrine, folklore, popular fiction, and anecdotal evidence, we are taught the virtue of generosity and the dangers of greed and selfishness. Most of us agree in principle that "it is more blessed to give than to receive" and cherish altruism as a character trait, yet we practice it rather poorly.

We even give an affirmative nod to the words of Eliza Doolittle's father. In *My Fair Lady* he sings that we ought to help our neighbors but if we're lucky we won't be home when they need us.

Weighing the Issues

As we scurry about, frantically getting all we can, we seem able to rationalize that giving will deplete our store of goods and energy and thereby interfere with our personal pursuit of happiness. In the quest for security and satisfaction, we are generally willing to let others provide for themselves and reluctant to assume any responsibility as care-givers except for family members and our most intimate friends. There were times when charity was extended more easily and with a broader frame of reference. We need to think back only as far as our own country's origins to recall how a sense of community and mutuality of interest was a fact of life in colonial times and in the struggle for independence from England.

Our American tradition has embraced "the best interests of the majority." Indeed, the whole concept of a *middle* class once reflected the acceptability of being average—"neither too humble nor too great," as poet David Mallet put it. It is certainly also true that many generations of Americans have endorsed a work ethic that was expected to guarantee their security and independence. However, even though personal achievement was admired in many respects, extravagant flaunting of one's gains had been generally seen as "putting on airs." Attempts to rise too far above the median standard of living of "good and decent folks" marked an individual as different, prideful, and therefore uncharitable. Well into the twentieth century, social mores demanded a one-for-all-and-all-for-one philosophy that encouraged the sharing of one's bounty with those less fortunate. In fact, paying attention to the concerns of others and lending appropriate support to the needy have been important factors in the mutual bonding that has helped individuals, families, and entire communities to survive in mainstream America.

Recent history has clearly shown that the familial, ethnic, and social commitments that once characterized American thinking have given way to a self-absorbed individualism that has seriously threatened our traditional foundations of giving. The volunteerism and sacrificial spirit of the past have yielded to such cultural realities as the fragmentation of family life, changing economic trends, liberalization of moral and religious values, geographical mobility, rebellion against authority, and the cult of the "me" generation. The result has been a tremendous increase in getting more for self and giving less to others.

The movement from a concern for the group to a focus on self, from the rule of laws and values to expediency, from self-sacrifice to self-indulgence, has had both advantages and disadvantages for the individual and society. On the one hand, giving more to self has facilitated a breaking away from the confines that rigid traditionalism can impose. A cultural emphasis on competition, personal excellence, and even the goal of becoming "number one," has encouraged a reliance on the self that increases the potential for unusual growth. Thinking for oneself, as opposed to blind obedience to external controlling forces, requires considerable maturity—the kind that many immigrants to this country felt in leaving behind the tyranny of their homeland. Somewhat ironically, self-development can also impart new energy and direction to our efforts on behalf of others. As we break free of dull routine and narrow thinking, we are enabled to view ourselves and our world more realistically and with a broadened perspective.

On the other hand, *exaggerated* focus on the self has led to an ever-widening tendency to ignore social obligations and the very traditions, values, and ties to the past that sustained our growth. People who are eager to get all they can out of life often find justifications for giving less and less to others. As they smugly enjoy their gains, they develop a reluctance to share the rewards of their cleverness, ambition, and earning power.

To a certain degree, such tightfistedness is self-protective, but we also withhold if we are unconvinced that giving always helps the recipient. Because it sometimes seems that charitable acts merely encourage laziness, we come to suspect the motives of those who claim to be in need. If our suspicions predominate, whether accurate or not, we are discouraged from giving.

As we are bombarded with stories or televised accounts of social injustice, street violence, drug-related crimes, and governmental or private profiteering, we become more and more apathetic, convinced that some problems have no solution—or at least none that our personal efforts can further. It then seems logical to withdraw our benevolence from the world at large and focus on pursuing our personal interests. Hints of graft and corruption within specific charitable organizations cause us to doubt whether anyone has actually found relief through our giving. If we do not actually witness a grateful response, giving becomes a depersonalized and meaningless act—and we are likely to conclude that it is best to forgo the whole complicated process.

We also give too little if we learn from experience that volunteering time or energy in one area merely leads to more and more requests for our help. The old army adage about never volunteering for anything seems particularly valid when we realize that offering our services virtually guarantees that we will be called upon again. So we slump down in our seats at school, church, or civic meetings in hopes of not being asked to lend a hand. Doing a good job as a committee member one year usually assures our nomination for a more demanding assignment in the future. Because others applaud our efforts, we know we will feel guilty if we say no. In these instances, we fear that giving obligates us to continue giving, and we resent such intrusions on our freedom.

The argument can be made that most of us are not really unwilling to lend a helping hand; neither are we necessarily selfish or indifferent to the causes at stake. It may be simply that we are already as busy and burdened as we think we can handle. We are reluctant to find the time or energy for nonessential effort, especially when we have set limits to the commitments we will make. This reasoning, of course, has considerable merit. Between holding down a job, raising kids, fixing the car, mowing the grass, running to Cub Scouts, and so on, most of us barely have time to sit down and catch our breath.

On the opposite side of this debate are the voices of those who decry the growing public apathy to the plight of others. It is a valid conclusion that most people are cooperative and altruistic only if it is convenient. Far too often, self-interest plays too dominant a role in how we spend our time and money. Psychologist Paul Wachtel puts these concerns into accurate perspective: "In the pursuit of efficiency and productivity, we have promoted the expectation that each will view his home, school, and community primarily as a launching pad for the purpose of rising to his appropriate level."[1] Wachtel raises an important issue here. If a gift is only *incidentally* for the benefit of others, he argues, we are losing touch with the deeper meanings of community, tradition, and emotional-social rootedness in our lives. No matter how rich we become under these conditions, we are actually becoming diminished. Life with little or no anchoring in filial and agapic love is tragically impoverished.

Part of the reason we may withhold our care from others is the discomfort that arises when we empathize with a person in need. It is normal to avoid pain, but putting ourselves in someone else's shoes implies that we are willing to share his or her burden of suffering. Many people find that very difficult to do, especially if the relationship is not particularly close. It is perhaps understandable why many in our era of self-aggrandizement have chosen to "travel light." Caring about others' welfare makes us more vulnerable to discomfort, because it adds their problems to our own. Being "cool" engenders minimal risk to self—a strategy designed to avoid the pain that can come from involvement in the life of another person.

Declining Family Involvement

It is also very obvious that we do not give as freely at home as we should. The theme of increased self-focus and decreased attention to the needs of others has affected the family, the very center of our society. As we have thrown off the constraints of public opinion and traditional family values, many of us have come to treat commitment to marriage and the family as a secondary priority. Family cohesiveness is difficult to maintain if its members are constantly rushing off to varied events, all of which are described as crucial to their personal happiness. Old and young alike eat on the run or alone—when the urge hits and the busy schedule allows. The family dinner hour, a traditional time of gathering, is too often sacrificed because of outside activities. Parents and children view their work schedules, school tryouts, television shows, and friends' company as more essential for their well-being than family bonding. Thoughts of giving time, helping out, and exchanging ideas at home wane in importance.

If a marriage and the family it has created are taken for granted, personal commitment subsides. Even while we give token affirmation to involvement with our loved ones, our behavior may say otherwise. When family involvement is not consciously viewed as important—when each member is not nourished and valued—attentions wander and energies are given to other concerns. The job, the social club, the sporting interests, all come to be objects of focus that can detract from attachments to the home.

The decline in efforts to maintain family ties must be evaluated in light of the interpersonal dynamics between the architects of the home—the marital partners. To understand why mates come to give so little to each other, we need only look at what typically happens in too many homes. Once the marriage vows are spoken, the husband becomes even more intent on establishing his career, thereby proving that he is an exemplary provider and head of the household. A man who does not take these assignments seriously is considered irresponsible, even in an era when wives are increasingly joining the workforce, out of economic necessity or in search of careers of their own.

Traditionally, husbands and wives accepted the responsibilities of marriage more gracefully. When spousal roles were clearly defined—husband as breadwinner and wife as nurturing homemaker—it seemed easier to maintain a sense of working in tandem toward mutually accepted goals. Marriage "for better or worse" called for teamwork and perseverance through tough times. Sacrificing personal dreams for the good of the family was a principle rarely questioned—and "identity crisis" was a term not yet invented. Even when spouses felt a pinch of resentment over their responsibilities, they generally looked cheerfully ahead to a better future, willing to wait patiently for a less demanding and more pleasurable period of life. Today, because needy mates want more immediate rewards, duty and long-term commitment are hard to sell. If the self is lost to the demands of home and job, there is an impulse to reach out indiscriminately for personal affirmation. That kind of relief is all too often imagined to be found in an extramarital relationship.

Intimacy with a new companion, someone who has the time and interest to respond, is a powerful elixir for tired mates. The returns are instantaneous and the obligations are negligible. It feels good to once again see someone smile back and show interest. Suddenly the participants are reliving the carefree excitement of courtship. They may have forgotten how great those days were as they struggled with the everyday realities of adult responsibility, but the old feelings quickly return.

Male-female interactions are especially exhilarating when they are unencumbered with children, mortgages, a history of arguments, and the demands of permanent commitment. Lovers suddenly feel young again, joyous for the first time in years. Because, for many, these feelings rekindle a sense of self that has been lacking for so very long, breaking the rules of marital fidelity may seem excusable, even necessary for their emotional well-being. The very fact that sharing one's selfhood with a lover is not "obligatory" can surround an affair with feelings of personal validation, a celebration of the right to freely choose one's mode of satisfaction. Both giving and getting are more pleasurable when they are spontaneous and uncluttered by thoughts of duty. When mates give generously to each other, they are maintaining positive and open communication patterns. But, if either partner gives too little, he or she is depriving the other of emotional nourishment and creating a hunger that may seek satisfaction outside the marriage. So long as spouses give too little love, commitment, and attention to each other and to their children, marriages will falter and family life will be shattered. Both individuals and the wider community can be expected to suffer irrevocable damage if family life—the building block of any stable society—is allowed to vanish in a sea of "me-ism."

Giving Too Much

Because most of us agree intellectually that giving too little is unkind, insensitive, and even unwise, we would hardly want to be known as selfish or stingy. But is it possible to give too much? Is it necessarily a compliment to be described as overly generous? Again, what we are really examining is the concept of balanced giving-and-getting.

As we have already seen, any act of generosity has two participants, so it must be evaluated on those terms. It should be fairly obvious that giving is imprudent if it exhausts the giver's resources or is inappropriately motivated, but also if our giving indirectly harms the receiver or misuses the relationship.

First, from the giver's perspective, if we begin with the hypothesis that the "stronger" we are, the more goods or energy or love we have available for others *and* ourselves, we see that a giver must be careful not to deplete those inner stores. It follows that we give most sensibly out of strength, not weakness. Giving that drains the giver of emotional energy, without replenishing it, interrupts the normal cycle of intake and output that maintains general well-being.

Charles is a mid-level manager in an accounting firm who is in danger of losing his job because the productivity of his department is below company standards. Known as "good-time Charlie" because of his easy-going ways and eagerness to help others, Charles has gradually spoiled the workers he supervises. When they are late, Charles smiles and says, "You really ought to watch it." If production is particularly low on a given day, he stays late to cover the shortfall himself, rather than asking the staff to remain. Charles is friendly, generous, and well-liked at the office, but the breezy overindulgence with which he treats his staff has undermined his managerial ability.

An analysis of Charles's psychological makeup and lifestyle reveals that he is not very strong emotionally. Being "Mr. Nice Guy" at work is an ill-considered attempt to sweep away his self-doubts and bolster his level of confidence. Here is a needy man who wants so desperately to be liked that he gives from weakness, not from strength. This is a classic example of giving "too much," for—by overlooking the need for discipline in the workplace—he is limiting his professional progress and thereby ignoring his own best interests.

When times are good and much is taken in, most people tend to be generous because they have a great deal to offer. When the rate of return decreases, our level of giving may need to be adjusted. This kind of self-monitoring helps maintain our inner equilibrium by ensuring that we retain enough strength to give more later. A sound principle of both physical and mental health is that we must rest and nourish ourselves.

Excessive giving seems so unnecessary—even foolish—to most of us. Yet we all deplete our resources in benevolence at one time or another. Why do we sometimes give too much? One reason is that most of us assume that being overly generous is always an act of kindness. In our haste to convey a caring message to the object of our indulgence, we overlook some of the considerations that should govern our giving. For example, when we want very much to impress someone of importance to us, we are tempted to overdo it a little. Although we usually do not fault someone for trying hard to please, we should realize how often such efforts backfire and will leave the donor frustrated, if not angry. How often we say, "I knocked myself out, but . . ." to describe our disappointment in the outcome of our generosity. The expression itself should be enough to tell us why such giving fails to accomplish what we intended. If we harm ourselves in our giving, there is no chance for us to feel our efforts are worthwhile, especially if they seem unappreciated.

We must be careful not to evaluate the merit of our efforts in terms of the returns we expect. Many people pay too little attention to both the reasons they give and the effect on the recipient. Apportioning our generosity according to what we *hope* to get often leads to disillusionment.

One problem with giving is that we sometimes do not understand what it is we expect to accomplish. Guided by some vague inner need, we act more often from urge than from reason. Our motives frequently stem from subconscious desires that are predominantly self-serving, rather than genuinely altruistic or productive.

Parental Pampering

Consider the prime example of excessive giving seen in parental overindulgence. When we give children too many material pleasures or unsupervised freedom, they invariably get into trouble. Whatever the intent, spoiling a child will turn him or her into an obnoxious kid and probably an irresponsible adult. The patterns of parental overindulgence are easily rationalized. Mom and Dad never had much as kids, so they want their children to make up for their own deprivations. Or Dad is rarely home, so he assuages his guilty conscience by giving his teenager a flashy car and too much spending money. Or, more commonly, "We love our kids so much that we want them always to have the very best."

When parents give too much to their children, they overlook two important points. First, they are building a false view in their offspring of what life is really like. Children who believe they will always be unconditionally indulged will later feel abandoned and at a loss for answers to life's inevitable adversities. Having been conditioned to expect filet mignon, it will not be easy to adjust to ordinary lunch meat. Coping mechanisms are rarely learned through pampering. Because spoiled kids tend to expect others to solve their problems and gratify all their demands, they fail to develop the inner resources that would carry them through tough times. Children grow up lacking in self-reliance if they are unfamiliar with the process of struggling for answers. Solving problems builds character; being "on the take" encourages helplessness.

A second unfortunate by-product of parental indulgence is the jealous reaction of the children's peer group. When other kids go home and complain about what Johnny has, they are hurt and angry when their own parents say "No!" and may take out their resentment on Johnny. On the other hand, indulged teens (in particular) who are generous in sharing their bounty may find themselves the center of attention among their peers. But, since friendships based on such selfish motivation are hardly genuine, many a "poor little rich girl or boy" leads a rather lonely existence.

Indulgent parents, by trying to ensure their children's present happiness, often create future problems for them. For example, it is not uncommon for the children of overly generous parents to grow up with a sense of guilt, especially when the parents have gone without to provide the youngsters with trivial pleasures. Even if the elders do not play a martyr role, the children may feel as if their gain has been their parents' loss, a debt impossible to repay. In the extreme, this kind of guilt can seriously impede future successes.

Parents do well to teach their children that giving is a necessary facet of societal living and, indeed, part of what defines us as "human." But parents must be careful to explain that generosity must be controlled so as not to deplete inner stores too rapidly. True, it feels good to give, and it *is* good to give, just as it is satisfying to receive, but excess in either direction is inappropriate. Children who have a healthy self-image and learn to balance giving and getting—increasing or decreasing their output based on sound judgment—will not be in danger of giving either too much or too little.

Some children quickly take advantage of a playmate who gives too much and expects too little of others. Quite frequently, a child who is insecure may try to "earn" the friendship of peers by being overly generous and too submissive in give-and-take play situations. This sends a message of innocence and vulnerability to which many will respond by taking advantage of the helplessness it implies. Children who have been properly taught the virtue of "sharing" will also realize that they, too, have territorial rights. Otherwise, they may be manipulated by other children, fleeced of their toys and their dignity, and discarded with contempt when the goodies run out.

Manipulative Generosity

We have seen that giving too much is often motivated by an unstated wish to get something specific in return or to compensate for some realistic or unjustified sense of guilt. Excessive generosity is even more self-serving if it is used as a means of establishing control over another individual. It is manipulative in that the giver does not make a direct request for a favor or affection (which might be refused), but instead hides the wish under the gift—thus establishing "credit" with the beneficiary. Yet, because this kind of trickery is essentially hostile, givers will make it difficult for the recipients of their apparent altruism to return the favor. The uncollected debt then acts as a social I.O.U. whose intent is to prolong the relationship between the two parties. More importantly, it bestows on the giver a degree of power he or she may previously have lacked.

We can see such a problem in the case of a twenty-year-old college student who is at risk of being dismissed from his fraternity house for failing to meet its grade-point requirements. Jerry tries very hard to be liked. He helps anyone in need: lending out his typewriter even if he needs it himself, giving ideas for term papers when his own are not yet written, even volunteering to do the housework when it's not his turn. Jerry seems to assume that the less for self, the better he will be able to maneuver others for approval. But his tactics to gain popularity frequently backfire leaving him with less, not more.

An analysis of this young man's history shows his birth order plays a strong part in the development of his social behaviors. Born between an older brother, whom his father favored, and a younger sister, who was Mom's pride and joy, Jerry never felt bonded to either parent. He was neither strong enough to compete with his brother nor the right gender to gain his mother's favor. Though no fault of his own—or his family, for that matter—Jerry just seemed to "slip through the cracks" of family ties to drift on his own. He learned early to adapt to inadequate family bonding by becoming overly attentive to everyone he met. In his saccharine attempts to be helpful, he has made people intuitively sense there is something phony about his style of care. As he has become depressed he has accepted a recommendation by his parents to see me.

In our therapy sessions Jerry also tries to manipulate me to like him. He tells me many examples of his benevolence, as if expecting me to praise him for his ways, but I do not. He begins every session by complimenting me on my clothes or how my office is decorated, and he ends every session telling me how much I am helping him, but I do not act pleased. If I do, he will be locked into believing *I* will take care of him and he will not learn to stop manipulating out of fear. After trying to please me on a number of occasions, Jerry and I get into the following exchange:

"You look sad today, Jerry," I begin.

"Oh no, it's nothing. I'm fine," he replies, covering his sadness as if he must be upbeat to please me.

"You don't seem to want to acknowledge your down mood," I reply.

"I'll be all right," Jerry replies with a half smile.

"Jerry, I get the feeling that you don't want to bother me with your sad feelings."

"You're doing a great job, Dr. Rottschafer. Why should I be down?"

"Sometimes when we want very much to have people like us, we try extra hard to be pleasant to be sure everything is OK. I feel you are trying to do this right now," I answer.

"Why should I bother you with my moods? You must have really difficult cases to deal with. I don't want to add to your hard day."

"You seem worried that being truthful with me will burden me, and I may be annoyed with you," I answer to reflect what he is saying.

"Well, you know, ah, I've got to have somebody on my side," Jerry replies with tears forming.

"It's really hard to believe someone could like you for just being Jerry, isn't it."

"I'm sorry for slobbering like this," he apologizes through his tears. "Guess I never quite believe people could accept me unless I earn it."

"And if you give more and more they can't turn you down?" I ask.

"Exactly—like they sort of owe me and I'm in control," he replies.

Those who extend generosity solely for the purpose of controlling other people are really to be pitied, for they usually want only to be liked and admired. But such manipulation is both ingenuine and socially naive, for relationships based on indebtedness rarely remain intact for long. Therefore, although the surge of power experienced by deceitful givers may somewhat ease their feelings of inadequacy, any temporary gain in self-esteem is illusory, since it is won at great cost to personal integrity.

Through either material gifts, flattery, or servility, those who give too much are paying for the grateful attention they hope to receive. This exchange may dull the receivers' pain of being put upon, especially if they are unsuspecting of the hidden motives. Some manipulators may be unaware of their own secret agenda, but it takes skill to stalk a target, administer some sugar-coated poison pills, and keep the victim happy enough to ensure compliance with future requests.

Excessive generosity is often rooted in a sense of inadequacy that makes the giver dependent on others for affirmation. Consider the kind of play-acting needed to guarantee that others will provide the desired attention. The giver must be careful to appear caring and solicitous, must be docile and avoid making outright demands, must downgrade his or her own personal strengths, and must constantly evaluate how the receiver feels so that the relationship is preserved. The magnitude of this effort is exhausting!

When carried to such extremes, giving can be very painful. In fact, psychologist Shirley Pankin describes the excessive giver as being martyr-like: enjoying helplessness. In *The Joy of Suffering*,[2] Pankin describes masochism as an emotional disturbance that can begin in infancy if a mother provides inconsistent care. By granting only off-again/on-again nurturance, the mother is teaching her baby to wait patiently for relief of its needs. Though protesting helplessly, the infant becomes conditioned to the idea that the pain of suffering is a necessary prelude to the joy of relief. Then even going without takes on an associated quality of pleasure, a lesson that may be carried into adulthood as overgenerosity or other masochistic behavior.

Giving is such an important way of relating to others that we must not allow anything to interfere with this purpose. When our goals are worthy, we must be honest about them, asking for what we need and giving only from the heart. Using others by deceptive generosity violates our relationships and renders our gifts meaningless. Better to be open with our demands and risk a turndown than getting what we want by pretense.

10

Giving to Our Children

The Parental Self

> But there's no vocabulary for love within the family . . . love within
> the light of which all else is seen. . . .
>
> T. S. Eliot

It should now be fairly obvious that healthy giving represents a balance between the self and others—with the nature of the gift and the underlying motivation expressing that equilibrium. Most of us insist on "fair play," so it is not easy to give because of genuine concern for the recipient and without recording how much we get in return. Such idealistic concepts do, however, usually frame the generosity we extend toward our children. But even parental love is not perfect, since it, too, can be distorted by our own emotional inadequacies.

Although few people would refute the idea that parental love is the purest and most altruistic of human emotions, explanations vary as to why this is so. Biologists, for example, would refer to this nurturing urge as "genetic" or "instinctive" and point to its universality among all species of animals. Anthropologists would probably cite archaeological discoveries proving the existence of strong family ties in mankind's earliest societies. Theologians might emphasize the inevitability of positive parental

141

feelings in beings who are "created in the image" of a loving and paternal (or maternal) deity. Students of human behavior might care to mention that some of the aspects of parental care result from identifying with our children—that, in reality or fantasy, when we give to our children we also give to ourselves and thereby live forever through them.

But parents require no such complicated analyses. Most simply say that they love their children more than anything else in the world and would give their lives to protect them (although some do not always act that way). Giving to our children is more than a duty; it is a joy. For that reason alone, we can gain additional insight about the process of giving by examining parent-child bonding and behavior.

Patterns of Maternal Giving

Because the earliest and most constant presence in a child's life is Mother, it is not idly said that "the hand that rocks the cradle rules the world." Indeed, the quality of maternal care we experience will to a large degree determine our physical, mental, and emotional development and therefore how we relate to the world in which we must live. For most people, the word *mothering* is synonymous with loving, nurturing, and protective behavior. Yet, though linked to the structure and hormonal activity of the female body, the so-called maternal instinct is mysterious and not fully explainable on a physiological basis. In fact, we impart a spiritual quality to motherhood somewhat akin to "godliness" or "good-ness"—powerful, but not subject to complete analysis.

What we do know with certainty is that motherhood is intimately intertwined with "love"—another phenomenon that is essential to life but hard to define accurately. We revere Mother as a noble symbol of generosity—searching for her qualities in our mates and friends and call-ing out for her in time of trouble or from our beds of pain.

Obviously, one of the first acts of generosity by a mother is to provide food—to sustain the newborn's life by continuing the process of physical nourishment begun in the womb. An infant's early experiences with the feeding process help shape its attitudes about giving in general. We tie our sense of security to how regularly—even how lovingly—food is given by our mothers. So many things can go wrong in the feeding process that we may wonder how any of us grow to maturity with a healthy connec-tion between how we have been fed and how we come to give. There are matters of allergy, what the child is fed, regularity in feeding schedules, the question of who does the feeding, and whether the infant is fed in its mother's arms or has a bottle propped up with a pillow.

The act of nursing is thought by some to be an important determinant of a child's learning to give. Women who nurse give something more to their babies than perfect physical nourishment. Breast-feeding, by its very nature, ensures the close physical contact thought by most developmentalists to be essential in establishing an infant's sense of security. For a variety of reasons, a woman may be unable or unwilling to nurse, but a desire to do so is one indication of her maternal generosity. That is not to say, however, that a bottle-fed infant is necessarily being "deprived," so long as the feeding process includes a liberal amount of the cuddling and indecipherable babytalk that convey peace and loving acceptability to the infant.

Part of the inner strength and impulse to be generous to her child is determined by the history a woman brings to motherhood. Was she nurtured lovingly in her own infancy? Did her childhood experiences foster a sense that giving was a positive pattern of behavior? Was the moral concept of generosity taught in her home? What is her attitude toward pregnancy and the value system she will use to raise her children? Preparation for motherhood begins long before marriage.

All those factors, and more, will shape a mother's motivation to give selflessly to her child, but her spirit of maternal generosity will also be affected by the infant's behavior. When a woman has carried a child within her body for nine months and been preoccupied with the hopes and joys, as well as the pains and burdens, of pregnancy, she has every right to expect to be rewarded. Every woman wants a healthy, happy baby who will give her much joy and little trouble. Obviously, few babies fit this description.

When an infant is hurting, a mother is distressed, especially if she does not know what is wrong. Whether due to illness, injury, allergies, or developmental problems, a baby's discomfort produces crying or irritability that can quickly wear a mother down. It is not unusual for an otherwise loving mother to resent a sick, crabby baby, not just because of the extra work and worry, but because the baby is not responding to her in the positive ways she hoped.

L. Rosenbloom and M. Lewis describe how an infant's arousal level influences the interaction between mother and child.[1] Active infants demand, and therefore get, more food, care, and time than babies who are relatively lethargic. Similarly, responsive, sweet, happy infants elicit different maternal behavior than do youngsters who sleep a great deal or are not very sensitive to their surroundings. When mothers and babies receive little attention from each other, they may give less in turn.

These generalizations not only underscore some of the determinants of maternal behavior but show how easily an infant can be conditioned toward or away from generosity. The first year of life is a crucial time to learn about giving. We will next consider what is perhaps the most important influence on maternal response: the gender of the child.

Mothers and Daughters

Ideally, what a mother gives to all her children in equal doses is the kind of love, affirmation, discipline, and instruction that prepares them to be independent adults. At some point in the nurturing process, every mother faces the inevitability of letting go of her fledglings. But there is much truth in the observation that "my son's a son till he gets him a wife, but a daughter's a daughter the rest of her life." Even today, in an era when the principle of gender equality makes it easier for young women to attain financial independence, mothers continue to react differently to their daughters than to their sons. A mother tends to identify more naturally with a daughter and therefore clings more tightly to the ties that bind them together. In many respects, a daughter is expected to remain a little girl forever.

In *The Reproduction of Mothering,* Nancy Chodorow writes that "mothers of daughters tend not to experience infant daughters as separate from them in the same way as do mothers of infant sons."[2] Since she is the same gender as her daughter, a mother easily empathizes with her female child's emotions and experiences. Because this child's joys and sorrows are so deeply shared by her mother, a daughter is often vigorously encouraged to pursue the activities that the mother has already found rewarding in her own life. Conversely, mothers will warn their daughters to avoid situations in which they themselves have encountered failure or pain. Because they see their girls as extensions of themselves, mothers may be overly cautious about their daughters' future.

If a woman accepts and likes herself as is, she is quite comfortable with sharing herself with her daughter. Then her sense of maternal adequacy and personal maturity allow her to be generous, because giving will not be felt as a loss of self. But if her own insecurity makes her jealous or resentful of her daughter, a mother may withhold her care, become too critical, and in many other ways avoid cementing the normal mother-daughter relationship. It is difficult for a mother to give of herself when her own needs have been unsatisfied and take priority over those of her child.

Consider the case of a woman who finds herself unable to get over her divorce of some five years earlier. Deeply hurt when her husband left her for another woman, she broods over his betrayal and feeds on an ever-widening sense of resentment and insecurity. When her daughter returns from weekend visitations with her father and his new wife, the mother bristles with emotion. Morbidly curious about her former husband and the second marriage, this woman grills her daughter for details of the visit—especially how he treated his wife and how she acted toward the daughter. Although the mother at first brightens noticeably as her daughter tells of how much fun she and Daddy had together, she is very disappointed to learn that the stepmother behaved impeccably and, in fact, participated in the weekend's activities. So Mom makes such comments as, "Be careful, honey, you can't trust your dad. He can be a snake in the grass." Since she still loves her ex-husband and misses him terribly, she is jealous upon hearing of how well the new marriage seems to be going and that the daughter has accepted the second wife. Now adding to her shame, hurt, and anger over being left for someone else is the "disloyalty" of her daughter. This mother has come to therapy to work through the love/hate ambivalence toward her former spouse that is contaminating her feelings toward her daughter.

Perhaps because motherhood is sometimes depicted (unfairly) as endless giving with little reward, the popular sentiment is that mothers have some deep-seated sense of direction that keeps them functioning in a consistent manner over a long period of time. A woman's general attitude toward mothering is mainly developed in the context of her personal history, especially in the quality of the relationship with her own mother, beginning in infancy. The tenderness, protection, sensitivity, and consistent handling she received as a baby will deeply impact on her future role as a mother, which explains why even aunts, grandmothers, great-grandmothers, and other women who have shaped us in our early years have had a hand in our destiny. Patterns of both sharing and withholding continue to pass down through the generations and influence a woman's disposition to give. But at the core of a woman's inner history of giving is the mother-daughter bond.

Regardless of its sacrosanct qualities, the relationship between mothers and daughters has always been fraught with contradictions. In her best-selling *My Mother/My Self,* Nancy Friday opens her first chapter, "Mother Love," with these words:

> I have always lied to my mother. And she to me. How young was I when I learned her language, to call things by other names? Five, four—younger? Her denial of whatever she could not tell me, that her mother could not

tell her, and about which society enjoined us both to keep silent, distorts our relationship still.[3]

The lies mothers tell to their daughters stem from their efforts to protect them from the reality of a stark and sometimes cruel world. In that world are men who are often preoccupied with their sexuality or the urge to dominate, the temptations to rebel against mother and form a separate identity, and the secret envy that mothers and daughters harbor against each other. Friday writes that "we are raised to believe that mother love is different from other kinds of love. It is not open to error, doubt, or to the ambivalence of ordinary affections. This is an illusion."[4]

A mother's bias is to hold her daughter close while letting her son go. Although some mothers "possess" and therefore seriously damage their sons—as will be explained in the next section—most mothers let loose of sons at an appropriate time. Mothers usually give their sons a sense of freedom, but they tend to place their daughters under a sometimes subtle, sometimes obvious, bondage. In that symbiotic tie, the mother gives herself the link she once felt (or sought) with her own mother. Women who had a weak relationship with their mothers now try to set things right, to find what they did not have. A mother may erroneously assume these bonds are signs of love, yet be blind to the fact that the daughter's independence is being sacrificed. Even when she rummages through her daughter's purse or closet, she feels her intentions are loving. "It's for your own good, dear," she tells her daughter when her spying is discovered.

Sometimes mothers bind their daughters by making the girls their special confidantes. As mothers speak of their marital struggles and confide their inner problems, they draw their daughters too close for comfort. These uncomfortable ties violate the natural boundaries between adults and children and force young people to deal with emotional baggage they are not ready to handle. Children need to be free to rely on adults for nurturing and guidance and should not be forced into premature reciprocity toward the parent.

And yet, despite the importance of giving a daughter time to be a child, unburdened by adult themes, a mother must still train her daughter to be alert to the dangers of the real world. Law enforcement agencies and mental-health experts are aghast at the increase in child sex abuse cases, the majority of which are perpetrated against females—often very young females. No doubt both parents should discuss with their sons and daughters criminal acts of physical and sexual abuse. However, since daughters may come to their mother more easily about these matters—as well as topics of sexual behavior and procreation—often the mother is the one who talks about sexual issues.

As a mother tells her daughter about growing up, there perhaps is no more important message than the one of understanding and interacting with males. Of course, the best example is a mother's behavior with her husband. But a daughter also needs to know what is important to males and how to relate to them. Daughters need to appreciate the details of the male psyche: the balance between the aggressive hunter and the little boy, the importance men put on food and sex as proof of love, the awkwardness most men feel when they are being tender and emotional, the fears they hide regarding incompetence and failure. Since daughters grow up to spend most of their lives with a husband, the lessons learned from Mom about being a female and relating successfully to males are crucial.

Many women have told me of the deep resentments they hold over having been expected to share in maternal responsibilities in the home. Mothers may have careers to cope with, but young girls should not be assigned the part-time job of raising their siblings. Such adult duties rob them of their own chance to be children. Even teenage girls should not be forced into more than occasional care of the family. The narcissism of adolescence requires that they attend rather exclusively to their personal interests and needs. When this self-focus is substantially interrupted, the teenage girl may come to resent her mother's demands and the very idea of parenthood.

Women often discover in psychotherapy how deep are their hungers for their mothers. Even if those feelings are buried beneath resentment or anger, many women sense that they have never been able to satisfy their yearning for their mothers after leaving home. "My husband finds some of his mother in me," a woman tells me, "but I cannot find my mother in him. Since he is but a man, I'm left unsatisfied." She, like many other women, complains that when she does go to her husband for tenderness, empathy, and emotional nourishment, he misinterprets her overtures as a desire for sexual intimacy. "Sex is fine," she relates, "but that is not what women seek when they hunger for mothering. In fact, when we have sex I often feel I am doing something *for* my husband, as if sex is a service I give. So once again I'm left needy."

Whatever differences may exist in the styles of mothering and in the personalities involved, it seems that much of the strength of the maternal urge lies in a multigenerational link between mothers, their own mothers, and their own daughters. As these women hold each other's hands, they silently transmit the mysteries and techniques of maternalism between themselves.

Mothers and Sons

Sons also require a mother's loving care to become mature, and in some ways a mother's childrearing approach is the same for her son and daughter. However, mothers see some aspects of raising a son as a special challenge that is different from their responsibility toward a daughter.

A mother's task in raising a son is complicated by the fact that she is female. She is at a disadvantage in the sense of not knowing what it is like to be a male. Despite this handicap, she must operate in ways that will nourish her son and prepare him to leave her eventually.

How a mother treats her son is strongly affected by her general attitude toward men. Many of her deepest feelings and values have been formed during her early years through contact with a father and one or more brothers. Ideally, during the years of childhood and adolescence, a daughter goes through her various developmental stages in the presence of a father who loves her and personally guides and encourages her intellectual, emotional, and social maturation. Daughters learn what men are like directly from male family members and indirectly from their mothers' responses to them. Male acquaintances and boyfriends also provide a collection of impressions about the opposite sex that help shape a woman's future maternal responses to sons. However, the most important link between her past experiences with males and her future attitude toward sons is found in a daughter's yearning for a fatherly presence.

A daughter comes to sense at an early age that her father is near but not always close, someone she can love but not possess. Because fathers are typically busy with their jobs and male interests, they convey to their daughters that their availability at home is limited. They may love their daughters very much, but fathers are usually not as chummy with their daughters as mothers are. Although daughters may excuse their fathers' preoccupation with other matters by saying to themselves that Daddy is very busy, they sense that something is missing between them. When daughters yearn for a closer rapport with their dads, they can easily suppress the desire and later transfer the unsatisfied hunger to males whom they *can* possess—their sons.

A mother's basic longing to possess her son can be her undoing. Freud theorized that every little girl grows up competing with her mother for Daddy's attentions and cannot wait to have a beloved male all to herself.

Since most husbands will not allow their wives to possess them (part of the natural male drive to be independent from female domination), a wife may seek that kind of unswerving devotion by attaching herself too strongly to her baby boy. Freud maintains that the firstborn son is typically experienced subconsciously by the woman as a reincarnation of her father—a male that is all hers, unshared with Mother. Usually she enjoys his dependence on her for a while but lets go as he approaches adulthood—because of social pressures and the child's demands for autonomy.

As a mother interacts with a son, she teaches much about the "softer" qualities of life: gentleness, kindness, tact, deference, patience. Sons who grow up imitating these tender qualities bring a richness to their character that makes them more human, easier to be with, more appealing. The "hardness" of male aggression requires the critical balance of these androgenous qualities a mother can model for her son. A mother does well to instill these virtues in her son, but she must also be careful not to go so far that she interferes with the development of male interests.

A woman consults me about her seven-year-old son's problems with neighborhood friends and peers in school. Often he comes home crying because other boys pick on him. When I ask how she responds, she tells me how she gathers him in her arms and soothes him with gentle words.

"What do you say to him?" I inquire.

"I tell him that the other boys probably didn't mean to be so rough and that tomorrow things will be better."

"Are they?" I ask.

"Well, not really. Usually he gets hurt. Either they play rough or argue or call him names. Why do they have to act that way?"

"You seem to be bothered by the typical rough-house play and hostilities that boys engage in."

"I am. I didn't raise Jimmy to be uncivilized. Why can't these children just play nicely and respect each other?" she responds.

"Well, what have you taught your son about being with other boys?" I ask.

"I want my son to be pleasant and friendly. I firmly believe that when you are nice to someone else, or share with them, they will be nice to you. I've tried to instill in him the ideas of cooperation and fair play."

"And your hope is that by teaching Jimmy to be a little gentleman, he will grow up to be a decent citizen?" I query.

"Yes. Is that wrong?" she asks.

I assure her that while her goal is not wrong, there are other aspects about being a boy that we have to talk about: fighting, playing guns, and talking dirty. As if annoyed with me for even suggesting that hostility and sexuality are all part of being a boy, this mother—a genteel, elegantly dressed woman—sternly says:

"I didn't plan on raising a little barbarian. Is crawling through the mud, shooting toy rifles, and using foul language mandatory for a normal boyhood? What is he going to be like twenty years from now?"

In subsequent sessions we explore the expectations she took to the task of raising a son. She discovers that hidden resentments against her aggressive father have led to a distorted image of her little gentleman son who will become what her father was not. She differentiates between her feelings about her father and her expectations for her son and soon begins to accept her son more realistically. She learns to prefer her son's growth rather than her own satisfaction. Gradually she becomes more comfortable with the need for her son to be assertive and masculine. She passes on those feelings to her son as she allows him to assume, with her blessing, male interests and behavior. This does not mean that she cannot encourage and reward gentleness, manners, and artistic interests. Indeed, she must reward these "softer" ways along with permitting the more aggressive male behaviors. But before her son can be tender he must know how to be tough.

In her book *Mothers and Sons*, Carole Klein explains what a mother must begin doing in her son's infancy to encourage him to become independent, assertive, and sexual. It is Klein's opinion that mothers "urge a boy onto the path of growing much sooner than she would his sister, and as a result he gets hurt earlier and more often than she does."[5] Mothers seem to make the erroneous assumption that this encourages independence and self-control. Paradoxically, says Klein, when a boy's dependency needs are satisfactorily met in childhood, he will then be better equipped to "become more independent and less emotionally demanding of others as a man."[6] She reminds mothers of the "delicate balance" between too much and too little mother love. Boys who get too much maternal coddling may become overly attached to their mothers and hence "unmasculine." If they do not have *enough* mothering, they can grow up excessively dependent and passive, detached and/or afraid of women, or hostile and demanding.

Klein also theorizes that mothers feel more personally responsible for their sons' happiness and worldly success than for the well-being of their daughters. If that is true, mothers of sons are more vulnerable to guilt feelings. While believing in their own "impossible omnipotence," mothers may simultaneously caution themselves about being too protective and involved in their sons' lives—a double-bind that can cause distressing doubts and self-blame. "There are a seemingly infinite number of ways in which a mother's passion for her son invites guilt feelings," states Klein.[7]

The most important gift a mother can bestow on her son is encouragement to be a male. Part of that gift is her acknowledgment of his sexuality. We know about a young boy's sexual interests—his delight in running around naked, his propensity to fondle his penis and to experiment with it proudly, to see how far and long he can urinate, to feign ignorance so he can ask his Mother about an erection—and so on. A modest mother may wonder how she can ever caution and punish her son enough to make him stop such unabashed displays. Although, of course, a boy must learn there is a time and a place for everything, she threatens his growth as a male if she inhibits his sexual expressions too severely.

While accepting of her son's sexual curiosity and expressiveness, a mother must also give her son the message that she herself is off limits as a sex object. By being careful not to arouse him with her nude body or by walking around the house in her underwear or transparent nightgowns, she tells him that she is *Daddy's* woman, not his. He will then be encouraged to respect her as his mother and subvert the urge to use her as a source of sexual fantasy. A parent has the responsibility to direct a child's natural sexual instinct away from the family and into the world at the appropriate time.

It is common for mothers to be curiously naive about the sexual impact their nudity can have on their sons. Some swim programs for children and mothers allow boys up to age six to undress, shower, and dress in the same communal room with the mothers and female instructors. These women are usually shocked to hear my explanations about how they are acting "seductively." They always admit, however, that it would be totally wrong for their husbands to act in the same way with a daughter or to allow their daughters into the home bathroom when Dad is showering—the way some mothers do with their sons.

Mothers give sons their manhood by letting them go into the world without her. To fail in this crucial task is to seriously jeopardize his maturation. Consider a thirty-year-old man, still living with his widowed mother, who comes for psychotherapy because he is depressed over being the only unmarried member of his peer group. He reports that his life has been totally dominated by his overpossessive mother, a woman who so deeply loved her father that for years she bypassed her husband's needs and focused on her son's. Ever since her husband died, she has lived in fear that her son will marry and leave the family home.

After years of bickering, the son has finally found the courage to leave his cloying mother—despite her financial bribes, feigned heart attacks, and even threats of suicide. But she has not given up easily. She has hired a private detective to keep track of his whereabouts and whom he might be dating. She also leaves plaintive messages on his answering machine, such as, "I suppose you are out with that slut again! When you find me dead of a broken heart, you'll have only yourself to blame."

Granted, this woman is more than overpossessive—she is very troubled emotionally. However, there are many less disturbed mothers who are unwilling to release their sons from their control and thereby interfere with their sons' ability to form meaningful relationships with other women.

The possessive mother unintentionally raises her sons to go from one woman to another, in search of either freedom from her clutches or, ironically, someone to duplicate her powerful image. In both cases, for most mother-dominated sons, there is still the problem of what to do about Mother. There is a sense of being afraid to be finished with the symbiotic ties they have maintained. A "mama's boy" is both comforted by this bonding—that is, consoled, indulged, and protected (often from a hostile father)—and frightened by its intensity. He fears the power of his mother's neediness, the sense of being captured by her sadness. Nevertheless, because the mother-dominated son finds some enjoyment in his preferred status, he does not always want to change. He may be willing to sacrifice his independence in exchange for the rewards of being her "pet." If he did not cooperate, she would have little power over him.

Patterns of Paternal Giving

An examination of how a mother gives of herself reveals that she is the primary nurturer from the moment of birth and continues to give all through the developmental years and even into adulthood. Her parental role is usually more constant and influential than the father's, but patterns of paternal giving also figure crucially in a child's maturation process.

The most common myth about parents is that mothers give love and care while fathers give money and discipline. Up to about the middle of the twentieth century, the father's main responsibility was seen as providing the labor needed to earn a paycheck that would ensure his family's survival. When Dad arrived home, his work was considered finished, because Mom was expected to manage the home front. The father's paycheck more or less guaranteed his right to escape from work until the next day.

But fathers have also been stereotyped as chief disciplinarian in the home. The maternal warning to "wait until your father gets home" breathed fear and trembling into many who were raised in earlier times. Father was the "heavy," the provider of correction "for the child's own good." Since he was the family's authority figure and could be less manipulated by his children than Mother, he became associated with the task of providing discipline, whether or not he liked this assignment.

Today's fathers are shedding the traditional role of harsh policeman of the family. Modern parents share more equally in every aspect of child-rearing, including the disciplinary process. This is not to say that all parents have ruled out the iron fist that was regarded as good parenting in our more authoritarian past. But the negative publicity surrounding child abuse has made corporal punishment all but outlawed on the home front.

As both mothers and fathers increasingly share in providing as well as in discipline, the father's role may not be as clear-cut as it once was. What, indeed, should a father give to his children to best ensure their growth toward maturity?

In a general sense, a father must be as deeply involved with his children as a mother—giving love, understanding, guidance, and discipline. This heartfelt participation in their lives provides a sense of security for his children, but it also announces who he is and what he stands for. As a father gives of himself, he allows his children into the inner core that represents his values, interests, feelings, and beliefs. Youngsters may be less interested in the specific nature of a father's attitudes than in the fact that he is willing to open his mind and heart to them. That type of intimacy binds both generations together, whether Dad is playing baseball with his son, showing his daughter how to make a birdhouse, telling what it was like when he was a boy, or helping with a school assignment.

What children need perhaps more than anything else from today's busy and often absent fathers is a guaranteed period of togetherness each week. Even if it is only for an hour, it does not matter what they do together, so long as there is a genuine and heartfelt sharing of emotion and interest between them. Silently watching television together from separate chairs is of minimal value. Instead, there should be deliberate choosing of a program that will stimulate conversation during and/or after the viewing. Any time together should involve smiles, touch, comment, and other emotional expressions of *personal* contact. There must be a clear sense that Dad truly enjoys being with his beloved child.

Fathers (and mothers, too) must also teach a child what they do at their jobs. It is amazing how many children do not know what specifically a father does at work all day, let alone how he feels about his profession or life in general. There is usually no need to give details about how to become whatever he is—carpenter, lawyer, or truck driver—but the father should provide information and opinion about what a good worker is expected to do. He should talk about paying attention to the details of the task, following orders, sensing customer or employer needs, dealing with troubles and problems, preventing failure, overcoming low morale, communicating with people, and so on. All these descriptions of the parental effort can be translated by a child into survival and success in his or her own immediate world of school and social relationships. Children look up to Dad for this kind of guidance, especially if he is the only breadwinner in the family.

Fathers, of course, still give discipline and are therefore symbols of social order and authority. Their jurisdiction over the child's behavior at home reminds the child of the government's power to enforce its laws. When a father (or a mother, for that matter) does not adequately represent the world of discipline, he prevents his children from being prepared for the challenge of living in the wider society. Children cannot survive in a complex world if they have no respect for society's harsh realities and no awareness of their civic responsibilities. Many of today's teachers blame the shocking lack of discipline at home for the disrespectful attitude of children toward rules and the rights of others. It is obvious that an employer or a society has rules and will not tolerate what indulgent or neglectful homes allow.

Fathers and Sons

A father's main responsibility toward his son is to provide positive examples and explanations that teach what manhood is all about. A mother can reinforce her son's growth toward masculinity, but she cannot be a role model. A father or suitable male substitute must be available to teach a boy about using head and heart, being tough and tender. Many fathers have a great deal of trouble with this apparent contradiction. Some cultivate gentleness and love but avoid teaching their sons how to be strong and tough when those qualities are appropriate. Others attempt to make macho sons who reinforce their own distorted ideas about being male. Whether male or female, children must learn when to be strong and when to be gentle in their relationships with others. When television's "Mr. Rogers" comes on the air with his effeminate manner- isms and gentle voice, "Have you ever made friends with a feather?" he may be reinforcing tender qualities of children, but he certainly is not balancing his efforts with an example of the mindset children need in today's world. Tender compassion is what links us together in the human family, but this mutuality of interest does not imply that children will not require tough-mindedness to compete with peers and defend themselves from danger. Being "nice" does not necessarily make a child innocent and vulnerable, any more than being "assertive" means being rude or otherwise antisocial.

A family comes to see me with an eight-year-old son who has been beating up on other children at school and has been expelled recently for kicking his teacher. In the waiting room before their appointment, the father and son engage in "play" that is rough enough to disturb my ses- sion in the office. As I come out to see what is going on, the two are swatting each other with rolled-up magazines and laughing gleefully. When I ask them to wait quietly, the father says to his son with a wink, "Okay, tough guy, we'll have to cool it for now, but I'll getcha later." At this moment I have pretty much completed my diagnosis of the child's problem even before we meet formally.

There is a hostile potential between a father and his son. Perhaps it is because all males, even in the animal world, are more aggressive and competitive than their female counterparts. As they stake out their terri- tories and fight for control, there is a hidden element of violence. Whether because a father is essentially protecting his sexual interests in his wife or because he fears losing authority over his son, father-son clashes are legendary and their truces uneasy. When a father calls his son to him with the word *son,* he is usually not just requesting his presence; he is also reminding the son of his subordinate position in the dyad. (Fathers rarely address their female child as "daughter.")

Because fathers were once sons themselves, they remember first- hand the rebellious urge, the confrontations, the show of force, the Oedipal competition. Of course, a son has the potential of growing stronger physically—and often educationally—than his father. Sons will also have the advantage when their fathers are too old and weak to be controlling. All fathers know the day is coming when their sons may surpass them, and for some fathers the fear of that day rests uneasily in the back of his mind.

Wise and emotionally mature fathers will naturally want their sons to exceed their own accomplishments. Such fathers want to share their strength with their sons and help them succeed. But a father who is ruled by vanity and an unresolved sense of inadequacy cannot allow his son to get ahead of him. Even though a father's pride can be greatly enhanced by a son's productivity, not all fathers can overlook the threat to their own self-esteem that their sons' achievements seem to represent.

Father-and-son business ventures are notoriously unstable and failure-prone. A thirty-three-year-old man consults me about his recurring nightmares of being chased by a monster whom he tries unsuccessfully to escape. He has often awakened so distressed that he cannot get back to sleep. This man works for a father who owns a machine shop. They clash constantly because the father is intimidated by his son's progressive ideas. He is too proud and stubborn to admit that his son has learned about modern advances in engineering school—technology the father is not familiar with. The father, guarding what he has built by himself "the old-fashioned way," is angry because he had no one to help him get started long ago. He does not take lightly to his son's readiness to jump in at the top. The father's resentments are obvious. He is not as well-educated as his son and secretly envies his son's ability to progress rapidly because of advanced training and a high level of confidence. So he puts many roadblocks in his son's path and is very critical of his efforts.

Inevitably the son has two choices: let the father rule, or break away and form his own company. Since the son is still emotionally dependent on his father's approval, he finds many excuses to stay subordinate and believes it would be disrespectful to leave the business. Yet their clashes promote neither mutual respect nor productivity. I ask him to bring his father to the next session.

When they arrive, the son is wearing a business suit; the father wears a short-sleeved sport shirt and casual slacks.

"Terry, would you mind much if I ask you to take off your jacket and tie?" I begin. "Let's get more comfortable." Terry quickly catches on and also rolls up his shirt sleeves.

"I'm delighted you are here, Mr. O'Rourke. Terry has told me a lot about the great things you have done to build up your business. He really admires your gumption, the way you started from scratch and now have twenty employees."

"Well, it wasn't easy," says the father.

"I'm sure it wasn't," I reply, mindful of the father's deep need to feel important. Later on I discuss ways the business might advance. This allows me to usher in the topic of his son as an asset rather than a threat.

"I can't help but admire your foresight in sending Terry off to engineering school," I comment. "He can really be a tremendous asset to the company, especially since I'm sure you don't want to work forever."

"That's for sure," replies the father with a smile.

We are now in position to talk about cooperation and mutual respect between these two men. The father has to realize that as he gives more to his son, he will invariably get more. Once he stops treating his son like a competitor, the business will thrive and the father-son ties will be strengthened. In turn, the son will be freed from his father's domination—and the "monster" will no longer haunt his dreams.

Males often define manhood in a variety of ways: being competitive, using tools, engaging in contact sports, protecting those in need, feeling their sexual prowess, and so on. However, perhaps Sigmund Freud best outlined the task of finding mature adulthood as learning to love and to work. Historically these two tasks were split between the two parents: mother teaches us how to love and father teaches us how to work. Ideally today both parents model these two behaviors; fathers now need to be adept at talking about doing one's work *and* loving other people, especially women.

The amount of love and affection he shows his wife is a father's best example of how to treat women. He sends an important message to his son in acts of kindness, respect, tact, and physical affection to his wife—an example that will dramatically affect the son's adult married life. If dads also talk to their sons about the details of endearment, protection, support, task-sharing, and physical as well as emotional intimacy, they will effectively pass along the important elements of being a man.

To summarize, a father primarily gives love to his son by encouraging the son's total development. This gift is best accomplished when a father gives deeply of himself through personal attention and appropriate training. Although fathers must see their sons as individuals with separate identities, when they affirm their sons' adulthood they have an opportunity to identify part of themselves in their sons. They can even transcend their own limitations through their sons' accomplishments. As fathers give wisdom and strength to their sons, the sons become gifts of joy in their fathers' lives.

Fathers and Daughters

A father's challenge in raising a daughter is different from that which he faces with a son. A father feels toward a daughter somewhat like a mother does toward a son. Because both are aware that the child is the opposite sex, a certain awkwardness or lack of empathy prevails. The discomfort is far less if the father has been raised with one or more sisters, but his task is still complicated by the fact that he is neither a female nor a daughter. His special mission, beyond providing love and guidance, is to form a relationship with his daughter that conveys his sincere interest in her growth and development. A daughter, no less than a son, needs to feel that her father loves her very much and is truly willing to be involved in her life. Despite his not knowing what it is like to be a girl, he must offer his full attention to her needs, learning about his task as he goes. However, in his interactions with his daughter, a father must be mindful that she is different from him and from her brothers in many ways.

A father has to be careful not to treat his daughter like Dresden china—fragile, pretty, on display. It is unwise to set her on a pedestal to idealize her or otherwise act as if she required constant protection. Treating a daughter too gently can polarize her personality structure into being "all fluff and no tough," as one father told me.

A daughter is in need of male guidance if she is to understand and develop all aspects of her personality—the tender and the firm, the weak and the strong. In that sense the father provides an image that contrasts with the feminine image gleaned from the mother. Each parent contributes in ways that shape an androgynous self-portrait whereby the daughter can identify both her male and female components. This modern view of the female temperament is far more acceptable now than it was in the first half of the twentieth century, when women were to expected to play the role of "weaker vessel." Nevertheless, as the first man in his daughter's life, a father has the special task of introducing the idea of gender differences by noticing and encouraging her femininity. Although most girls go through a tomboy stage that seems to deny their femininity, they usually should do so briefly and then resume their female role.

Although a father has a special opportunity to affirm his daughter's femininity, he must be mindful of setting limits to his expressions of male approval. It must be clear that his affection does not imply a sexual interest, that only Mother—his wife—is entitled to such attentions. Although a daughter may "strut her stuff" to see if Daddy is admiring her, she will be frightened and confused if he looks at her lustfully. A father must be especially careful to respect his daughter's need for privacy when she enters adolescence. Jokes about her bodily changes are entirely inappropriate, although a father's *refusal* to acknowledge her young womanhood is felt as rejection by this important man in the girl's life. A teenage girl needs to be treated with courtesy and sensitivity to her feelings during this perplexing time, and her father should make sure his son also complies with her wishes in that regard.

It goes without saying that there is absolutely no room for a sexual type of interaction between a father and daughter. A father's task of raising his daughter is severely compromised and their relationship permanently damaged if he crosses over the line of sexual impropriety. This barrier must include an awareness that even dirty jokes convey a sexual tone when told by a father to his daughter. Children and adolescents are terrified by paternal sexual interest and intimate contact, although some victims comply with a father's advances out of a sense of duty or lack of understanding of what is happening. Incest is finally being punished as the serious crime that it is.

A father does well to give both his daughter and son signals that he and their mother love each other and are sexually active. It is healthy for children to realize that their parents go out together, have fun, smooch, and lock the bedroom door. The traditional notion that children must never know that their parents have a sexual relationship is unfortunate. Not only do expressions of sexual love bind the marriage together, but they remind the children that they do not have to fear incestuous intrusions. Freedom from this fear allows children to develop their own sexuality without anxiety over parental stimulation or response.

A couple brings their thirteen-year-old daughter for counseling because she is excessively hostile toward her parents. She frequently bad-mouths both of them and treats them with intolerable amounts of disrespect. After several sessions with her, it becomes obvious that this young lady is worried about her parents' marriage. In essence, she is creating an unpleasant scenario that will force them to stop going their separate ways and consult with each other over their mutual "problem." I instruct the parents to come alone next time.

During that session I suggest to the parents that they play a "family game" with their children. On the next two Friday nights they are to get all dressed up and leave together on a date without telling anyone at home where they are going or when they will return. Under no circumstance during the week are they to reveal the details of their night out, even under intense questioning by their children. I encourage them to smile and say, "That's our little secret."

When they return two weeks later, the parents report with amazement how curious their daughter has been about their secret dates. "But she always has this faint little smile when she questions me," reports the mother. The parents tell me at length about where they have gone and what they have done, even forgetting to tell me how their daughter has been acting. "Oh!" they say when asked, "She's much better."[8]

It is a gesture of strength for a father to demonstrate respect and love for his wife. Through spousal affection, he teaches his daughter to identify with her mother in a positive way. He is also making a subtle announcement that he is no more important than Mother in his daughter's life. If a father undercuts a mother's authority and significance, he does a great disservice to his daughter, for it is through identification with her mother that she finds her womanhood.

It is all too common for a daughter to compete with her mother for Dad's attentions. A father should understand that all mothers and daughters have a natural rivalry and that he must not side with the daughter to gain superiority in unresolved marital conflicts. If he continually pits mother and daughter against each other, everyone will lose.

Nancy Friday illustrates how daughters tend to struggle with mothers and to idealize fathers because Dad is absent, male, mysterious, and does not handle routine discipline:

> Daddy is godlike, not just because he's distant and has this attractive sexual quality, but because . . . mother has to do the day-by-day discipline. We argue less with him . . . because we don't have this long-standing battle with him over a hundred things.[9]

Although a father may be an object of idealized love, this is only temporarily so (or it should be)—for a daughter is expected to leave her father eventually and find her own man. This truth is symbolized in the part of the traditional wedding ceremony where the father "gives" his daughter away. This ritual reminds both parents, the bride and groom, and the audience that the father's special place in her daughter's life is over. He will always be her father, but another man will now be more important to her. The father thus gives the world a new couple to begin the wondrous life cycle all over again—truly a gift of substance and of love.

The Love Connection

In conclusion, one may wonder if there are lessons to be gleaned from the example of parental love that would help us all treat each other more generously. Even the best of parents make mistakes, of course, and many emotional and social problems are rooted in faulty parenting. Yet there is something so special about how parents love their children that it is appropriate to use such acts of love as guidelines for learning to love other people both wisely and well.

If we could see other people as connected to us, somewhat like we are connected to our children, we might be able to love them more. There is a choice here, for we must be *willing* to see others as part of the human family—the brothers and sisters under the skin who are our companions along life's journey. This sense of being united in purpose and function may serve to encourage us to give more freely as individuals. The familiar saying "what goes around, comes around" implies that "you value me, I value you / you help me, I help you." As we keep an eye on others, looking for opportunities to be at one with them through a smile or a helping hand or other act of generosity, we reinforce our mutuality of interest. This willingness to be more humane—and less competitive, hostile, and alienated—can be expected to decrease the distance we feel between ourselves and others.

If giving is to have an implicit quality of self-healing, we must be able to perceive generosity as being just as beneficial for the giver as it is for the receiver. It is not wrong to look for the fulfillment of our own needs and purposes when we give, whether to our family members, friends, or strangers. If we see something of ourselves in others, and they in us, we learn more about who we are, and we resolve much of our existential loneliness in deep interpersonal oneness.

11

Whom to Serve

The Spiritual Self

May the love of Jesus fill me
As the waters fill the sea.
Him exalting, self abasing:
This is victory.
Kate B. Wilkinson (1859–1928)

In the process of becoming civilized, we have established various institutions to assist in the control of the self. Because we have acknowledged that individual desire is not always in the best interests of society, we have subscribed to the wisdom of allowing social, governmental, legal, familial, and other institutional rules to govern us. By acknowledging the tension between the self and others, good and evil, impulse and restraint, we have attempted to improve our search for overall satisfaction by restricting the self's autonomy.

Commitment to Self and to God

One of the dominant institutional forces in society has been the church. (By "church," I am referring to organized religious activity, whether at the denominational level or in the local parish, in the pulpit or in the pew.) Since our Pilgrim beginnings, we Americans have placed our religious institutions, and the freedom to worship within them, near the top of our system of values. Describing ourselves as a "God-fearing" people, we have traditionally submitted ourselves to religious rule and therefore have looked both to God and to spiritual leaders for guidance and control. However, religious leaders and believers alike have found submission of the self to be increasingly uncomfortable in an era of self-assertion.

The scene has been set for confusion as believers listen to two different and often differing voices—to self, with the thrill of achieving personal, self-serving motives, and to an institution that claims to speak for God. In their uncertainty over how much of each—self and church—should be followed, believers have congregated into groups that articulate their own predilections. Believers who espouse predominantly self-enhancing goals tend to join more liberal religious groups or to disagree (openly or silently) within the conservative church they may attend. Worshipers who lean toward more strict, self-denying beliefs align themselves with more conservative institutions. Each group seeks to answer the question of what to do with the self while embracing religious and spiritual values.

The fastest-growing churches in modern times have been conservative, whether the more moderate evangelical wing or the strict fundamentalist and charismatic movements. These conservative churches draw many followers because they offer relatively direct guidance and rule at a time when values and rules are not clearly articulated in the society at large. Conservative believers seem willing to submit to institutional control despite the fact that, according to a 1978 Gallup poll, 80 percent of Americans believe "an individual should arrive at his or her own religious beliefs independent of any churches or synagogues."[1]

Conservative believers attempt to resolve the question of what to do with self and still remain committed to a religious tradition by denying the self's importance. They attempt to ignore the self and its urges, believing firmly in selflessly following God while serving others. Meanwhile, more moderate and liberal church members have attempted to balance their heightened individualism with their important religious beliefs. Some have found success, but many have been troubled. As moderate and liberal religious people have enjoyed the freedom to get more and more for themselves, they have struggled with troubling questions of whether individual, self-fulfilling goals are spiritually justified.

Some have preferred to focus on how their religious beliefs can serve themselves rather than considering how best to serve God and others.

Robert N. Bellah and his associates have addressed this relationship between commitment to self and to others in their excellent book *Habits of the Heart: Individualism and Commitment in American Life.*[2] The authors examine the ways that Americans have come to understand the beliefs and practices that they use to make sense of their lives. As Bellah evaluates what people are doing in their marriages, jobs, civic activities, and religious practices, he concludes that individual pursuits have seriously undermined commitments to the very institutions that have made our country flourish. Yet he in no way suggests that the pursuit of individual growth and freedom should end.

How then, one might ask, can the individual and our institutions support each other more constructively? Bellah writes that the question is not just a matter of resolving the "profound impasse" between individual and institutional goals, but of considering "whether the older civic and biblical traditions have the capacity to reformulate themselves while remaining faithful to their own deepest insights."[3] Bellah concludes that "[a]nything that would violate our right to think for ourselves, judge for ourselves, make our own decisions, live our lives as we see fit, is not only morally wrong, it is sacrilegious. . . ."[4] After all, religious freedom continues to be one of our most cherished values.

Still, there is evidence that the more conservative branches of today's religious institutions have had considerable difficulty in allowing their members as much individual freedom as they might like. Furthermore, conservative institutions have found it difficult to reformulate their deeply held beliefs so as to accommodate the striving of their members to get more personal freedom and worldly goods. Acknowledging that, spiritual or not, Americans are indisputably enamored with "the good life," few conservative authorities still believe in self-imposed austerity. Most would agree that financial success and material increase do not necessarily constitute a challenge to Christ's admonition to "lay not up for yourselves treasures upon earth . . . (Matt. 6:19 KJV). Furthermore, most religious believers agree, for the most part, that it is their personal, as well as God-given, obligation to develop themselves to the fullest.

However, despite the expansiveness of the vision of self-development in a land of religious freedom, many sincere believers use spiritual teachings to prevent personal growth, as if they cannot spiritually justify such self-focus. The question of whom to serve—God or self—rests uneasily in the hearts and minds of many. They are aware of the uncomfortable contradictions between putting self last on Sunday while hastening to put it first on Monday. The question of whether the self is good or bad, crucial or detrimental to spiritual practice, demands answers.

This chapter will address the pressing issues of how evangelical and fundamentalist Christians deal with the self and the process of getting and giving. In specific, this chapter will evaluate the furtive call for self-avoidance heard especially in conservative religious circles.

We will consider the basis for such a call, its misinterpretation by both the parishioner and the theologian, and the way to resolve the apparent conflict between service to God and to self without undue guilt. I will defend the thesis that the Bible clearly spells out a message of developing and loving the self so that our inner strength can be used to love God and each other in ways that he commands.

I will preface my remarks by stating that I have been born, raised, and educated as an evangelical Protestant and have now come to examine critically, albeit lovingly, what appears to be serious deficiencies in religious thinking about how the self does and ought to function. My association with parishioners, other professionals, and religious patients in my clinical practice tell me clearly that there is considerable guilt and confusion among believers concerning what Scripture teaches about the self and its role in religious life. My purpose is to help relieve some of the confusion surrounding these issues.

Avoiding One's Self

Judeo-Christian beliefs emphasize that God is to be loved, obeyed, and worshiped above all persons, deities, and things, and that other people should be loved more than we love ourselves. Christ summarized the Old Testament law by stating: "'Love the Lord your God with all your heart and with all your soul and with all your mind.' This is the first and greatest commandment. And the second is like it: 'Love your neighbor as yourself'" (Matt. 22:37–39). At first glance it would appear that since the self is less important than God or others, it should be minimized if one is to be properly spiritual.

A twenty-three-year-old man consults me with symptoms of depression, confusion, and vocational apathy. After graduating from a conservative, Bible-based college two years earlier, he took a sales job where essentially he had to talk people into buying his company's products whether or not they needed them.

"I'm caught in a dilemma," he tells me. "I'm supposed to push products these people probably can't even use. I have to convince them against their will."

"Sounds like you feel you are doing something wrong," I reply.

"Absolutely," he answers. "I look into their eyes as I talk, and I see myself almost harming them. Is this how a Christian should act?"

"And if they buy, you are guilty of . . ."

". . . forcing my will on them," he interrupts. " My home, my church, and my school have taught me to put others ahead of myself. If I'm supposed to look out for their interests ahead of my own, I just can't do this job in good conscience."

I explain to this young man that the Bible does not rule out being assertive or convincing; nor is it un-Christian to overcome sales resistance. However, if he cannot believe in his own heart that his products are beneficial to people, and if being in sales violates his conscience, then he should look for another kind of job. He agrees that sales are not for him and also agrees to look further into the issue of integrating assertiveness into his belief system.

Although a careful exegesis of Scripture does indeed proclaim self to be last, the Bible by no means shows the self to be unimportant. Scripture, in fact, clearly teaches that God created people in his own image—hardly a sign of unimportance—and that he sent Jesus Christ, his only Son, to die for and redeem those who accept him as their Savior (John 3:16).

The Bible also teaches that God the Father has sent his Holy Spirit, the third person of the Trinity, to strengthen, direct, and intercede for us—again, a message of unending compassion. The most prevalent theme of the New Testament is God's love for people, and even though God also demands justice according to his divine law, he is primarily described as a God of boundless grace. Despite our weakness, God's purpose is to direct us upward toward a richer, fuller understanding and enjoyment of life's full potential. The human struggle toward the ultimate perfection of eternal reward, while not attainable on this earth, is still a deeply significant movement toward enlightenment and joy. By God's grace, we are able not only to deal with life's trials but to find a sense of happiness. Yet, despite the Good News, as the gospel is called, and the awareness of God's loving messages to mankind, many seem to persist in dealing with God as though they are not the redeemed but the condemned, not under grace but under the curse. Ignoring God's grace, many seek to decry the value of his finest handiwork and avoid the joy of self-development.

The Laymen's Dilemma

Many sincere believers feel confused because they hear sermons and read Bible passages stating that God loves them and still feel awkward about loving themselves. Although they also believe that God wants them to develop their talents to the fullest, they somehow feel that humble self-negation is the best spiritual posture.

"Self," to many religious conservatives, is equated with a rebellious questioning of authority, an indulgent preoccupation with one's own desires, and a spirit of worldliness that differs from traditional biblical teaching. Some believe that self-care or self-confidence makes one "smug," "cocky," "vain," "selfish"—a denial of one's dependence on God. They deeply fear that the development of self apart from strict rule and constant examination will lead to a haughty pride that eventually will overshadow spirituality. The more conservative the religious believer, the more emphasis will be put on firm *control* of self via guilt and punishment. The self will be restricted with scriptural prohibitions and warnings to subdue any passions and ambitions. References to "worldliness" or "the flesh" will be aimed not merely to control impurity but to prevent self-reliance. The underlying assumption is that self-esteem—even personal confidence—risks potential rebellion against God or other authorities. Of course, there is little room to love a self that has such a potential for evil!

Strict conservative believers are more likely to stress imperfection and to advocate suppression of impulses and passive obedience. Pastors warn parishioners against self-centered and lustful drives and they, in turn, attempt to warn the public at large. The more fanatic have bumper stickers threatening that "the wages of sin is death." Some even sit in the end zones at nationally televised football games so they can hold up placards with Bible verses on them. These efforts may be personal reminders to control the self tightly, but they also reinforce a very negative worldview: Self is evil.[5]

Control is necessary for morality and the maintenance of spiritual beliefs, but some churches control the mind in the form of anti-intellectualism. People who think too much, read secular books, or attend nonreligious (even nondenominational) colleges are seen as jeopardizing their salvation. There is an obsessive fear of being seduced by "the world"—a word churches often use to describe anyone who does not agree with their specific belief system. To maintain the purity of the faith (that is, to keep their constituents under firm control), some church groups insist on forms of confession and disclosure that border on brainwashing. Some churches threaten excommunication for whatever they decide is disobedience, as if expulsion from the local church were tantamount to exclusion from heaven. Others demand public admission of wrongdoing, with guilt, shame, and punishment the necessary prerequisites for reinstatement. These acts reflect an obsessive fear that individuation breeds rebellion, that satisfying one's personal wishes and ambitions risks embracing a way of thinking that could lead one astray.

A woman consults me with barely suppressed anger. She tells me that her pastor ordered her and other members of their church to leave their homes for unrestricted use by various denominational leaders who were coming to the community for a week-long conference. When she complained to the pastor, he upbraided her lack of faith; when she said she wanted to take time to decide before surrendering her home for a week, he said she was disobeying God's will.

We talk about what her church means to her and conclude that she will have to succumb to the pastor's mandate if she wants to remain in the church. We then shift to how she will deal with her anger, recognizing that if she buries her anger, her spiritual and social relationships will suffer.

It is interesting that in a land of individualism and freedom, people will still seek, or at least tolerate, such rigid control systems. Many conservative religious groups provide a hiding place where, in the name of righteousness, the "evil" self can be subdued. It is ironic that those who control these followers are not at all as passive, or even obedient, as they demand others to be. The higher up the ladder some leaders climb, the more they use aggressive, self-serving behavior to carve out and defend their territories. If questioned, they can claim divine guidance, as did Oral Roberts in explaining why his followers had to send in more money to build a new hospital. God had given him a "vision"—one that apparently did not include the fact that the area was already overbuilt with hospitals and that his would probably always operate in the red. The actions of Roberts, Jimmy Swaggart, and Jim and Tammy Bakker have amply demonstrated a spirit of self-service that belies the words they preach to others.

Those who see the self as "a problem" tend to emphasize Old Testament themes drawn from God's firm—even severe—handling of the wayward Israelites. They select those passages that emphasize control and seem to portray God as an angry parent. Even the New Testament message of love and grace is carefully culled to accentuate those passages that stress how evil "sinful" people are. A favorite admonition is 1 John 2:15–16: "Do not love the world or anything in the world. If anyone loves the world, the love of the Father is not in him. For everything in the world—the cravings of sinful man, the lust of his eyes, and the boasting of what he has and does—comes not from the Father but from the world."

Conservative Christians buttress their arguments against the self by reminding others that Christ urged his followers to be "gentle and humble in the heart," as he was (Matt. 11:29), and to renounce all earthly signs of power and acclaim. Christ, they say, urged a believer to forsake everything else (Luke 14:33) and to deny himself (Mark 8:34) with deference, meekness, humility, sacrifice, gentleness, and self-restraint. And, in his Sermon on the Mount, Christ describes the blessed as those who are poor in spirit, mournful, meek, and persecuted (Matt. 5:3–5, 10). Another argument used is based on the scriptural paradoxes citing that "many who are first will be last" (Matt. 19:30) and that one must be humble as a child to enter the kingdom (Matt. 18:3–4). The implication drawn is that we must lose self (life) if we are to preserve our souls (Mark 8:35). Taken from this perspective, the Bible clearly does seem to urge humble self-negation as *the* sign of spirituality. As I have noted elsewhere, many Christians have thus identified themselves with an image of passivity and submission in an attempt to be "pure."[6]

Self, then, is seen by many conservative Christians as evidence of worldliness, as if the self is yet untouched by grace and unredeemed by Christ's resurrection. Self is at odds with God, so enjoyment is suspect. Some zealous believers define individualistic appetite and a drive for personal achievement as "dangerous." At the bottom of their anxiety seems to be the fear of being seen as replacing God with self—an act that increases fears of divine abandonment. Their fears are similar to what children feel after being naughty—that they will be punished and rejected.

Educated Opinion

When conservative believers look to their leaders for words of authority about the self, there is little encouragement. Sunday worshipers hear many sermons about the self, but the messages typically include warnings about its evil side and/or exhortations toward altruistic, self-effacing service. Very few conservative ministers preach on self-esteem, being responsible to one's self, or the value of strengthening and loving the self so as to enhance our service to God and to others. In sum, the self is seen as selfish and thus carnal, not spiritual.

David F. Wells, professor of historical and systematic theology at Gordon-Conwell Theological Seminary, calls self-esteem "the new confusion."[7] Perhaps it is more accurate to say that confusion about the self is not "new" but currently under new consideration. Christians have always had trouble deciding what to do with the self. In the past, self was smothered under denial and submission; in modern times, self is more prevalent and assertive. Wells calls the love of self "the essence of sin" and asserts that true self-esteem only results from Christian salvation.[8] For Wells, what is sinful apparently is the love of selfish goals apart from the requirements of divine and human responsibility. Wells, I am sure, knows the difference between healthy and unhealthy self-love, and some of his readers may, too, but the rank-and-file layperson reads into such statements the same meanings so many have always heard: Thou shalt not love thyself—it is sin.

C. S. Lewis, a foremost religious writer, also has chronicled the insignificance of the self. "Self-renunciation is thought to be, and indeed is, very near the core of Christian ethics," he writes. "[Jesus] says that a true disciple must 'hate his own life.'" Lewis goes on to say that "the self . . . which is called *I* and *me* . . . puts forward an irrational claim to preference. This claim is to be not only hated, but simply killed; 'never,' as George MacDonald says, 'to be allowed a moment's respite from eternal death.'"[9]

Powerful words. Lewis further describes the self as "God's creature, an occasion for love and rejoicing. . . ."[10] But these positive words about the self are lost to the reader when commingled with his negative statements about the self.

The confusion about what to do with self is reiterated by John R. W. Stott, director of the London Institute for Contemporary Christianity, an organization designed to help the clergy and the laity interpret the Bible. He wrote for *Christianity Today* an article entitled, "Am I Supposed to Love Myself or Hate Myself?"[11] The very question suggests that Stott senses what is in the heart of countless conservative believers. He proposes an altogether reasonable answer to his own question (as will be seen later), but before he does, he manages to utter many of the anti-self statements other religious writers present.

Stott begins by quoting Bonhoeffer: "When Christ calls a man, he bids him come and die." Then he adds that "Christ call us to self-denial," which Stott defines as the kind of thing Peter did in denying Christ: "He disowned him, repudiated him, turned his back on him. So we must do to ourselves."[12]

To his credit, Stott does not stop here—indeed he cannot, if he is to be true to an accurate exegesis of the Bible. He adds that Christ also calls people to self-affirmation; therefore, we are to value (although not to love) ourselves, because there is good in the self. He refers, of course, to the biblical teachings about being created in God's own image, loved by God, and redeemed by him at a great price. This, says Stott, is the self we are to love: the redeemed self. What we are to deny is our sinful ("fallen") self, "our irrationality; our moral perversity; our loss of sexual distinctives; our fascination with the ugly . . . our selfishness . . . our proud autonomy."[13] Already the tone shifts. Most everyone can agree that irrationality and perversity are wrong, but is it sinful to be selfish? Is there not also a healthy selfishness? Is there not justifiable pride in self as well as virtue in autonomy? Is it not spiritually sound to love ourselves, to proudly esteem ourselves, to rise to levels of self-management that encourage independence?

Stott confuses the reader with his choice of words, for he does not explain clearly enough what self-care includes. The worst comes when, elsewhere, Stott writes that even "when we affirm our true self in Christ we find we are not free to love ourselves, but rather to love him."[14] Once again self is the culprit: Getting is greedy, self-care risks selfishness, love of self can overrule love of God.

Wells, Lewis, and Stott are excellent writers whose publications are eagerly read by many believers. No doubt their essential purpose is to extol God's magnificence and to keep the self in its proper perspective compared to a sovereign God. However, in their zeal to praise God's greatness, they reinforce the conservative believer's opinion that we should continually minimize the self to win God's approval. They do not clarify for the reader that a healthy appreciation of the self *strengthens* us for the task of filial and agapic love.

Resolutions

The avoidance of promoting the self's value while serving God and others is rooted in *fear*. This apprehension is so deep-seated that it has successfully interfered with the spiritual and personal growth of religious conservatives of all faith systems. At the heart of the issue is the fear that becoming our full selves will risk our security with God—that like our ancient predecessors, Adam and Eve, we will be self-willed enough to risk paradise and lose again. Torn between the natural urge for self-development and the fear that they will offend God—possibly even deny him—many devout believers opt to minimize the importance of self, snuffing out any chance of self-care, even at the cost of personal enhancement and growth. This fear is needless, tragic, and totally at odds with a loving God's stated desire. "I have come that they may have life, and have it to the full" (John 10:10b).

The fear of becoming our full selves is erroneous on three counts. First, God loves and values the self; second, a strong self is crucial to making a significant impact in life; and, third, God wants us to love ourselves so that we can love others. Let us examine each of these three points.

God Loves and Values the Self

The height and depth of God's love is evidenced in his description of mankind as image-bearers, partakers of his covenants, and objects of his redemption, compassion, and intercession. But more: God values us so deeply that he gives us the freedom eventually to be ourselves. Consider what happened in Eden, where God considered Adam and Eve's freedom to choose between good and evil as even *more* important than their being perfect (sinless). In allowing us to assert ourselves, God knew fully what our choice would be and how much it would cost him to bail us out of our just deserts. Nevertheless, because he values the idea of a self that has the ability to think and decide, he grants us the freedom to "be." When the psalmist grasped this truth he wrote, "You made [man] a little lower than the heavenly beings and crowned him with glory and honor" (Ps. 8:5). Similarly, Paul was so overwhelmed with God's immeasurable love that he was convinced nothing—not even death, nor angels, nor any earthly power—could separate us from God's love (Rom. 8:38). This is a creature of great value, this human being—a "me with a mind of my own."

Scripture shows consistently that God values the self through his loving-kindness, patience, and forgiveness. God wants us to succeed, to use the talents he gave us, to struggle and thereby grow, much the same as loving parents desire for their own children. Christ dignifies the believer by stating, "I no longer call you servants. . . . Instead I have called you friends" (John 15:15). He promises that if we remain in him and he in us, we will be able to do even *greater* things than he did (John 14:12). Paul urges us to assert ourselves with strength (Eph. 6:10) and to use our power as a gift from God (2 Tim. 1:7).

The essence of the argument for a strong and valuable self perhaps is best seen in the New Testament concept of *grace*. Traditionally, grace has been defined as "God's gift of love to the undeserving." Christian theology explains that, since the fall from perfection in Eden, mankind has forfeited any claim on God's favor or eternal reward. In our helpless, lost condition, we have no chance to transcend eternal hell except through a merciful God who, in the covenant of grace, has forgiven us and restored us to full rights and privileges as heirs of the very kingdom we had eschewed. In Christian theology, the creature's task is simple: Repent, believe, and accept God's gift.

My own understanding of grace, however, is that grace is *more* than God's gift to the undeserving. Grace also includes coming to our true purpose in life by serving God with our entire being. That being, the self, is therefore of such value that it must be enhanced to its maximum capacity. In fact, if we do not develop ourselves fully, we remain too weak to carry out God's intent for us. Grace *is* an unearned gift, but grace, once accepted, allows us to get up boldly and confidently from our penitent, frightened, helpless knees. We do not earn this special status; it is unilaterally given to us as a gift to be used for the development of the very self that will then fulfill God's purpose in us.

Grace theology, then, bolsters the argument for the valuing of the self and shifts away from a preoccupation with mankind as creatures "lost in sin." Our status under grace changes from worthlessness to covenantal image-bearers, from lost souls to heirs of the kingdom. We thereby lose the bondage of fear and accept the freedom to grow as persons. We are now allowed—in fact, encouraged—to celebrate our full selves, to think and experiment on our own, and to be genuine and authentic. Grace is not something God *does* for us but *is* for us.

J. Harold Ellens, pastor, theologian, and clinical psychologist, probably has done more to illuminate us about grace than any other writer in the past twenty years.[15] He states:

> We do not begin to realize or to appreciate the radical, unconditional, and universal nature of [grace] until we begin to acknowledge that grace as God personally articulates it in Scripture certifies you and me as saints in the middle of our brokenness, in the process of our pathology, in spite of ourselves.[16]

Grace is "radical" because we can insist that God give it to us despite our unworthiness; grace is "unconditional" because there are no "ifs" on God's part; and grace is "universal" because it is for everyone. Says

Ellens: "The theology of grace is the most healing intervention ever undertaken for the population of this planet."[17]

If it is our fears, and the elaborate strategies we concoct to defend against them, that keep us from being healthy selves, then we desperately need an answer that we can appeal to for peace. For effective relief, this answer must be beyond the limits of the fragile self. Richard Rhem summarizes the answer well:

> A profound sense of God's grace brings one a very great freedom, freedom from fear and defensiveness, freedom from the anxiety of what the future holds for human development, scientific or philosophical formulation. Grace brings freedom and creates openness. There are no questions we dare not ask, no perspectives we fear to bring to expression.[18]

A Strong Self Is Crucial to Making an Impact in Life

A second resolution of the believer's fear of being an authentic self comes from realizing that the self is crucial in our outreach to the world at large. God's plan is that we become strong enough to deal with all aspects of life so that his purposes can be manifested through us. The bigger the sense of self and the more adequately that self is developed, the more God has to work with—as evidenced in the assertive, strong-minded biblical characters God chose to get his plans accomplished. It is a mistake to interpret Christ's advice to lose one's life (Mark 8:35) as meaning we are to throw self away.

The issue seems best understood as one of perspective, of not losing *self* but *self-centeredness.* The self only becomes a problem when self-deification overshadows caring relationships with God and others. All through Scripture self-deification has been punished forcefully. "Sin" is partially defined as the action of a haughty self that needs no one else and is above even God. Christ is urging us to lose our self-centeredness but not ourselves, for God requires us to develop ourselves so that his purposes can be manifested through us.

The biblical perspective is clear that the self must have limits. In Exodus 20:4–5 the ancient Israelites are warned that no one and no thing is to replace God's preeminence: ". . . for I, the LORD your God, am a jealous God, punishing the children for the sin of the fathers. . . ." Christ told his disciples that he himself was not first of all his own self but was here "to do the will of him who sent me and to finish his work" (John 4:34). Our relationship with God firmly puts God ahead of and above us, and history shows that those who have tried to replace God or usurp his power have become doomed. This is dramatically illustrated in Steven Spielberg's film *Raiders of the Lost Ark*.

When the theologian says that self-denial leads to self-discovery, we must remember what is meant: We find our peace and perspective as we lose our preoccupation with satisfying and saving ourselves. Self-centeredness makes us anxious to act as our own savior, as if our lives were totally in our own hands and we must earn the hereafter on our own merit. Such a prospect leaves us in inevitable despair, for we sooner or later must admit we cannot manage our own life and destiny totally by ourselves. Our generic neediness binds us to helplessness and fear—as poets, philosophers, theologians, and thinkers throughout the ages have attested. It is as we look upward to God for help that we begin to lose our self-centeredness and gain our selfhood.

We seek religious answers to find relief from the stress of feeling helpless and needy. With a perspective that includes God and others, we find a readiness to live more fully. Then we can finally look out beyond the limits of the self and into the vast opportunities of personal relationships with God and each other. Focusing on the self as an end goal is simply too limited. Losing self-preoccupation is a relief because the world is so vast compared to the limited world of the self. We only discover who we really are as we branch out beyond ourselves.

A critical issue preventing self-discovery is the fear that reaching out to the world at large will be uncomfortable—even dangerous. Although we read that God will never leave us (Heb. 13:5, cf. Deut. 31:6), we are like children who want to ride our bikes down the block but no farther, lest we lose sight of our house. Because a world-view requires self-confidence, many religious believers do not want to venture into the unknown, despite Christ's injunction to spread his Word throughout the world (Mark 16:15). Peering deeply into the mysteries of relationships and new ideas is fraught with chances of failure, so emotional guardedness seems like a safe alternative. The price for that safety, however, is one of dependency and immaturity. Those who do not find the self are trapped in childish themes that should have been outgrown long ago.

Clinging to God in childlike dependency risks developing a naive and too-humble innocence that interferes with personal maturity. Many subconsciously seek God as either a nourishing surrogate mother, an authoritative father-figure who punishes naughty children for sin, or the loving "Daddy" adored in childhood. Many believers find it difficult to face an adolescent individuation process for fear of having to wrestle with life on their own.

When we do not let go of our naiveté, we make innocence seem like a virtue, says Rollo May in *Power and Innocence*.[19] May points out that the word "innocence" is derived from the Latin *in* and *nocens,* that is, "not harmful." It is tempting for us to fearfully avoid the imagined danger involved in mature self-discovery and to draw back from the risks inherent in disagreeing, rebelling, breaking free, and thinking for ourselves. May calls this perspective "a childhood that is never outgrown," one that results in a "utopianism" where real dangers are not seen.[20] He concludes that innocence prevents us from developing the kind of realism that allows us to handle our own destructive capabilities: "[Innocence] actually becomes self-destructive. Innocence that cannot include the daemonic becomes evil."[21]

For many religious persons, the denial of self is not at all the honest self-negation they may claim it to be. Rather than becoming a true search for humility and service to God and others, it is only a sham, a pseudo self-denial, a cover-up of hidden desire. Thus, when believers play the role of sweet, innocent, obedient children who are denying the unacceptable parts of the self, they are keeping themselves too weak to put their hidden urges to rest. As the self remains weak, it demands *more* attention.

Innocence is an *ungodly* attempt to be more "spiritual" because it actually leaves us too weak to do God's work. It bears repeating that, although God does not need anyone or anything to help him out, he nonetheless works through the vehicle of the person. When the self is puny, that work is compromised. The self-denying believer becomes the object of some of Christ's most condemning words—"salt that has lost its savor," "a light under a bushel," "a house built upon sand," "a tree bearing bad fruit." Promoting the growth of the individual fosters self-confidence and maturity—traits that, in turn, can enhance the desire for spiritual expression.

God Wants Us to Love Ourselves—and Others

We have already considered that resolving the conflict over what to do with the self while living a spiritual life begins with an acceptance of our worth as persons loved and valued by God. A second source of resolution comes from reaching out to the world to exert ourselves as a force for good. We will now consider the third point: how loving ourselves keeps us in a healthy relationship with God and with others.

Most religions teach that we are able to love because of God's presence in all creatures. The Bible puts it this way: "We love because he first loved us" (1 John 4:19). Love, then, is more than a sentiment or an attraction; love is a dynamic response flowing from God's presence within us. Because he empowers us to love, we can reach out in acts of personal interest in others, utilizing our will to love to create independent loving behavior. We are free to choose with whom we will form special love bonds and how much love we shall expend, but our love does not flow from an empty vessel. Nor do we love solely in response to divine instigation. In understanding how or why we love, we must consider that we love others out of our love for ourselves. In fact, if we do not love ourselves, we cannot love others.

We have the capacity and opportunity to love ourselves because of our power to love. The justification seems clear: Not only do we love the self that God loves in us, but we follow his command to love each other as we love ourselves (Matt. 22:39). Once fortified with self-care, we have enough inner substance to share.

The importance of loving the self is underscored by the fact that as we relate with others we owe them a self of some substance. Thus, if we develop our character with a sound self-acceptance, we can better act as a friend to others. When we take good care of ourselves and interact with a sense of pride and confidence, we offer a more personable and interesting someone with whom others can relate.

A young woman comes for psychotherapy, depressed and heartbroken because her boyfriend has ended their relationship. She cannot eat or sleep, her work is suffering, and she has no interest in life's pleasures.

As we talk about what went wrong in the relationship, she tells me she often found it hard to believe her boyfriend really loved her. It was hard for her to smile when he gave her compliments, and she accepted but did not seem responsive to his affection.

"I don't know why I didn't respond," she reports. "I just found myself in this cautious mood when he was nice to me."

"Had he ever hurt you in some way?" I inquire.

"Not really. I just couldn't seem to let go with him, even though I wanted him to love me," she tells me.

"It seems you felt undeserving of his love," I reflect.

"I think you're right," she says. "I always wondered why—with so many other girls around—he would pick me."

"So, in your doubts about yourself, you found it hard to enjoy his love," I respond.

"Yes," she answers with tears forming. "Why would a good guy really want to love me?"

As our treatment continues, we discuss her low self-esteem and find that she has a long history of talking negatively about herself. Over the years she has attempted to improve herself by having an in-the-head critic compile and review her weaknesses. She has had good intentions, but her efforts have been at the expense of self-worth, for it is hard to love ourselves when we are too critical of our own faults.

Loving ourselves does not mean embracing our faults. Rather, we acknowledge the role of our shortcomings and pry deeper to understand their meaning. Only then can our decision to do better be effective. What we fear about examining our less acceptable parts is owning a truth even Augustine and Paul had to face—there are times when we do not necessarily *want* to be good. Although we are often more than willing to do as Adam and Eve did to achieve our desired goals, this does not mean that we must hate ourselves for our sins. It is in self-awareness and self-acceptance that we can better appreciate what we must do to produce genuine change.

If we acknowledge and accept ourselves as is, we can then encourage self-esteem while working to understand and correct any inappropriate behavior. This self-esteem precludes worry about deeper issues of worth-lessness or rejection. Freed from fear of our unlovability, our minds can then move on to question what we are doing wrong. In such an atmosphere, it is far easier to change our ways.

In sum, we promote our growth by accepting our worth, developing a powerful outreach, and loving ourselves for who we are (thereby allowing us to love others). As we accept God's plan for us to come to our fullness, we reduce our fears that becoming our true selves will jeopardize our relationship with him. When the self is "abased," as urged in the hymn cited at the beginning of this chapter, there can be neither an exaltation of God nor a victory for the person. Our commitment as believers is to both God and ourselves.

Spiritual Limits for Getting and Giving

Given the encouragement and the freedom to grow to our full potential, are there limits to "getting" as we seek also to maintain our spiritual commitments?

In the middle of a speech to a conservative religious audience on the importance of getting as well as giving, I was aware of a sudden hush over the audience. I waited for what seemed like an eternity until one brave soul said, "But we've always been taught that we should give; it is wrong to get for yourself." Spotting the minister in the audience, I asked him to explain if that is what he or the church at large meant in teaching that "it is more blessed to give than to receive" (Acts 20:35). He may have been surprised to hear his parishioners confess their confusion on this point, but he should not have been.

From the beginning of Christianity, giving has been extolled as spiritual, worthy of blessings both in this life and the next. Christ advised the rich young man: "Go, sell everything you have and give it to the poor, and you will have treasure in heaven . . ." (Mark 10:21, cf. Matt. 6:19–21). This message has been widely associated with religious belief and, indeed, with spiritual piety.

On the other hand, Jewish and Christian teachings describe getting as carnal, a sign of self-service. The Old Testament warns that if we love money and what it can buy, we will never be satisfied (Eccl. 5:10–12). Again and again Solomon warns that trusting in riches brings failure and ultimately unrighteousness (Prov. 11:28; 13:8; 28:22; 30:9). The New Testament, too, is replete with dire warnings about the evils and risks of getting much for oneself. Paul instructs Timothy: "People who want to get rich fall into temptation and a trap and into many foolish and harmful desires that plunge men into ruin and destruction. For the love of money is a root of all kinds of evil . . ." (1 Tim. 6:9–10). His fear is that being rich makes one high-minded, that is, self-contented and oblivious to the demands of God and the needs of others. The apostle John warns against the same evil: "For all that is in the world, the lust of the flesh, and the lust of the eyes, and the pride of life, is not of the Father, but is of the world" (1 John 2:16 KJV). Christ speaks frequently of the risks of materialism: "But the worries of this life, the deceitfulness of wealth and the desires for other things come in and choke the word, making it unfruitful" (Mark 4:19).

The biblical prohibitions against greed, lust, covetousness, selfishness, and pride are designed to safeguard against putting the temporal over the eternal, self over God. Christ patiently tells his followers over and over that they cannot serve both God and material goods (eg., Matt. 6:24). In emphasizing the primacy of our relationship with God, Christ advises that if we are distracted by anything that would come between us and our Maker, these distractions should be avoided regardless of cost. He states dramatically, "If your hand or your foot causes you to sin, cut it off and throw it away. It is better for you to enter life maimed or crippled than to have two hands or two feet and be thrown into eternal fire" (Matt. 18:8).

Church leaders often cite the story of a young man who comes to Jesus and asks how to find eternal life. Jesus tells him to follow all the commandments, but the man says he has already done that. "What do I still lack?" he asks. When Jesus tells him to sell everything he has, give to the poor, and follow him, the man goes away sad, "because he had great wealth" (Matt. 19:22).

Some believers try to follow these words of Christ to the letter, whether by owning nothing and taking vows of poverty or by at least giving enough money to the church to feel less troubled by their affluence. Others, however, are so troubled by worldwide hunger and poverty that they cannot justify simply letting others help the poor. They believe in giving to the point where everyone is taken care of, surely a lofty goal! Ronald Sider's book, *Rich Christians in an Age of Hunger,* answers the question of how much one should give: "until there is equality."[22] Sider suggests that true believers should share by means of a graduated tithe (the more earned beyond basic needs, the more one should give away), by living sparsely, by fasting, sharing with neighbors, making one's own clothes, even by communal living. "The crucial test," Sider says, "is whether the prosperous are obeying God's commands to bring justice to the oppressed."[23]

There probably are very few Christians who will go without or live meagerly, as Sider suggests, just to help the poor. But where should conscientious believers draw the line? Can we justify our many luxuries when so many are starving in the world? What are the limits of compassion? How far should we go in following Christ's words regarding getting and giving? Sider suggests that when all of this is put into perspective, we must conclude that God does not ask people to stop seeking *more*, but does demand that success be shared with those less fortunate.

My own position is that the development of a full self is not only allowable, but it is commanded biblically. Nowhere in the Bible is success or affluence prohibited. In fact, Christ makes it quite clear in the parable of the talents that if we have the ability to succeed and do not, we will be punished (see Matt. 25:14–30). God is happy to see us succeed and displeased if we neglect or squander our abilities.

Of course, success must be kept in perspective. Christ's warnings mean we have to be careful not to be *distracted* by our successful getting. Distraction comes in the form of selfishness—in not sharing reasonably with others, especially the poor. Proper perspective is also lost when there is haughtiness—the kind of smug, self-congratulatory pride that Christ spoke of in his story about the foolish man who tore down his barns to make way for his huge increases, but forgot to nourish his soul, which was to be taken from him that very day (Luke 12:16–21).

Because Christ knows how easy it is to get hooked on material goods and personal success, he reminds his followers that "it is easier for a camel to go through the eye of a needle than for a rich man to enter the kingdom of God" (Matt. 19:24). Here Jesus says something very insightful about human nature: our tendency to lose sight of true goals as we are preoccupied with all that we get. We too easily believe we can handle success without being distracted, but such beliefs are deceptive.

It seems fair to say that left to ourselves, we would *not* pursue God's interests for us—nor even our own balanced perspective—bent as we are on the pleasures of self-certification. But, except for God's unending love, we would come to naught. It is from this viewpoint that the self takes its meaning. Whom do we serve? We serve self with God, so that we can serve God with self.

12

Becoming Fulfilled

The Satisfied Self

Hold fast the time! . . . Hold every moment sacred. Give each
clarity and meaning, each the weight of thine awareness, each its
true and due fulfillment.

Thomas Mann

Billionaire John D. Rockefeller, Sr., was once asked how much
money is enough. His reply, "Just a little bit more," reveals more
than this aggressive achiever's constant hunger or even the driving
force of human greed. We all seem to live our lives in search of just a little bit more of everything.

Most of us think a lot about personal fulfillment and what it takes to
raise our general level of satisfaction. Pollster Daniel Yankelovich
reported in the 1980s that approximately three-fourths of all Americans
have frequent thoughts about this process—a rather remarkable number,
in light of our nation's history of sacrifice, duty, and social responsibility.
His research shows "tens of millions" of experiments with self-fulfillment, all focused on reducing stress and improving the quality of life.[1] It
seems fairly obvious that the desire for self-improvement is universal.
What better explanation can we offer for the downfall of communism
than the individualistic demand for more satisfaction on a daily basis?

Even decades of harsh suppression were not able to erase the basic human desire to live more enjoyably and have personal control over achieving that goal.

In preceding chapters we have described this search as multifaceted: meeting our various physical and emotional needs, indulging our particular wants, expressing our urge to be productive and creative, reducing our sense of personal inadequacy, bringing meaning to our lives, establishing interpersonal connections, and meeting spiritual needs—in short, discovering our identity in relation to the universe.

Rather than aimlessly taking all that we can, or giving up the search because we do not have the money or energy to join those more clever or capable, we need to know what we can do right now, on our own, to satisfy ourselves. And it is possible for most people to proceed without special training or professional guidance.

We will now consider some specific approaches to getting more satisfaction out of life. By understanding how we become satisfied and practicing certain techniques, we can enjoy our lives more and reduce the frantic and undirected strivings that lead mainly to frustration.

There are three key ways by which we can increase our satisfaction. All three begin with the letter A—AWARENESS, ABSORPTION, and APPRECIATION. (I have come to refer to the three as "A1, A2, and A3.") The more competently we utilize these techniques and the more deeply we understand their underlying principles, the more fully will the hungry self be satisfied.

Awareness

We cannot begin to satisfy ourselves until we recognize our needs and wants. By correctly using our physiological and psychological sensors to become aware of precisely what we seek, we provide information to the brain that can be translated into appropriate action. Focused awareness puts us in touch with both our inner selves and the world around us. Unless we accurately evaluate our complicated physical and emotional requirements and know what is available for relief, we will be unable to sustain life, let alone find satisfaction. When we are vaguely unhappy, yet act in self-defeating, unreasonable, or unpredictable ways, it often means that we are not conscious of what we actually need or want.

Although accurate self-awareness is a critical prelude to finding gratification and solving problems, we must also be aware of what the environment has to offer. The brain must match an inner request with what is available in the outer world if that desire is to be fulfilled. Without a realistic appraisal of the supplies available to meet our needs and wants, we are forced to go without or make unnecessary compromises. Either outcome is frustrating. The more accurately we recognize a fit between demand and supply, the better our chance of fulfillment.

We sustain our lives and find satisfaction by responding to certain internal messages. Many of these responses are reflexive, as in the quick withdrawal of the hand from a hot stove or the surge of adrenaline in a threatening situation. Sometimes we are not consciously aware of an urge, much less the reasons why a particular need or want is present. Still, maintaining awareness at some inner level, whether conscious, subconscious, or intuitive, is the first step in finding whatever it is we seek.

Our awareness of the *external* world comes about through the use of our five senses—seeing, hearing, smelling, tasting, and touching. We see the danger and react to avoid it; we smell the food cooking and prepare to eat it; we are touched lovingly and respond in very specific and complex ways. As one sense is activated and others are brought into play, we stop focusing exclusively within and, instead, contact objects outside of ourselves. For example, when we smell a flower, we direct our attentions outward and may also look at the flower and touch it. Such attention provides information that is brought inward to enrich our total experience.

To be fully aware requires that we flow out to the object of our interest, surround it with our senses, and then take our perceptions back into ourselves. This round trip from self to object and back again to the self should be as sensually alive as possible for maximum fulfillment. Thus, when we eat, we must bring every one of our five senses into contact with the food. As we hear the steak sizzle, smell its seasonings, see its colors, note its tenderness, and taste its juicy, delicious flavor, we will be aware of having eaten to our satisfaction. If we talk or watch television while eating the same steak, we are compromising that eating experience and may have to substitute quantity for quality by eating too large a portion or snacking later. The more we focus specifically on our sensory experiences, the more we increase awareness and feel content.

We can use our senses to fill ourselves from many sources: interpersonal, materialistic, intellectual, spiritual, or our own creativity. All of these sources of satisfaction are inexhaustible and simply wait for us to discover and utilize them. There are always people nearby with whom we can relate; literature, art, and music available for our enrichment; the good earth at hand to nourish, inspire, and console us. There will also always be new ideas to absorb, new areas of life to explore. We need only notice and respond to them.

The broader the sources of our awareness, the more effectively we can utilize them for gratification. Our interests will vary. Some days we find fulfillment in work, others days in play. One hour we seek food, the next we want to be close to someone we love or perhaps to meditate. It is in this endless process of choosing from a rich and varied menu of possibilities that we best fulfill our various needs and wants.

The Costs of Inattentiveness

Psychotherapist Fritz Perls used to tell his students, "Awareness is everything."[2] He explained that as nature abhors a vacuum, so the mind seeks to avoid incompleteness. The mind strives to relieve the tension that has accumulated because of unfulfilled desires. Part of Perls's gestalt therapy (*gestalt* is the German word for completion) was to set the stage for a patient to become so aware of every part of his or her problem that the solution would be self-evident. If a patient's hands were tightly clasped, for example, he would ask the person to notice those hands and have them struggle against each other more actively. Perls would use every sigh, every movement, every scrap of a reported dream, to lead the patient into a deeper consciousness of what the "wisdom of the organism" was saying. The patient, finding no place to hide, could either face his or her inner truths or be sent away as unwilling to cooperate. To facilitate change, all Perls asked of a patient was to be as fully aware as possible.

When we are unaware of what we really need or want, we are tempted to fill our lives with plastic substitutes that do not satisfy. We resort to fantasies, prejudices, lies, and distortions so we do not have to face our feelings. We may blame others rather than ourselves, but we swallow our anger and create an ulcer rather than risk rejection from open confrontation.

Or we simply close our eyes to the obvious, like the woman who sat across from me during our first meeting and looked out the window at a beautiful fall landscape. Multicolored leaves swayed in the breeze, the mums were gorgeous, children leaned over to splash happily in the courtyard fountain. Yet she said, "There is nothing to live for; I want to end my life."

When asked, she admits seeing the things I have mentioned, but she says they have no meaning for her. She is so filled with depression and pain over her father's death five years ago that she has room for no other sensation. In the back of her mind, death is preferable to life because it would mean rejoining her beloved father, so she is inattentive to external stimuli. Since she has not yet taken her life and (according to her psychological test results) will probably not do so in the future, she will continue to suffer by being half-dead emotionally unless she finds a reason to notice and enjoy life's pleasures.

After months of exploring the deep impact her father has had on her life, and how she has chosen to search only for his presence, she gradually learns to let go of him. I know she is making good progress when one spring morning she looks out my window and says, "Do you notice how beautiful the tulips are?"

Only if we face our problems and inquire deeply into the essence of a dreaded thought or experience or memory can we infiltrate our fears with new ideas. This infusion of information usually results in relief—because even unpleasant facts are more realistic than our fears. Using new data, we develop insight and begin to think or feel differently about our problems. Since improving our awareness forces us to be more honest with ourselves, we can avoid the lies and phony solutions that short-circuit our satisfaction.

It is puzzling that we often do not give awareness more than a cursory nod. Although we prize free choice and subscribe to the idea of self-improvement, we may be inattentive to the very steps necessary to expand our minds. Students often hurry to get through school rather than try to learn anything. Many adults seem so security-minded that they keep plodding along a rigid course rather than spend the time and risk the effort or money needed to open themselves to life. It is surprising how easily we believe in tradition for tradition's sake, afraid that an expanding awareness will entail loss. Fearful of change, we censure others for trying something new, as if their flexibility reminds us how stuck we are in our own lives.

We live in an era when we seek more of everything and want it *now*, yet we pay too little attention to what exactly we want and why. So we seek instant knowledge with cram courses, immediate wealth with state lottery tickets, total love with new partners. Although aware that we are unsatisfied, we seem blind to the importance of gathering data to reach specific goals—changing our minds and altering our habits according to those facts. Inattention to such details can cost us our dreams.

Enhancing Our Awareness

Maintaining awareness is such a vital part of achieving satisfaction that we must be careful to avoid anything that would interfere with the process. What can we do to enhance our awareness and thereby become more fulfilled as individuals?

First, we must open our minds and senses. We must go beyond our narrow routines and adopt a mind-set that places value on sensual experiencing and allows us to react more honestly to whatever life brings. Many people deliberately reduce their level of awareness, preferring to avoid unpleasant facts and stay entrenched in old habits. In *The Closing of the American Mind*, Allan Bloom reminds us that we must open ourselves to life's great issues if we really want to take life seriously. He lists various dichotomies—"freedom-necessity . . . good-evil, body-soul, self-other . . . being-nothing . . ."—that should be important to us, explaining that:

> A serious life means being fully aware of [these] alternatives, thinking about them with all the intensity one brings to bear on life-and-death questions, in full recognition that every choice is a great risk with necessary consequences that are hard to bear.[3]

Bloom believes that Americans have chosen to avoid confronting serious questions: "The old tragic conflicts reappear, newly labeled as assurances: 'I'm OK, you're OK.'" We have dulled our awareness to avoid having to choose. "America has no-fault automobile accidents, no-fault divorce, and it is moving . . . toward no-fault choices."[4]

The tragedy of inhibited awareness is that it stunts our intellectual and emotional growth. If we close our minds to life in all of its breadth, we are ignoring the data with which to better understand ourselves and the world at large.

Awareness increases our initiative and excitement because we are less restrained by innocence and the fear it often produces. Looking at life through eager eyes, we make new interpersonal relationships, see our jobs in a fresh light, and discover so much more than we had previously known. As we explore the external world of thoughts and ideas, we reach more deeply into our inner hearts and minds, each time expanding our consciousness. We need new habits, new goals, new feelings, if we are to break out of our routines and learn not to take life for granted.

Second, we must be willing to learn something new. I routinely recommend a weekly news magazine such as *Time* or *Newsweek* to my clients when they report feeling dull and having "nothing to talk about" with family and friends. Reading is a crucial way to learn. When we read good books, magazines, and the daily newspaper, we expose ourselves to the wide variety of events and ideas that affect our lives.

Other mind-expanding behaviors include taking on-the-job training or a class or two at local high schools and colleges that offer adult-education programs. Educational television also has a great deal to offer us, if we prefer to learn in the comforts of home. If we are willing to switch from being merely entertained or amused—giving up maybe one or two hours per week of the mindless drivel featured in so many television programs in favor of reading, taking classes, or watching the Public Broadcasting System—we will expand our awareness and our lives.

Third, we must pay attention to the details of our surroundings. That means noticing things we have taken for granted and correlating what we apprehend with what we comprehend. There is too much at stake for us not to be constantly alert. The driver whose mind wanders as a sharp turn approaches, the student who does not hear the announced exam date, the investor who misses the news flash of a sudden event that will influence the markets—all are at risk because they are not fully aware of important data.

If we fail to pay close attention to our immediate circumstances or deny our impressions of what is happening, we will too quickly rely on others' observations and yield to their demands. For example, at work we may let our own accurate perception of problems with management or fellow workers be totally overruled by what other people want or by our reluctance to speak up. We may see the mistakes that someone ought to be correcting—the waste, the indifference, the discrimination, the stealing—yet close our eyes to these problems because of our fears of being disliked or even fired. "What can I do?" we shrug. "It's not my problem." After a while we may not even be aware of grossly inappropriate conditions because we have habitually "adjusted" to them rather than taking action.

It is each person's responsibility to notice fully what is happening, to attend to the details of each situation, and to follow through with appropriate actions. Of course, acknowledging one's own perceptions and acting on them does not negate the importance of keeping the rules or taking due note of the opinions of others. Instead, this kind of vigilant attention brings the self and its awareness to every situation in which a decision is needed.

Fourth, we must free ourselves from narrow-mindedness. Although it is natural to enter every new situation with some idea about what to expect, it is counterproductive to let only those preconceived opinions determine our actions. How often we say automatically, "It'll never work, so why try?" or prevent ourselves from attempting something new simply because *someone else* has decided the venture is unrewarding. It is as if we subconsciously look for reasons why we should not expand our lives.

Remaining closed to new experiences is easier, but it means that we are allowing negative thinking to dominate our choices. When we expand our awareness, we drive out the rigid preconceptions that keep us uninformed and indecisive. Seeing matters in a new light will release us from the biases and fears that so often restrict our activity.

In essence, awareness is the means whereby we bring ourselves into total contact with reality—our private, internal world as well as the people, objects, and experiences around us. The more accurately we are aware of what is within us and what is around us, the better equipped we are to find satisfaction.

Absorption

When the Chicago Bears won the 1985 Super Bowl, superstar running back Walter Payton was asked how he felt about his dream come true. "I don't know," he replied. "It hasn't really sunk in yet." Payton was having difficulty absorbing the full impact of victory, even though he was fully aware of what had happened.

To "absorb" an experience is to take our awareness of it so deeply into ourselves that the happening becomes acknowledged and accepted. Internalizing the data we gather is harder than most people imagine. In fact, none of us absorbs all the stimuli that bombard our senses. We selectively attend to the stimuli around us, often choosing only those that we *want* to comprehend and ignoring the rest. Whether consciously or not, we react to sensory information according to our subjective impressions of how capable we feel of dealing with the experience it represents.

Some experts believe that the brain absorbs everything it perceives and permanently records these stimuli. Much of that stored material is of little importance and will probably never be recalled. But I am not talking about that kind of absorption, important as it may be. Instead, I am referring to the internal processing through which we extract something meaningful from an experience and use it for personal enrichment. By taking in an experience in all its dimensions, we edify or teach or excite ourselves in some way, thereby adding to our growth. Just as food must be assimilated into the bloodstream to be useful, so too with our experiences. We must open ourselves fully to every experience—first allowing it into our conscious awareness ("A1") and then absorbing its mental and emotional relevance ("A2").

A thirty-eight-year-old attorney consults me with symptoms of depression. He feels empty despite his successes, bored even though, by most people's standards, he has an exciting life. Although recently returned from a vacation in the Caribbean, he says he is impatient and irritated, not at all refreshed by the experience.

"What did you do on your trip?" I ask.

"I don't really remember," he replies. "I guess we had fun, but I feel something should have happened that didn't."

"Tell me how a typical day went," I prompt.

"After breakfast I'd walk to the newsstand to pick up *The Wall Street Journal* and give my investments the kind of time they don't get when I'm busy at the office. After lunch I'd catch up on some law briefs I brought along. Then we might swim or stroll a little until it started getting dark and we dressed for dinner."

Having been to the same island, I was excited just thinking about some great things my wife and I had seen and done there. Of the three or four I mentioned, this lawyer remembered only one. In other words, he was not impressed by much of anything—the exotic flowers, the iridescent water, the native cuisine, and the local sights. He was there, but he absorbed virtually nothing to enrich himself.

Many objects of our involvement are meaningful for a short time and soon forgotten. Our lives are full of such events—a fine dinner, a beautiful sunset, a special Christmas present. These experiences touch us as they happen, so we internalize their importance momentarily and move on to the next event. Despite their brevity, these experiences have been growthful or meaningful in some way, even though we may not remember them in detail. By contrast are the larger events of life that we have absorbed deeply because of their impact on our lives. We do not forget graduation, our first love, or a moving experience, because we have extracted permanent significance from such events. We recall them often, each time re-absorbing some of the feelings associated with them. Even if the event was unpleasant, our assimilation of its impact becomes part of who we are.

The Excitement Factor

When we absorb an event, there is a noticeable interaction between the self and the experience. This interaction has excitement to it because something dramatic is happening. There may be at least two explanations of what that "something" is.

Some of the excitement is in the act of *being drawn into* the event at hand. As the curtain goes up on the drama, the action takes us in and commands our full attention: The self is momentarily lost in the lights, color, and dialogue. According to this explanation, we are expecting the object of our attention—a person or the event itself—to *make* us respond.

Because we want to be impressed by "good" objects, we expose ourselves to a number of potentially enriching experiences in hopes that they will do something *to* or *for* us. That explains why buying bigger and better goods, finding zestful experiences, and meeting "better" people will help increase our satisfaction. Conversely, when we expect an event to absorb and enrich us but it does not, we blame the situation or the other people involved. We become disenchanted with books, friends, restaurants, vacation spots, and the like if they do not "do anything" for us.

A second explanation for the excitement found in an act of absorption is that *we take into ourselves* the event or experience before us: The self does the absorbing. Consciously or not, deliberately or not, the individual allows the internalizing to happen. Thus, the "goodness" of a movie or friend or job is experienced because we permit the self to enjoy the person or situation at hand, whether or not it has intrinsic worth. Here, since the emphasis is on the act of valuing whatever is available, we retain some degree of control over what we absorb.

Whichever explanation takes priority in a given situation, it seems fair to conclude that the excitement of absorption lies in the act of bringing together subject and object so that some pleasant aspect of that event is internalized. Even if the interaction is negative, something dynamic is happening to us at an inner level of emotional and/or cognitive awareness. Whether we absorb an experience or are absorbed by it, there are changes within us that can be used to promote personal growth.

Awareness ("A1") and absorption ("A2") go hand in hand. The more we are aware of what is going on around us, the more varied are our sources from which to absorb meaning. When we combine "A1" and "A2", we experience a deeper degree of satisfaction than if we had failed to get all that could have been obtained from some event. Ironically, most of us get far less than we could be getting because we ignore the pleasures that are available to us at any given moment. Our sense of emptiness has little correlation with the skills or opportunities or good fortune we have (or lack) at the time. This idea may bother us, since we like to blame our unhappiness on circumstances rather than recognize it as a function of how callously we ignore all that we have. The fact is, we feel deprived and needy primarily because we take in only a fraction of the love, attention, joy, success, and pleasure that each day brings.

Satisfaction depends on our *willingness* to deeply internalize life's goodness. While it is human nature to want all we can get, it also seems true that many of us suffer from emotional bulimia. We have a tendency to chew up and swallow our good times and regurgitate them soon afterward. Perhaps, by paying only brief attention to our joys, we hope to keep alive our passion for acquiring even more—oiling our "mean and lean working machine," as one high achiever described himself. Many of us are so afraid that absorbing our successes will lead to complacency that we internalize good times just long enough to acknowledge them and then move along in search of more.

Some people who give life's joys but scant attention are subconsciously saving themselves from imagined loss. They associate success with potential loss, as if winning is but a prelude to losing. It is not that they have so few good times, but that they do not *keep* them. It has been my professional observation that much of the depression experienced in this "land of plenty" relates to the quick disavowal of hard-earned happiness.

Increasing Absorption

The more we internalize whatever is pleasant, or "victorious," the more we will be satisfied. But how can we increase our absorption of positive experiences? There are two basic ways to do this: an easy way and a more difficult one.

First, the easier way: We absorb more from our experiences when we are *willing to enjoy* what these circumstances have to offer. As a starter, you might look around right now to see what your surroundings can provide. If you are reading in bed, notice the good feelings that can result from lying down on a comfortable bed in the security of your own room. If traveling on a plane, consider how great it is to be able to afford jet travel. Give yourself permission to enjoy the excitement of going off to a new place; acknowledge the importance of living in a country that provides such luxuries.

We improve our absorption considerably whenever we notice the details of our current situation and feel their importance. A sunny day, a tasty lunch, a warm coat against the snow, the smile of a friend—all deserve our willingness to extract pleasure and meaning from them. As we take in more and more from whatever is available, we expose our very being to the potential joys of the experience. The decision to absorb takes place right after noticing fully what is available ("A1") and right before opening ourselves to the experience. We must allow the feelings to flow between the event and our inner being so there is full contact. That permission is sometimes a conscious decision whereby we choose to become totally "involved." But often the choice is first seen in an involuntary expression of joy or amazement that signals us to pay full attention. Whether deliberate or not, it is relatively easy to absorb life's goodness, once we permit ourselves to be open. As we linger and savor the experience, even as we recall it later on, we extract something meaningful and feel more content.

A more difficult way to increase absorption involves *summoning the courage to grow,* since the more of life's experiences we internalize, the more we mature. Yet much can go wrong to impede this kind of growth. Foremost is the fear of change.

A couple in their late forties comes for marriage counseling after having been separated for a year. The wife had gone back to college for an M.B.A. degree after their children became established on their own. She now has a well-paying and interesting job that has expanded her definition of who she is and what she wants from life. The husband, threatened by his wife's newfound independence and decreased subservience to his dominance, has done nothing to support her personal growth. When his insulting remarks and other negative responses to her choices got bad enough, she separated from him, telling him she could not continue her self-development while putting up with his complaints.

With infinite patience and a loving heart, this woman has tried unsuccessfully to encourage her husband to grow with her, or at least share the excitement she is experiencing. Because all he sees are the unsettling changes in his life, he gripes continually about "liberated wives who ought to stay home where they belong." He refuses to visit his wife at her apartment, seeing her absence only as a threat to his male dominance. Unwilling to absorb her self-development as an asset in their relationship, he continues to avoid her buoyant spirit and nurse his wounded male pride. Since he perceives even marriage counseling as a threat to his control, it soon becomes evident to me that his fear of change—his unwillingness to absorb anything positive from his wife's growth—will sabotage our progress. After several visits, he refuses to return.

The courage to open ourselves to new experiences comes harder if we are too firmly entrenched in familiar habits, even destructive ones. Many people would rather stay with what they have than face the fears inherent in making new choices. If the potential benefits of change do not outweigh the risks, it is difficult to surrender control and drink more deeply from life.

It may seem strange that we hesitate to internalize our hard-won victories. Surely life is difficult enough without needlessly suffering the pain of diminished rewards for our efforts. Why would we not do all we can to enhance our sense of pleasure or success? Some clinical psychologists fault the rampant narcissism of our times, citing the shallow inner core of those whose primary goal is self-aggrandizement at the expense of others. This vacuous center, they say, requires constant feeding because it is too poorly developed to hold on to the very profits the narcissist lives for.

As plausible as this explanation may be, I believe the primary cause of inadequate absorption is our fear of personal growth. All through our lives we have developed step by step, building on our familiar and secure bases, yet cautious about making the bold leaps needed for adventurous living. To avoid disapproval, we gear personal development to our expectations of what others will think of us. And to prevent the pain of failure, we typically choose to operate from a view of life as harsh and difficult rather than full of unlimited potential. We have allowed our fears to overshadow our desires to expand.

It is neither immature nor pathological to embrace security as a central dynamic of our existence. Certainly in our stressful world we need to know where our safe harbors lie. But it is unsatisfying to remain in peaceful havens, sheltered from the excitement of the open sea. To remain too dependently attached to old habits and beliefs is to avoid life's important adventures. People who are preoccupied with the tried-and-true often reject new experiences that could have developed their inner fiber. They restrict their ability to grow and cannot trust others or themselves—simply because they do not summon the courage to push on, despite their fears.

As we decrease our dependency on the familiar, we open ourselves in good faith to whatever life brings us. We begin to trust our perceptions and proceed into new experiences with a sense of adventure. Then our primary focus becomes living in the here and now, noticing and taking in *everything*, moment by moment. Safe harbors are still important to us, but more as foundation than superstructure. We will neither consciously dwell on our sources of security nor evaluate each new opportunity on the basis of stereotyped thoughts or unexamined habits. By claiming our self-worth and believing in our accomplishments, we are fortified and find the courage to grab every opportunity for growth that comes our way.

Appreciation

Awareness and absorption are absolutely crucial in our search for satisfaction. But to stamp them in as deeply as possible, we must take one subsequent step: We must appreciate what we take in.

In his highly acclaimed research on the stress syndrome, Hans Selye found that the greatest reducer of physical and emotional stress was not power, success, security, pleasure, or even love; stress is best reduced when we feel *grateful.*[5] His findings may seem puzzling at first glance. Why should appreciation (a synonym for "gratitude") be so relaxing? Selye is not talking about a quick "thanks" or a religious prayer of thankfulness said by rote. What I read in his findings is that an honest, heartfelt sense of appreciation sets off a chain of internal events that touches even our physiological processes.

True gratitude is calming for several reasons. First, deep appreciation is *an admission to ourselves that indeed we have received something.* Appreciation confirms that we have made contact with the object of our search, and that some sense of fulfillment has occurred. Appreciation says "Aah! Great! Thanks!" In feeling grateful, we validate the reality of the fulfillment. By admitting, "Mission accomplished!" both mind and body can relax by letting go of tension.

There is a direct correlation between how honestly we feel appreciative and how effectively we can let go of our tensions. To *say* that we are grateful does not produce relief unless it reflects genuine appreciation. Likewise, to say "It's about time I won something!" has too many negative overtones to imply real gratitude that a specific goal is accomplished. When we have waited too long for relief, residual anger takes priority over our enjoyment of a victory.

A thirty-year-old woman consults me with symptoms of anger, hurt, and despair. She has just had two major aspects of her life come to an end: She has graduated from medical school and has become divorced. As might be expected, she is exhausted from the years of pressure, fear of failure, and endless hours of study. The demands at school kept her from any meaningful time with her husband and eventually wrecked their marriage.

"I am so angry," she begins. "If I knew then what I know now, I never would have gone to med school. It has not been worth it."

"It's been absolutely exhausting, hasn't it?" I reflect.

"Worse," she responds. "It's been dehumanizing. I had to literally give up my social and personal life to survive."

As we talk, it becomes obvious that this woman is suffering from more than anger over the rigors of medical school or the tragedy of a failed marriage. She also feels she has nothing to compensate for what she has been through.

"Is there nothing positive to warm you?" I ask "You must be grateful that you are now a physician, one of the most respected members of society. You have the ability to heal, let alone to command an excellent salary and a fine standard of living. Does that mean anything to you?"

She does not answer.

In the months ahead, we will have to work through her resentment and bitterness so she can get on with her life. Part of that task will be to sift back through her past few years and discover the good parts. It is essential that this woman balance her negative feelings with a realization that there were times of success, praise, friendship, excitement, discovery, and guidance. Because she has not been grateful for what she has received along the way, she is too bitter to feel positive about her accomplishments. Appreciation confirms that we have received something of value.

Appreciation has a second benefit in that *it sets the stage for happiness*. When we are truly grateful we rejoice, and we do so spontaneously from our inner depths. Feeling relief *should* make us happy. We clap with joy when the football team's defense holds at the one-yard line in a close game. We celebrate when we get our jobs back or when worry over an illness ends. Such celebrations are the natural outpouring of appreciation; happiness is a salute to whatever forces have provided our relief.

Some people act as if there is no need to be grateful when they have brought about their own success. After all, no one else did the job for them! This attitude overlooks the inherent benefits of *feeling* appreciative. It also fails to acknowledge that no one totally succeeds at any task without some external assistance. In every success, we are always indebted to a host of people, to fortuitous circumstances, and to God. While being the instruments of our accomplishments, we never carry out our tasks alone. When we appreciate the help we have received, we are expressing our relief in knowing that there are positive forces standing behind us. This, too, adds to our sense of happiness over the completed task and enriches our joyful celebration.

A woman sits silently weeping during our final session after months of treatment. She began therapy feeling that she was an emotional orphan, that her parents had never cared for her deeply, and that she would search endlessly for their love but never find it. Now that she sees more clearly what they have done for her, she feels united with them in appreciation.

"I never knew how much my parents really loved me," she relates. "I thought they were always doing things arbitrarily, for their good, not mine. I've spent so many years in unreasonable bitterness. My relatives always told me I was too hard on Mom and Dad, but I never saw it. Now I do. I'm so grateful to them—and to you for helping me recognize their love. My tears are of joy. Thank you so much." Her gratitude warms me deeply.

There is a third benefit of appreciation: *It confirms our worth, our ability to be effective.* When we celebrate an achievement and feel grateful that "good fortune" has come to us, we are admitting that we had a hand in making the success come to pass. When students earn an *A* on an exam, or athletes win a game for their team, there should be an implicit acknowledgment that the deed was done through their own efforts. Exaggerated expressions of humility that disown any claim to personal excellence and diligent labor are unrealistic (and rarely sound genuine)—even if it is God who is given all the credit. After all, God may have created us with certain innate abilities, but it is our responsibility to activate those skills and use our talents appropriately. Appreciation, by recognizing our personal accomplishments, increases our sense of self-worth and confidence.

Of course, no one applauds pomposity and brazen bragging, but it is hardly improper to say, "I'm really grateful for the skills I have, and it makes me feel wonderful to do so well." When we give ourselves credit for what we are or have done, we build the self-esteem needed to contribute more completely toward the accomplishment of any task.

On the other hand, being appreciative to others for what they have given us further confirms our worth by recognizing that we have been cared for. When we are grateful to those who died for our country as we celebrate Memorial Day, or when on Thanksgiving Day we appreciate God's goodness in providing another year of harvest, we are happily observing that others have been generous to us. We are then inspired to give something back to others. In this joyful exchange we reject the feeling that no one cares. An appreciative response to others' attention imprints the realization that life is good.

Those who cannot genuinely say "thank you" are unwilling to accept the fact that someone has given to them. True gratitude involves one heart touching another in a moment of encounter affirming that we are not alone. This acknowledgment of fellowship is satisfying for both parties. As eye meets eye and hand clasps hand, there is a sense of oneness, a kindred spirit.

Appreciation forms a social bond of love, whether it is filial love, romantic love, or spiritual union with God. Each act of appreciation touches one to another and reduces barriers of competition and enmity. That is the thrust of the biblical injunction to love neighbor as self. Love means opening up to each other and establishing a connectedness that involves us in a system of reciprocal care and contributes deeply to our sense of identity, security, and hope.

13

Reorganizing the Search

The Disciplined Self

"... God doth not need
Either man's works or his own gifts. Who best
Bear his mild yoke, they serve him best. ...."

John Milton

As we engage in our many acts of seeking satisfaction, we have to impose some sense of order on our behaviors if we do not wish to risk disappointment—even chaos. In this final chapter, we will examine the standards of conduct that will best ensure our maximum satisfaction with life.

Time magazine ran a cover story in the late 1980s that asked the question, "Whatever happened to ethics? Assaulted by sleaze, scandals and hypocrisy, America searches for its moral bearings."[1] The article was written in an era of scandal at all levels of public and private life. Foremost at the time was the crisis of the Reagan presidency. Not only was the Administration facing Iran-Contra charges rivaling Richard Nixon's Watergate scandal, but over one hundred members of the Administration had ethical and legal charges filed against them during Ronald Reagan's tenure in office. At the same time, daily headlines carried the scorching stories of the sexual escapades of presidential candidate Gary Hart, televangelist Jim Bakker, and the Marine guards at the U. S. Embassy in Moscow. Stories also revealed how drugs, illegal tips, and inside trading were rampant on Wall Street. And, in Chicago, "Operation Greylord" documented that the courts were corrupted with bribery.

Time pointed out that these and other issues are "merely symptomatic of the materialistic excess that has turned the 1980s into . . . a time when by one's possessions thou shalt be known and judged."[2] There is little evidence to suggest that the 1990s will be marked by a lessening in the pursuit of self-centered goals, whether by legal or illegal means. Psychoanalyst Heinz Kohut perhaps speaks for many social critics when he describes the modern psyche as "enfeebled, multifragmented, and disharmonious."[3]

Placing moral and ethical rules ahead of personal gain is obviously not altogether popular in our times. We Americans zealously guard our right to individual expression, often in defiance of conscience, external authority, and social values. Perhaps the popular view of what it means to be living in the "land of the free" is so steeped in seeking personal satisfaction that we forget that our roots—and our greatness as a people—are inextricably tied to a sense of moral law that reflects the will and best interests of the majority. In our exuberant self-focus, many of us act as if the self is more valuable and in need of protection than the rights of others. As we now witness the results of an era of self-expression outside the constraints of conscience and rules, it is imperative that we consider what might be done to reorganize our search for satisfaction.

We will now examine three principles that should govern the process of seeking satisfaction: a love ethic, self-discipline, and spirituality. It is obvious that we will probably continue to emphasize individualism and self-enhancement as the American way. However, something needs to be said about the need to refocus our sights on personal and social controls that are located *outside* the self—the values, standards, and rules that determine getting-and-giving behavior in any ordered and civilized society.

The rules I am proposing are not authoritarian do's and don't's. Instead, I am suggesting that total fulfillment requires us to acknowledge standards of personal and social conduct that have always brought out the best in people. We need to deliberately recommit ourselves to these principles which have stood the test of time. Bearing a controlling yoke is not easy, but it helps us avoid the pain and uncertainty of floundering without guidelines.

Developing a Love Ethic

Adhering to a love ethic has always helped us achieve the kind of emotional and social well-being that individual pursuits cannot provide. If we believe in and practice filial love, we redeem ourselves from what the Greeks called the deadly sins of greed, pride, and avarice. ("Avarice" has been defined as "excessive or insatiable desire for wealth or gain."[4] How apt for our times!) What is "deadly" about these sins is that in their practice we become lost in our own selfish ends and suffer an individual malaise that breeds interpersonal death. When trapped in an internal circle of stultifying self-focus, we are isolated from the ongoing process of being responsive to others that affirms our membership in the human family.

But, when we love, we avoid the death of self because we then provide ourselves with external objects upon which to focus our energies. In the context of transcending self-focus, "love" is not a personalized attachment (although such a feeling may be present)—it is an ethical, moral principle that shapes how we feel and think about ourselves in relation to others. A love ethic is ultimately growthful because it allows us to reach out and gather in new experiences that promote and expand our own welfare.

Healthy love does not require that we deny the self's existence or its needs, but it does imply an avoidance of self-preoccupation. When we love, we are reaching into the self as a base from which to operate, proceeding beyond self to focus on the object of our love. Unlike infatuation, where the self is negated in an adoration of the love object, when we love maturely we keep one hand firmly on the self, even as we reach out to grasp the hand of another. To love is to care about the welfare of the objects of our love, celebrating their joys, bearing their pain, making a space within our consciousness for them, and committing ourselves to a love ethic that maintains our involvement together.

Lawrence Kohlberg's theory of moral development helps us understand how a love ethic can guide us as we go about the process of getting and giving.[5] Kohlberg categorizes moral thought in three major levels of development, each of which contributes to social order. At the lowest level, behavior is modified only to avoid unpleasant consequences. Thus a driver might stop at a red light for fear of getting injured or ticketed by the police. The second level of moral development implies conformity to the rules and standards of a society so as to secure or maintain one's acceptance by others. Here the driver is motivated to stop at the red light by thoughts of what others might say if he or she does *not* stop.

Finally, at the highest moral level, people control their actions by voluntarily following social contracts that are based on principles of consistency, mutual respect, and trust. Here a person chooses to stop at a red light in consideration of others' welfare and to voluntarily maintain a sense of rightful behavior.

Kohlberg does not see concerns for social order as stemming from feelings of love. Rather, he assumes that emotions have "no significant role for identification or defense in the development of morality."[6] Kohlberg also rules out the influence of God's hand in individual moral choice. Instead, he dwells on *reason* as the means whereby we make our choices and sees the moral self as a by-product of the rational self. For Kohlberg, "love" and "morality" seem explainable in terms of acting reasonably, in anticipation of how one's choices may influence others, in other words, he explains love in behavioristic or humanistic terms.

Kohlberg's highest level of moral development would probably best express the kind of motives found in a love ethic. That is, when we make our choices with a view to acknowledging responsibility for others' welfare, we demonstrate the principles of love that best serve us all. An effective process of getting and giving therefore demands the guidance of a caring involvement with others, whether with family, friends, or people in general. Our love outreach encompasses empathy, kindness, patience, forgiveness, courtesy, respect, and all the other interpersonal behaviors that are reciprocally nourishing in their practice.

Henri Nouwen describes reaching reaching out to others in love as a movement toward fulfilling God's will. By moving away from hostility and toward hospitality, we create "a free space where the stranger can enter and become a friend instead of an enemy." Hospitality in this context is a filial love that offers people space to change themselves, to consider new options, to be liberated from fear, and to find their own God in their own way.[7] When we love, we set aside personal judgment, bias, and preoccupations that prevent new experiences with others. We become involved in people's histories, concerned with their lives, available for loving care, even willing to absorb their pain.

We may seek to protect ourselves from feeling the pain others experience, but we do so to our own detriment. Empathic caring may seem too costly, but ultimately it is life-giving to the self. Loving empathically strengthens the social-cultural-ethical fabric upon which we ourselves depend for survival. What is so conspicuously evil about crime, narcissistic self-indulgence, political enslavement, or any other form of activity that harms others is that such behavior sacrifices the good of all for the benefit of the few. It therefore violates all the rules of the love ethic and wounds the self by so doing.

It is even more corrupt to give lip service to the principles of love, fair play, and brotherhood while using these very principles as a shield behind which to promote one's own personal satisfaction. Few of us are innocent of that charge. The "bad guys" are not just the dictators who loot their countries and flee to retire in luxury—or the self-serving tele-vangelists, corporate inside-traders, dishonest politicians, and others who trick the public. Each of us tampers with the rights of others and flouts the legitimate demands of societal rules in many ways. Every thought-less, dishonest, unkind, and self-serving word and action we rationalize because "everyone's doing it" unravels the fabric of our social structure.

The love ethic is a reminder that there are claims on us as members of the human family. Since no one is totally self-sufficient, it is impossible to exist in isolation. Neither could any of us have survived this long with-out the efforts of those who have gone before us. We are who we are because of a host of people who have been personally involved in our early years: parents, siblings, relatives, friends, teachers, neighbors, reli-gious or community leaders, and anyone else who has had a hand in shaping our development. They all have a claim on us that must be repaid. We are also indebted to those who grow, process, and market our food and to those who keep our world functioning with efficiency and style—scientists, technicians, public servants, laborers, soldiers and law-enforcers, medical personnel, government officials, writers, and artists in every field. How could we survive without them? By looking after each other, we strengthen our senses of community and thereby promote the welfare of all.

Self-deification is the unrealistic (and uncivilized) belief that we are indebted to no one but ourselves, that only our own abilities and efforts are responsible for our achievements. Such an inflated ego ignores the fact that each generation is heir to the labors and wisdom of the past. Our parents and teachers were our nurturers and counselors; we, in turn, have the obligation to pass along the same tradition of caregiving. Our obligation to our forebears, our contemporaries, and those who will come after us is to live responsibly—which requires practicing a love ethic for the good of self and others. There is no more effective way to reinforce the essential values that bind us closely in human fellowship.

Maintaining Self-Discipline

Closely related to the importance of the love ethic in governing our search for satisfaction is the ruling principle of self-control. In an era of pleasure seeking, it is difficult to convince people to monitor their own behavior, much less to regulate it. Even a reminder that "discipline encourages success" does not necessarily persuade us that this formula need apply in every situation. If we believe, as many of us do, that we are basically well-intentioned—and that therefore the ends justify the means by which we attain them—we can easily convince ourselves that restraint is not always the best course. Because we tend to demand immediate gratification, we prefer quick fixes to the kind of well-considered planning that requires patient effort, and faith in the probability of being rewarded in the future. Many of us complain that self-discipline is too time-consuming, that depriving ourselves is an unnecessary waste of potential gain and forestalls good times and fun. "Do what you have to do," we urge others, thereby justifying our own code of expediency.

Aristotle called discipline the "hardest victory"—and rightly so. Controlling our own behavior demands patience, determination, and conscious self-denial. The call of our incessant desires tends to silence the voice of reason whenever we choose to honor personal gratification over sensible constraint. If we have jettisoned the controls provided by group consensus or by conscience, we will feel very anxious when slowed down by the restrictions of self-discipline. The philosophy of immediate payoff has been elevated to dizzying heights; many would rather ignore the promise of long-term gains than deny here-and-now pleasures.

Yet, we claim to admire those who lead disciplined lives. We readily admit that the professional athlete, for example, has had to live for years under the yoke of instruction, practice, self-analysis, and hard work. We know that no athlete achieves success without following very stringent rules and standards of performance. Furthermore, in many sports, team-work plays such a crucial role that no one can be a star in isolation. Even the superstar must cooperate with other team members and subordinate personal goals that conflict with the team's best interests. We do not even question this demand. Similarly, most people would agree that any accomplished musician or actor or scientist has reached the heights of professional ability only by being dedicated to a program of training and a denial of many personal pleasures. To achieve the greatest satisfaction, professionals in any field must be committed to their task, willing to sacrifice temporary gain for long-term rewards. Their efforts are all guided by a voluntary decision to maintain self-discipline. Athletes, musicians, and scientists can serve as models as we strive to become productive, "professional" persons. Their examples show us that the way to excel *as a human being* is to structure our lives around a studied discipline that is manifest in almost everything we do. There are a number of ways we can develop this principle in our own approach to life.

1. *"Professionals" discipline themselves with a sense of purpose.* They set long-range goals toward which they will direct themselves and then find interim satisfaction by keeping those ultimate objectives in view. This farsighted approach is in sharp contrast with the sense of immediacy found in the undisciplined. If our goals are reasonable, they will serve as guidelines to keep us on target and will provide encouraging rewards along the way. What keeps the college student going is the delightful awareness that someday there will be a graduation and new possibilities. Each passing grade or term paper returned with a "well done" comment, every friendship established, is a prize that reinforces his or her aspirations. Between the now and the then, however, stands a significant amount of self-discipline—or else that special day may never arrive.

2. *"Professionals" show self-control by considering how their behavior affects other people.* Because disciplined people think things through carefully, they avoid acting impulsively. They measure the effects of working, spending, speaking—all that is gotten and given—in terms of the impact these actions have on self *and* on others. Their patterns of behavior are modified by a social ethic that accounts for close intimates as well as for casual acquaintances and even strangers. Being people-oriented reflects the biblical command to avoid becoming a "stumbling block" to others (Rom. 14:13).

3. *"Professionals" exhibit self-discipline by competing fairly, that is, by respecting the rights of their competitors.* Although cynics may claim that "nice guys finish last" and winning is all that matters, such advice denies the need for moral directives in everyday living. It is no victory to win by destroying someone else's reputation, by abusing, cheating, lying, or bribing others, or by taking an advantage through clever manipulations. If we are truly human, we do not want to succeed "at any cost." When we

discipline ourselves, we compete in ways that respect self, others, and the ties that bind us together.

4. *"Professionals" follow rules.* That means much more than obeying the laws of the land. "Rules" refer to the moral and ethical standards that lend cohesion and stability to a given culture. When we play by the rules, we are underwriting order and fair play and therefore discouraging social unrest. Knowing that others share our standards also provides a degree of predictability to human behavior that heightens our sense of overall security. Rules are cognitive, not emotional, yet they promote the maturation needed to bring impulse, hostility, and self-serving emotions under firmer control. Without rules of acceptable behavior, any society would collapse into anarchy.

Rules of order are implicit in the social graces. Courtesy, tolerance, patience, and other such expressions of mutual respect have eroded badly in the self-serving focus of our narcissistic times. President George Bush captured the truth of this observation in his inaugural address, when he urged us to become a "kinder and gentler America." In our dash toward personal glory, we often trample on the softer virtues of civilized living.

Personal commitment to inner discipline keeps in sight the nobler qualities of the human spirit that the apostle Paul refers to as the "things above" (Col. 3:1). We all instinctively recognize these higher virtues—compassion, trust, honesty, kindness, forgiveness. These lasting ideals have come to constitute a rule of decency that all peaceful people affirm in their hearts, if not in their actions. Swiss psychiatrist Paul Tournier writes in *The Whole Person in a Broken World*, "It is not what men produce that unites them, but rather the eternal verities which they can lay hold of only with the heart."[8]

Perhaps the term *faith* best captures the idea that getting and giving have to be anchored in the deep soil of what we believe in, if either activity is to be satisfying. Faith is not identical with logic, reasoning, morality, or even spirituality. James Fowler points out in *Stages of Faith* that faith is "more verb than noun, [and] is the dynamic system of images, values, and commitments that guide one's life."[9] Faith imparts meaning and value to life itself. I suggest that personal discipline must include an internalization of the principles of love and morality at a level so deep that we habitually govern our acts according to those ideals. Such a commitment is not situationally determined; it will operate in every circumstance because it *defines* what we believe in and therefore how we will live.

Making the shift from total self-absorption gives us access to a broader perspective of existence that establishes a rationale for maintaining control over our impulses. Often to our surprise, self-discipline actually enhances our overall satisfaction, because it brings a liberating sense of inner peace and personal wholeness.

Affirming the Spiritual Dimension

There is a third guiding principle that, when put into practice, enhances our satisfaction. Central to the unifying truths that promise fulfillment for our deepest cravings is the spiritual dimension of life. Mankind has always appealed to supernatural forces to decipher the mysteries of the universe and thereby prescribe a remedy for human inadequacies, fears, and anxieties. Yet psychologist Perry London predicted in the mid-1960s that religion would be eclipsed by the mental-health expert as secular priest.[10] And about the same time, Nikita Krushchev prophesied that by the 1980s not one church would remain open in Russia.[11] Neither of these commentators took into account the urgent human desire for communion with an unseen supreme being.

If there were no God, we would attempt to invent one, for we could not bear the terror of a life-journey without the presence of a transcendent source of comfort. Our lives take on richer meaning within the context of the spiritual world, fortified by the strength, guidance, and consolation it provides daily—and reassured by belief in a loving Creator who awaits our final return to him.

Throughout this book, the life-journey has been described as sufficiently perilous for us to constantly crave satisfaction as a remedy. The dangers of life are not found merely in tragic or disappointing circumstances, but in the very act of *being* alive. All human beings experience a constant, underlying "angst"—a nameless fear that never fully ends. We learn to accommodate that anxiety or we perish, and it is by accessing the spiritual dimension that we facilitate such an adjustment. "Without God, fear rules," writes Tournier.[12] He reminds us that there can be no meaningful adventure into life without some inner acceptance of the image of God that is freely offered to all. It is our spiritual practices, he explains, that provide a sense of direction and purpose in our life-journeys.[13] If we hold fast the image of a God who both guides us and loves us, we talk to him in prayer, think about him in meditation, and worship him in fellowship with others. All these "religious exercises" clarify who we are and why we exist.

Each religion proposes a different format for how the life-journey is to be executed. Arthur DeKruyter speaks aptly for Christianity when he states that "of all the religious leaders and prophets and philosophers, Jesus is unique." Whereas the Greeks urged us to know ourselves, the Romans to rule ourselves, the Chinese to improve ourselves, the Buddhists to annihilate ourselves and our selfish desires, the Brahmans to lose ourselves in the world's soul, and the Internationalists to commit ourselves to peace, Christ encourages us to first commit ourselves to God's purposes, and then all else will follow.[14]

Although we resist being told how we should live, even by the very institutions we create and maintain to provide moral and spiritual direction, we all seek an inner peace that only the spiritual self can experience. Many of us stop short of making a spiritual commitment, either to God or to a specific religion or church, because such a commitment is seen primarily as restrictive. We often misconstrue spiritual principles and the demands of religious practice as burdensome impediments to happiness. Christ reminds believers that indeed there are obligations thrust upon those who would follow him, but that such a yoke is "easy" and the burden "light" (Matt. 11:29–30), when compared to the weariness of aimless wandering in existential fear. Expending our spiritual energies uncovers hidden solutions to our daily problems and ultimately restores the self to full vitality.

Andres Niño draws from Augustine's *Confessions* to spell out the psychological and spiritual aspects of that restoration.[15] He begins with the observation that psychology and religion enjoy a far more cordial relationship than in the past and are now in a closer dialogue about the ultimate purpose and meaning of life. This rapprochement is the inevitable product of acknowledging that many in our society feel empty and disoriented despite considerable achievement and financial success. Niño sees our struggles with the fragmentation of the self, a lack of inner depth, and an inability to rise above our anxieties as grounds for seeking personal coherence in a spiritual dimension. With God at the center of our being, we are better able to interpret the details of our experiences and find meaning, direction, and comfort in that knowledge, as did Augustine nearly sixteen centuries ago. Niño writes, "By reconstructing and organizing the narrative of his own experience, [Augustine] sets the foundations for a new idea of personality that includes individuality, introspection, and the capacity of transcendence."[16]

In an attempt to discover and restore his essential self, Augustine begins—as must we all—by examining the details of his life. "It is in my heart that I am whatever I am," he writes.[17] He first interrogates his memories, acknowledging the various aspects of his inner experiences that have been ignored or denied. Augustine discovers that he has been deluding himself, that he has substituted performance for real living, doing for being, false goals for real substance. "I was greedy to enjoy what the world had to offer, though it only eluded me and wasted my strength. And all the time I had been telling myself one tale after another."[18] What Augustine is admitting is that he has been living according to the pleasure principle and has eschewed deeper truths. When he finally opens himself to question life's essence, he painstakingly realizes that he has been lost in self and hiding from God. Augustine comes to the moment of truth about his life as he concludes in prayer: "You made us for yourself and our hearts find no peace until they rest in you."[19]

Niño reminds us that Augustine's quest for peace is not merely spiritual, for he must face his disillusionments with the soul-searching hard work of sorting through the complex feelings and thoughts that regulate his life. Niño's conclusion is that we, like Augustine, must reconsider "our views and interpretations of the world, our dreams, plans, and particular ways of self expression."[20] We must acknowledge our inconsistencies, the conflicts between our desires and our values, the urge to take more than we give. By placing pressure on the self, we are brought into inner harmony and find interpersonal contentment.

Niño interprets Augustine's description for finding God as follows:

"1. A fundamental openness to God's presence to the self" whereby we trust God and abandon our desire to hide as we face ourselves.

"2. A dialogue which flows with a wealth of nuances in a genuine personal language." As we communicate with God, we examine our lives and bring our memories and histories to him. As we tell him who we are and what we have been doing, we open ourselves to the impact of *his* voice, *his* ways within us.

"3. A coherence of past, present, and future structured around a matrix of individual meaning." As we allow God into our lives

and accept his prescriptions to love him, others, and self, then
we operate as creatures who have a core motive in life. We interpret life's events from this internal matrix of meaning; we evaluate the past events of our lives and our present desires and goals
with a sense of internal clarity and direction. The future is therefore seen from a perspective of certainty—not of what indeed
will transpire, but what we must do to transcend our various
problems and remain emotionally and spiritually intact."[21]

As we find God and solidify our lives around him, we are better able
to transcend the boundaries of the self and cast off our obsession over
personal gain. We then move beyond the narrow limits of the self to
develop meaningful relationships with others. Niño states that "relationships constitute . . . the central force that animate [our] search . . . and
shape the process of [our] restoration."[22] Put in the language of this
book, as we develop and know ourselves, we are then in a better position
to love by communing even more deeply with God and each other. To
the degree that our experience of God and others is taken within, rather
than handled at a safe distance, reaching beyond our own personal
boundaries does not lessen the self but strengthens it.

A God-centered self is a more adequate self, improved and refreshed
by the power of God's empathic, guiding, enlightening, and corrective
care-giving. All of life's uncertainties can be accommodated—even if not
fully understood—by this God-fortified self. Establishing a personal relationship with God, the Eternal One, provides a permanence that anchors
us in peace. Even when doubts, fears, and conflicts appear periodically
in our lives, our ongoing sense of restoration is a source of strength and
security. Because God's claim on us is deeply personal, his will for each
individual is a level of self-development that glorifies him by acknowledging his constant presence. When we bring God into our lives, we pursue his eternal purpose, take his loving hand in gratitude, and grow to
full capacity.

Using spiritual principles to frame a religious belief system is enlightening, but beliefs that are merely conceptual are not internally experienced, much less life-changing. Authentic spirituality is rooted in a *personal* relationship with God. Just as acquiring knowledge about another
person is a prerequisite to establishing a meaningful relationship with
him or her, so too in forging a connection to God. Spiritual maturity
implies that we have focused our efforts on learning as much as we can
about God's qualities and what he expects of us. That kind of faith is

never static—it demands thought and study, acceptance, total mental and emotional involvement. When we acknowledge our inability to end our feelings of inadequacy, to erase our wrongdoing, or to earn an eternal reward on our own, we have no recourse but "an unconditional acceptance of God's unconditional acceptance," as J. Harold Ellens reminds us.[23]

The spiritual life is a constant beam of light that illuminates the direction and destiny of our lives. Not only will our temporal rewards take their meaning from that guiding beacon, but our ultimate goal becomes total oneness with God. There is "blessed assurance" in knowing that complete satisfaction will be ours in the *hereafter,* whether we envision that final destiny as preceded by some interim state of existence (as in beliefs of reincarnation or purgatory), as occurring after a Judgment Day, or as immediately following our physical death.

Those who believe that "heaven" and "hell" are experienced only in this life have rejected the great expectation that our joy and fulfillment will be infinite, once we are no longer encumbered by our human frailties. "Heaven" is our vision of an eternity in which we shall finally experience total relief from emptiness and imperfection—as the hymn writer so eloquently says:

> When I in righteousness at last
> Thy glorious face shall see
> When all the weary night is past
> And I awake with thee
> To view thy glories that abide
> Then, then shall I be satisfied.
>
> Frederic Bullard, 1864–1904

That hope of glory is the answer we are all seeking, for it rests on a promise that one day our search for satisfaction will be ended.

Notes

Chapter 1: *The Human Condition*

1. Paul Wachtel, *The Poverty of Affluence: A Psychological Portrait of the American Way of Life* (New York: Free Press, 1983), p. 18.

2. Theodor Reik, *Of Love and Lust* (New York: Jason Aaronson, 1974).

3. J. Harold Ellens, *God's Grace and Human Health* (Nashville: Abingdon Press, 1982), p. 69.

Chapter 2: *The Process of Getting*

1. James Masterson, *The Narcissistic and Borderline Conditions* (New York: Brunner Mazel, 1981).

2. Theodore Millon, *Disorders of Personality, DSM III, Axis II* (New York: John Wiley & Sons, 1981), p. 68.

3. Ibid., p. 73.

4. B. F. Skinner, cited in Ernest R. Hilgard, *Theories of Learning* (New York: Appleton-Century-Crofts, 1956), pp. 82–120.

5. Ernest Becker, *The Denial of Death* (New York: Free Press, 1973).

Chapter 3: *Contemporary Getting*

1. Paul Wachtel, *The Poverty of Affluence: A Psychological Portrait of the American Way of Life* (New York: Free Press, 1983).

2. Ibid., p. 17.

3. American Psychiatric Association, *The Diagnostic and Statistical Manual of Mental Disorders, Third Edition* (Washington: A.P.A., 1980), p. 315.

4. Otto Kernberg, *Borderline Conditions and Pathological Narcissism* (New York: Jason Aaronson, 1975), p. 228.

5. Aaron Stern, *Me: The Narcissistic American* (New York: Ballantine Books/Random House, 1979), p. 13.

6. Ibid.

7. Christopher Lasch, *The Culture of Narcissism* (New York: W. W. Norton, 1979).

8. Daniel Yankelovich, *New Rules: Searching for Self-Fulfillment in a World Turned Upside Down* (New York: Bantam Books, 1982), p. 31.

9. Ibid., p. 32.

10. Wachtel, *The Poverty of Affluence*, p. 234.

11. Rhoda L. Rottschafer, *"Narcissism as an Adaptation to Social Stress,"* unpublished M.S.W. thesis (Downers Grove, Ill.: George Williams College, 1985).

12. Robert A. Anderson, M. D., *Stress Power! How to Turn Tension into Energy* (New York: Human Sciences Press, 1978), p. 18.

13. Ibid., p. 14.

Chapter 4: *Dealing with Our Parents*

1. John Naisbitt, *Megatrends: Ten New Directions Transforming Our Lives* (New York: Warner Books, 1982).

2. Martin Mayer, *Madison Avenue, U.S.A.* (New York: Harper & Brothers, 1970).

3. Martin Mayer, *The Schools* (New York: Harper & Brothers, 1970).

4. Martin Mayer, *About Television* (New York: Harper & Row, 1972).

5. Charles E. Silverman, *Crisis in the Classroom* (New York, Random House, 1970).

6. Charles E. Silverman, *Crisis in Black and White* (New York: Random House, 1964).

7. Garry Wills, *Nixon Agonistes* (Boston: Houghton Mifflin, 1969).

8. Charles Reich, *The Greening of America* (New York: Bantam Books, 1971).

9. Ibid., pp. 241–42.

10. Ibid., p. 307.

11. Peter Schrag, *The Decline of the WASP* (New York: Simon & Schuster, 1971).

12. Ibid., p. 221.

13. Ibid., p. 194.

14. Ibid., p. 65.

15. Henry Van Dellen, Medical Advice column, The *Chicago Tribune*, May, 1972.

16. Schrag, *The Decline of the WASP*, p. 77.

17. e. e. cummings, "The Cambridge Ladies Who Live in Furnished Souls," in Mark Schorer, *The Literature of America: Twentieth Century* (New York: McGraw Hill, 1970), p. 280.

18. Herbert Hendon, *The Age of Sensation* (New York: W. W. Norton, 1975), pp. 2–3.

19. Asa Baber, *Playboy* 31/6 (June 1984): 37.

20. E. Robinson and D. Jedlicka, "Changes in Attitudes and Behaviors in College Students from 1965–1981: A Research Note," *Journal of Marriage and the Family* 44/1 (Feb. 8, 1982): 237.

21. G. Masnick and M. Bane, *The Nation's Families: 1960–1990* (Boston: Auburn House, 1980).

22. Jessie Bernard, *The Future of Marriage* (New York: Bantam Books, 1973).

23. Hendon, *The Age of Sensation*, p. 6.

Chapter 5: *Over-Getting*

1. Myron Cohen, "Everybody's Got to Be Someplace," RCA Records, re-issue, produced by Ethel Gabriel.

2. Karl Menninger, *Whatever Became of Sin?* (New York: Hawthorne Books, 1973), p. 14.

Chapter 6: *Under-Getting*

1. Christopher Lasch, *The Minimal Self* (New York: W. W. Norton, 1984), p. 175.

2. R. W. D. Fairbairn, *An Object-Relations Theory of Personality* (New York: Basic Books, 1954).

3. Carol Tavris, *Anger: The Misunderstood Emotion* (New York: A Touchstone Book/Simon & Schuster, 1982).

4. Melanie Klein, *Envy and Gratitude and Other Works, 1946–1963* (New York: Delacorte Press, 1975).

5. Heinz Kohut, "Self-selfobject Relationships Reconsidered," in A. Goldberg and P. E. Stephansky, eds., *How Does Analysis Cure?* (Chicago: Univ. of Chicago Press, 1984), p. 50.

Chapter 7: *The Process of Giving*

1. Daniel Yankelovich, *New Rules: Searching for Self-Fulfillment in a World Turned Upside Down* (New York: Bantam Books, 1982), p. 8.
2. Ibid.
3. Erich Fromm, *The Art of Loving* (New York: Harper & Brothers, 1956).
4. Edith Jacobson, "Self and the Object World," *The Psychoanalytic Study of the Child* (New York: International Universities Press, 1954), vol. 9, pp. 75–127.
5. J. Harold Ellens, Personal communication, 1986.
6. Rollo May, *Love and Will* (New York: W. W. Norton, 1969).
7. Ibid., p. 183.
8. Ibid., p. 213.
9. Fromm, *The Art of Loving*.

Chapter 8: *Restricted Giving*

1. J. Harold Ellens, *God's Grace and Human Health* (Nashville: Abingdon Press, 1982), p. 87.
2. R. V. Sampson, *The Psychology of Power* (New York: Pantheon Books/Random House, 1966).
3. Sigmund Freud, *The Ego and The Id* (London: Hogarth Press, 1927), p. 79.
4. Sigmund Freud, *Civilization and Its Discontents* (London: Hogarth Press, 1930), p. 70.
5. Sigmund Freud, *Group Psychology and the Analysis of the Ego* (New York: Liveright, 1922), p. 52.
6. Ayn Rand, *The Virtues of Selfishness* (New York: Signet Books, 1964).
7. Ruth L. Monroe, *Schools of Psychoanalytic Thought* (New York: Dryden Press, 1955).
8. Eric Berne, *Games People Play* (New York: Grove Press, 1964).
9. S. L. Halleck, "Family Therapy and Social Change," *Social Casework*, October 1976, p. 493.

Chapter 9: *Disproportionate Giving*

1. Paul Wachtel, *The Poverty of Affluence: A Psychological Portrait of the American Way of Life* (New York: Free Press, 1983), p. 69.
2. Shirley Pankin, *The Joy of Suffering* (New York: Jason Aaronson, 1973).

Chapter 10: *Giving to Our Children*

1. Leonard A. Rosenbloom and Michael Lewis, *The Effects of the Infant on its Caregiver* (New York: John Wiley & Sons, 1974).
2. Nancy Chodorow, *The Reproduction of Mothering* (Berkeley: Univ. of California Press, 1978).
3. Nancy Friday, *My Mother/My Self: The Daughter's Search for Identity* (New York: Delacorte Press, 1977).
4. Ibid., p. 3.
5. Carole Klein, *Mothers and Sons* (New York: Houghton Mifflin, 1984), p. 45.
6. Ibid., p. 49.
7.
8.
9.

Chapter 11: *Whom to Serve*

1. Dean R. Hoge, *Converts, Dropouts, Returnees: A Study of Religious Change Among Catholics* (Washington, D.C.: United States Catholic Conference/N.Y. Pilgrim Press, 1981), p. 167.
2. Robert N. Bellah et al., *Habits of the Heart, Individualism and Commitment in American Life* (Berkeley: Univ. of California Press, 1985), p. 2.

3. Ibid., p. 144.

4. Ibid., p. 142.

5. Ronald H. Rottschafer, "Grace and the Importance of the Self," *Journal of Psychology and Christianity* 7, No. 1 (1988): 3–13.

6. Ronald H. Rottschafer, "The Passive Christian," *Journal of Psychology and Christianity* 3, No. 1 (1984): 42–51.

7. David F. Wells, "Self-Esteem: The New Confusion," *The Reformed Journal* 33, No. 10 (October 1983).

8. Ibid., p. 16–17.

9. C. S. Lewis, *God in the Dock: Essays on Theology and Ethics,* ed. Walter Hooper (Grand Rapids: William B. Eerdmans, 1985), p. 194.

10. Ibid.

11. John R. W. Stott, "Am I Supposed to Love Myself or Hate Myself?" *Christianity Today* 28, No. 7 (April 1984).

12. Ibid., p. 26.

13. Ibid., p. 28.

14. John R. W. Stott, "Must I Really Love Myself?" *Christianity Today* 22, No. 14 (1978).

15. J. Harold Ellens, *God's Grace and Human Health* (Nashville: Abingdon Press, 1982), p. 69.

16. J. Harold Ellens, "God's Grace, the Radical Option," *Perspectives* 4, No. 9 (Nov. 1989), 7.

17. Ibid.

18. Richard A. Rhem, "The Continuing Adventure of Faith," *Perspectives* 4, No. 9 (Nov. 1989), 7.

19. Rollo May, *Power and Innocence* (New York: W. W. Norton, 1972).

20. Ibid., p. 49.

21. Ibid., p. 50.

22. Ronald J. Sider, *Rich Christians in an Age of Hunger: A Biblical Study* (Downers Grove, Ill.; InterVarsity Press, 1977), p. 173.

23. Ibid., p. 128.

Chapter 12: *Becoming Fulfilled*

1. Daniel Yankelovich, *New Rules: Searching for Self-Fulfillment in a World Turned Upside Down* (New York: Bantam Books, 1982).

2. Frederick Perls, *Gestalt Therapy Verbatim* (Lafayette, Calif.: Real People Press, 1969).

3. Allan Bloom, *The Closing of the American Mind* (New York: A Touchstone Book/Simon & Schuster, 1987), p. 227.

4. Ibid., p. 228.

5. Hans Selye, *The Stress of Life* (New York: McGraw Hill, 1976).

Chapter 13: *Reorganizing the Search*

1. *Time,* May 25, 1987.

2. Ibid., p. 26.

3. Heinz Kohut, "Self-selfobject Relationships Reconsidered," in A. Goldberg and P. E. Stephansky, eds., *How Does Analysis Cure?* (Chicago: Univ. of Chicago Press, 1984), pp. 49–63.

4. *Webster's Ninth New Collegiate Dictionary* (Springfield, Mass.: Merriam-Webster, 1983).

5. Lawrence Kohlberg, "Stage and Sequence: The Cognitive Developmental Approach of Socialization," in D. Goslin, ed., *Handbook of Socialization Theory and Research* (New York: Rand McNally, 1969).

6. Al Ducek, "Religion and Morality: An Evaluation of Kohlberg's Theory of Moral Development," paper presented at the Annual Convention of the Christian Association for Psychological Studies, 1979.

7. Henri Nouwen, *Reaching Out* (New York: Doubleday, 1966), p. 51.

8. Paul Tournier, *The Whole Person in a Broken World* (New York: Harper & Row, 1964), p. 32.

9. James W. Fowler, *Stages of Faith* (New York: Harper & Row, 1981), quoted from the inside cover flap.

10. Perry London, *Modes and Morals of Psychotherapy* (New York: Holt, Rinehart & Winston, 1964).

11. Sergei Nicolaev, speech delivered, 10-21-90, at Christ Church, Oak Brook, Ill.

12. Tournier, *The Whole Person in a Broken World*, p. 25.

13. Paul Tournier, *The Adventure of Living* (New York: Harper & Row, 1965).

14. Arthur H. DeKruyter, "Practicing Self-Control: What it Takes to be Happy," *The Pulpit of Christ Church*, Oak Brook, Ill., 1988.

15. Andres Niño, "Restoration of the Self: A Therapeutic Paradigm from Augustine's *Confessions,*" *Psychotherapy* 27 (Spring 1990): 8–18.

16. Ibid., p. 9.

17. Aurelius Augustine, *Confessions*, trans. R. S. Pine-Coffin, (New York: Dorset Press, 1986), X, 3, p. 209.

18. Ibid., VI, 11, p. 126.

19. Ibid., I, 1, p. 21.

20. Niño, "Restoration of the Self," p. 12.

21. Ibid., p. 13–14.

22. Ibid., p. 14.

23. J. Harold Ellens, *God's Grace and Human Health* (Nashville: Abingdon Press, 1982), p. 64.

Index